A S THE OWNER of a particular type of dog—or someone who is thinking about adopting one—you probably have some questions about that dog breed that can't be answered anywhere else. In particular, you want to know what breed-specific health issues and behavioral traits might arise as you plan for the future with your beloved canine family member.

The **EVERYTHING** dog breed guides give you clear-cut answers to all your pressing questions. These authoritative books give you all you need to know about identifying common characteristics; choosing the right puppy or adult dog; coping with personality quirks; instilling obedience; and raising your pet in a healthy, positive environment.

The dog breed guides are an extension of the bestselling **EVERYTHING** series. These authoritative, family-friendly books are specially designed to be one-stop guides for anyone looking to explore a specific breed in depth.

EVERYTHING
YOU NEED TO KNOW ABOUT...

Yorkshire Terriers

Dear Reader:

So, you're interested in the Yorkshire terrier? I'm not surprised! These compact dogs have it all—great looks and plenty of personality. But the Yorkie is not for everyone. This dog needs an owner who will lay down the law and dish out lots of care and affection.

In my own lifelong journey with dogs, I have experienced plenty of purebreds and mixed breeds. I can tell you that not everyone is suited to share life with a Yorkshire terrier. I've written this book to help you learn more about these smart, energetic, and sometimes stubborn dogs before you give your heart to one. In these pages, you'll find Yorkie-specific information on health, training, exercise and activities, travel, and more. Learn as much as you can, and you'll be prepared to enjoy a long, happy life with your own Yorkshire terrier.

Best of Luck,

Cheryl S Smith

EVERYTHING
YOU NEED TO KNOW ABOUT...

Yorkshire Terriers

CHERYL S. SMITH

D&C
David and Charles

A DAVID & CHARLES BOOK
David & Charles is a subsidiary of F+W (UK) Ltd.,
an F+W Publications Inc. company

First published in the UK in 2005
First published in the USA as The Everything® Yorkshire Terrier Book,
by Adams Media in 2005

A catalogue record for this book is available from the British Library.

ISBN 0 7153 2332 6

Printed in Great Britain by Antony Rowe Ltd.
for David & Charles
Brunel House   Newton Abbot   Devon

Visit our website at www.davidandcharles.co.uk

David & Charles books are available from all good bookshops;
alternatively you can contact our Orderline on 0870 9908222
or write to us at FREEPOST EX2 110, D&C Direct,
Newton Abbot, TQ12 4ZZ (no stamp required UK mainland).

BREED SPECIFICATIONS

- **Height:** Not specified, but the average is 7 inches at the withers.

- **Weight:** No more than 7 pounds and as little as 2 pounds.

- **Head:** The top of the head should be flat rather than rounded. There is a definite drop from the head to the muzzle.

- **Ears:** Dark, upright, and well set apart.

- **Feet:** Compact and rounded. May be trimmed for show.

- **Tail:** Docked to leave only a few inches. Tail may be held upright, straight back from the body, or anywhere in between.

- **Coat:** Hair should be fine and silky, never wooly, and as straight as possible. Blue on the body is a dark steel-blue, not silver, and has no other colour mixed with it. Tan is a rich, golden colour, darker at the roots.

- **Topline:** Back is level, but it should not be long.

- **Movement:** Moves with a relatively straight front and good reach and drive.

- **Temperament:** Busy and inquisitive by nature.

Acknowledgments

My thanks go out to the Yorkshire terrier owners, breeders, trainers, and enthusiasts who shared with me their knowledge, stories, and passion for the breed: Janet Jackson, president of the Yorkshire Terrier Club of America; Joan Gordon, founder of the breed in the United States; Darlene Arden for her toy-dog expertise; Pam Wengorovius and her agility Yorkies; Deb Gatchell and Raney; Pam Shelby and Desi; Beryl Hesketh and her Heskethane Yorkies; Tami Grinstead and Cleo; Joan Gallagher and Buttons; Arlene King and JP and Fergie; Paula Segnatelli and her Carnaby Yorkies; Bill Wynne and Smoky.

Contents

Introduction

ARCHEOLOGICAL EVIDENCE now shows that the human and canine species have developed together throughout most of their existence. The domesticated dog, *Canis familiaris*, now comes in more than 300 purebred varieties worldwide, plus countless mixes of those breeds. Dogs developed for specific purposes have largely moved beyond those original tasks to become simply loving household companions.

The Yorkshire terrier is one such companion beloved by many pet owners. This is not an ancient breed, but it is one of the most popular. Not many Yorkies still hunt down rats—except occasionally as a sporting event—but they do appear regularly in conformation, obedience, agility, and freestyle competitions. Because of their size and portability, you may encounter them on airplanes and in shops, marinas, apartments, and condominiums. However, don't misjudge this little dog as a bashful bundle of fur you can pop in and out of your purse and use as a fashion accessory. Yorkshire terriers are only small when it comes to size—they have big personalities and require authoritative owners to keep them in check. In the right hands, however, the Yorkshire terrier can be a splendid companion for you, your family, and even your other pets.

This book will acquaint you with the Yorkshire terrier's "big dog in a little body" attitude, as well as the Yorkie's specific needs, so you can decide if this is really the perfect breed for you. You'll learn the breed's history, including how it switched from a rough ratter to a loving lapdog. You'll find tips on housetraining, teaching good manners, maintaining good health, socialization, activities, and more. This book will lead you through your Yorkshire terrier's life, from puppyhood to old age.

I have also included information for the specialized Yorkie owner. Do you hope to travel with your dog? Would you like to train your dog in a particular sport? Would you prefer to prepare homemade meals for your dog instead of buying commercial food? This book will guide you down all of these paths and more. The Yorkshire terrier is a versatile and intelligent breed that can be taught to fit almost any lifestyle. With the right equipment and training (not to mention time and patience), your Yorkie can become your ideal pet.

Before you acquire a Yorkshire terrier of your own, you must understand that while these creatures may be small, they're still dogs through and through. They might indulge in any of the misbehaviors to which dogs are prone, including barking, digging, and chewing. But they can also provide as much love and companionship as any bigger dog. Plan on spending plenty of time with your Yorkie—this breed does not tolerate isolation. Your dog will want to be a full member of the family, supervising every moment of the day's events. His antics may occasionally drive you crazy, but they'll make you smile even more often.

CHAPTER 1

History of the Breed

THE YORKSHIRE TERRIER ranks first among the toy breeds and sixth among all breeds on the American Kennel Club's popularity list. Compact, companionable, and full of attitude, the Yorkie has been a widely favored housedog since moving out of the mines and mills approximately 150 years ago. The shining floor-length coat, sparkling eyes, and equally sparkling personality make the Yorkie impossible to ignore. It's hard to believe that the opinion of dog professionals was once that this little dog would never achieve widespread popularity.

While much about this breed has certainly changed over the years, its personality formed early and has undergone little modification. A Yorkshire terrier is not a fashionable toy to be admired and ignored, as many people believe. This dog requires a responsible owner who will remain committed to both his mental and physical upkeep. Like all dogs, the Yorkie needs dental and medical care, but the breed's long coat and special personality deserve extra attention. Daily grooming and training are among this dog's most important needs.

Origins in Britain

The Yorkshire terrier actually began its development in Scotland, not England. While all dogs owned by the working classes at the time were small—laws denied them larger dogs to keep them from poaching with the dogs on the expansive hunting lands—there were several variations of "small." The official requirement was that dogs owned by commoners had to be able to walk through a hoop that was seven inches in diameter. This led to the breeding of many short-legged, long-bodied dogs.

Weavers and miners in Scotland wanted a smaller dog to deal with the burgeoning rat population. They crossed a variety of terriers until they had a scaled-down dog that was still true to its terrier heritage. By today's standards, these early incarnations of the breed were oversized, weighing in at twelve to fourteen pounds. Some even say that the Yorkie's tan head and legs were selected because they made the dogs more visible in the dark mine shafts.

 Fact

It seemed that Yorkies would never gain true popularity because the wisdom at the time declared that both men and women had to be attracted to a breed for it to succeed. People deemed the broken-haired Scotch terrier too fussy and feminine to gain popularity. They were wrong. Today, the Yorkshire terrier is the preferred pet of countless men and women the world over.

The dogs were also used as entertainment. In a time when bulldogs were actually used to bait bulls in competitions (grabbing onto the nose and holding on), Yorkshire terriers were pitted against rats in miniature rings. Because the ratting competitions required little space, many pubs included them as part of an evening's merriment. The pubs also held many informal dog shows.

The Move to Yorkshire

When the weavers migrated to Yorkshire in pursuit of work opportunities, they brought their little dogs with them. At the time, they were called broken-haired Scotch terriers. They still served as ratters and as entertainment in staged fights against rats. But they soon gained other opportunities.

In those days, almost every animal was shown in some way. Informal competitions regularly sprang up to determine who had the best wool sheep, the finest cattle, the handsomest chickens, and of course, the best dogs. Even before kennel clubs existed, dogs were being shown against one another and judged by those present or by some local authority. In the early days of the kennel clubs, almost any dog could be shown because there were no long pedigrees and generations of registrations. At first, Yorkshire terriers were shown in a class for "Scottish Terriers," which could also include Cairn, Dandie Dinmont, and Skye terriers. But the Yorkie's continued existence looked doubtful, as those in high places proclaimed the breed unnatural and unlikely to be favored by men.

Creation of the Breed

The experts were wrong when they said that a breed had to be favored by both men and women to gain popularity. The small terrier became well loved by the women of the time. Thus, the weavers found themselves in possession of the secret to the Yorkie's breeding, with a valuable product to sell. The working-class men were soon selling puppies to the upper-class women and carefully guarding the lineage of their dogs. This secrecy surrounding their product is the reason there is so little firm information about the breed's early history.

The Waterside terrier was once common in Yorkshire. This dog was a ratter and a small breed with a longish coat, occasionally showing a blue-gray color. The Waterside terrier was crossed with the otter hound to develop the Airedale terrier. This may be how the Airedale came to be mentioned in the creation of the Yorkshire terrier.

The Paisley, Clydesdale, and Skye share a confused, intertwined history. The Paisley line eventually merged into the Skye terrier, while the Clydesdale simply disappeared, but not before note was made of the fine and silky coat of the dog. While the

Skye standard was in the process of being solidified, breeders occasionally threw in individual dogs that were prick-eared and had softer coats than the desired hard coat of the Skye. The Paisley and Clydesdale probably contributed color, as they are described as dark blue to light fawn. The Paisley actually got so far as to have a written standard, calling for "various shades of blue."

Essential

Though the origin of the breed dates back only about 150 years, the breeds that went into the Yorkie's makeup can only be guessed. There's certainly terrier blood, and the Waterside, Paisley, Clydesdale, Skye, and black-and-tan terrier are all mentioned as possible progenitors. Other hypotheses include the Leeds terrier, Manchester terrier, and Maltese. Some even suggest the Airedale terrier, though the first four breeds are by far the best guesses.

Rising Popularity

By 1875 the little dog was not being used much for ratting, but he was still rising in popularity among wealthy women. Even at his then-larger size, the dog was carried about as a fashion accessory. And while the women enjoyed the company of their little pets, the weavers continued enjoying the extra cash they made selling the ratters to the upper classes.

The small terriers started adapting themselves to their new position in life right away. They bonded well with their mistresses and tolerated being carried around. But they still snuck around when they could get away to search for rats in the kitchen and storerooms.

Name Change

When a dog named Mozart won first place in the variety class at a show in Westmoreland, a reporter suggested that since the breed had been improved mainly in Yorkshire, the dog should become known as the Yorkshire terrier. The Kennel Club was formed in Great Britain in 1873, and included among the original forty breeds was the "broken-haired Scotch and Yorkshire terrier." The Yorkshire designation stuck.

The breed crossed the sea to the United States at about the same time. The first known litter was born on U.S. soil in 1872, and classes were offered at shows from 1878 on. However, these dogs were not regarded as anything special through the first decades of the twentieth century, and they nearly vanished from the states during the world wars. But ever since the 1950s, the breed's popularity has been on the rise. The Yorkshire terrier first made the AKC's top-ten list in 1995.

Changing Standards

The original classes were divided by weight—dogs that weighed less than five pounds belonged to one category, and those equal to or more than five pounds made up the other. But breeders soon made the dogs consistently smaller, and they quickly averaged between three and seven pounds. The standard was rewritten to make seven pounds the absolute maximum weight. Additionally, more details were added about coat and color, solidifying the Yorkshire terrier's physical look.

Coat Texture and Color

The Yorkshire terrier's coat has also changed over the years. At first, as the original name "broken-haired Scotch terrier" would indicate, the coat was harsher—only slightly silkier than other terriers. But that changed quickly. The Yorkie's coat was soon described as "long, straight, and silky." Waves or harshness in the coat were considered serious faults.

The color pattern standardized more gradually; old photos of early show winners depicted dogs with darker faces or little color differentiation. Early reports described coloring as blue-gray, tan, or black and tan. But by the end of the nineteenth century, a body color of silver blue and a head and legs of rich tan were being called for. Only a few years later, the recommendation for "blue" changed to a dark steel-blue.

Photograph by Cheryl A. Ertelt

▲ **An adorable Yorkie**

As is common with most changes in dog-breed standards, this color modification brought with it some undesirable characteristics. The selection for "blue" in a coat appears to be genetically linked with some detrimental skin and coat conditions, the most common being color dilution alopecia (described in Chapter 12). Still, people were insistent when it came to the color of the dog.

🐕 **Fact**

The correct way to refer to your Yorkie's coloring is "blue and tan." You may think black, gray, or silver and gold is closer to reality, but blue-and-tan is the approved color description.

Unwavering Personality

Through all these changes, the terrier temperament remained true. The Yorkshire terrier was and is a highly personable, spunky little canine that is impossible to ignore. Today, it is the most popular toy dog in Britain, and third in overall British popularity ranking. The typical Yorkshire terrier is a bright, lively individual, always interested in finding something to do. The Yorkie keeps a close eye on the family and on the world outside, often climbing to the top of a sofa to gain a window view. If you find that your Yorkie comments a bit too frequently on what's happening outside, you may need to block the view in one way or another to avoid complaints from neighbors. Still, this constant interest and tendency to alert humans to what's happening makes the Yorkie a fine watchdog.

Question?

What does "Ch." signify?
The title of conformation champion is designated with the abbreviation "Ch." To qualify for this title, a dog must earn a specified number of points from different judges. Some of the wins must be majors, which signifies that victory in that class was over a certain number of dogs.

Many Yorkies bond more strongly to one person, usually their main caretaker. To avoid having the dog decide to "protect" the caretaker from other family members, everyone in the house should take part in some facet of the Yorkie's day-to-day life. There are plenty of opportunities to go around, from feeding and grooming to exercising and training.

One advantage of the Yorkie is that almost anyone can handle exercising the dog. While many Yorkies may pull on the leash, they simply can't generate the same power as larger dogs and drag the walker down the street. The Yorkie can even get a large portion of exercise indoors, practicing different commands, playing fetch, and chasing toys on ropes.

Training should be an important part of your Yorkie's life. Bright and inquisitive, they appreciate learning new skills and showing them off for you. However, the terrier temperament quickly allows them to become bullies if they are allowed to think themselves in charge. Training should start early and be ongoing throughout life. Find a good basic-manners class to start, and then you can go on to teach your Yorkie whatever you like—any of the many dog sports, a variety of tricks, and helpful behaviors like carrying the leash and putting away toys.

Notable Individuals

A dog named Huddersfield Ben, bred in 1865, gets mention as the pillar of the breed. Mozart, the dog that spurred the name of the breed with his variety class win, was a son of Ben. Ben's handler, Mary Ann Foster, worked to popularize the breed. She traveled through England and Ireland, showing her dogs and letting people come to know the Yorkie's small size and big personality. She used many of Ben's offspring in her breeding, passing on his features to the breed. Her dog Bradford Hero was influential on early American breed representatives.

 Essential

The very first dogs mentioned by name in association with the Yorkshire terrier breed were Swift's Old Crab and Kershaw's Miss Kitty. Crab, the male, was a black-and-tan terrier, while Kitty, the female, was a Skye-type terrier that was steel blue in color. Huddersfield Ben traces back to these two.

Famous British Dogs

British dogs were imported to improve American lines. Those important in helping to solidify the breed in the States include Ch. Little Sir Model (instrumental in the foundation of the Wildweir kennel, mentioned in the next section), Ch. Progress of Progresso (winning bests in England, Canada, and the United States), and Daisy of Libertyhill (who produced multiple champions herself, and her daughters and granddaughters did the same).

Much later, another Brit, Osman Sameja, founded Ozmilion Kennel and gained fame for spectacular Yorkshire terriers. In the 1980s, Ch. Ozmilion Dedication earned the title Dog of the Year All Breeds in Great Britain, with a group win at Crufts (England's most famous dog show) and more Challenge Certificates won than any other Yorkie.

Famous American Dogs

In the late 1800s, Americans were infatuated with everything Victorian, and Yorkshire terriers became part of that culture. Selling adult dogs was more common then, and the adults drew the highest prices. While Yorkshire puppies could be bought for $10 to $25 at the time, an adult male could fetch up to $150—a very considerable sum in those days. These dogs were considered fashionable, and a wealthy member of the upper class could afford (and would willingly pay) the high prices.

 Fact

The only Yorkshire terrier to go Best in Show at the prestigious Westminster Kennel Club show was Ch. Cede Higgins. This dog won the discriminating eye of a highly respected judge named Anne Rogers Clark in 1978.

Butch and Daisy, both owned by Charles Andrews of Illinois, had AKC registration numbers, but Belle was the first to appear in the AKC studbook in 1883. A New Yorker, John Marriot, was the first American breeder of record. The Westminster Kennel Club show of 1878 included thirty-three purebred Yorkshire terriers. The first AKC Champions of Record were Ch. Toon's Royal and Ch. Bradford Henry, both tracing directly back to Huddersfield Ben.

In the early 1900s, Canadian and U.S. breeders interchanged dogs freely, keeping the breed vigorous. British imports also added to the gene pool until the advent of World War I. Through the war, Mrs. Harold Riddick was instrumental in maintaining the breed through a time of low popularity.

After both wars were over, Janet Bennett and Joan Gordon started their Wildweir kennel. Their British import, Ch. Little Sir Model, became the first Yorkie to win a U.S. Best in Show. A dog of their own breeding, Ch. Wildweir Pomp N' Circumstance, could at one time be found in the pedigrees of two-thirds of all Yorkshire terriers that had won Best in Show. Bennett and Gordon are widely credited with firmly establishing the American lines of the Yorkshire terrier.

Question?

What is a studbook?
A studbook is an official record of the pedigrees of purebred animals. Though this term is primarily used in the discussion of thoroughbred horses, other purebred animals, including dogs, are also registered in studbooks.

Beyond the Show Ring

Of course, Yorkshire terriers have plenty of presence outside the show ring as well. In fact, some have gained a fair amount of fame. Many people over the years have heard Joan Rivers talk about her

Yorkie, Spike. The breed is also popular with musicians, from Mel Torme to Stevie Nicks to Barbara Mandrell. Also, Jai Rodriguez of *Queer Eye for the Straight Guy* has appeared in fashion shows with his two Yorkies. The breed's small size makes these dogs convenient travel partners—they take up very little space on planes, buses, and trains, as well as in hotel rooms.

Mascot in Combat

In the Pacific during World War II, Corporal William Wynne bought a tiny, obviously purebred Yorkshire terrier that another soldier had found in a shell hole in New Guinea. Though Wynne took the dog to the nearest Japanese prisoner-of-war camp, no one claimed her. The dog didn't appear to understand any words in either English or Japanese, and her appearance in the jungle remained a mystery. Smoky, as Wynne named the dog, quickly gained fame and was ultimately voted "Mascot of the Pacific."

Smoky flew twelve air-sea rescue missions and survived 150 air raids. She shared C-rations and Spam with the soldiers and bathed in Wynne's helmet. The Twenty-Sixth Photo Reconnaissance Squadron of the Air Force constructed a special parachute for her, and she jumped from the training tower. She even helped lay a telegraph wire by crawling through a seventy-foot-long pipe towing a guide line.

Wynne and Smoky toured all over the world, entertaining wounded soldiers at army and navy hospitals during and after the war. Smoky jumped through hoops, walked a tightrope, and performed other tricks.

Alert!

It is completely possible for Yorkshire terriers to get along with other canines in the home, as well as cats, rabbits, and other family pets. However, this does require a substantial amount of training and adjustment time. A large dog or cat could intimidate a small Yorkie, so you'll need to give the pets time to get used to each other.

The White House

The only Yorkshire terrier known to have occupied the White House, Pasha, resided there during the Nixon administration. While often referred to as the pet of Richard and Pat Nixon, Pasha actually belonged to their daughter Tricia. Pasha had canine company from Vicki, a miniature poodle, and King Timahoe, an Irish setter.

You can find photos of Pasha and the other dogs at the White House on the Internet at *www.archives.gov/Nixon*. They're pictured on the lawn in front of the White House, being walked by the president at Camp David, and in front of a White House fireplace at Christmas.

Current Conditions

While the Yorkshire terrier breed remains relatively healthy, it does face some genetic problems (as described in Chapter 12). Potential Yorkie owners should be familiar with these conditions. Some can crop up unexpectedly, but breeding lines that are clear of defects increase the chances of healthy pups. Proper nutrition and good choice of equipment can also hinder certain predispositions.

 Fact

Not only has the Yorkshire terrier become highly popular among the general public, it's also been the preferred pet of baseball players Joe Garagiola and Edgar Martinez, actors George Hamilton and Richard Burton, and famous television personality Johnny Carson.

Temperament has become an issue among many breeds, both large and small, and Yorkies are no exception. Follow the advice in Chapters 3 and 4 when choosing a breeder and an individual dog. Yorkies should be feisty, but never snappish. If not made a full member of the household, regularly interacting with all members, Yorkies have a tendency to choose one person as their own and may attempt to bully other humans. A Yorkie that growls at someone and is rewarded by having that person back off can quickly become a tyrant. You need to keep control of your feisty little dog but should never use physical punishment. Positive reinforcement has proven much more effective time and time again.

As Yorkies have become progressively smaller—individuals weighing only two or three pounds are common—dental problems have increased, and the ability to naturally whelp (give birth) has decreased. While you may be more attracted to the smallest individuals, these are somewhat more likely to experience health problems. Dogs of five or six pounds are preferable. You will appreciate a slightly larger dog that lives to a ripe old age much more than one that can fit in your purse but will pass away early.

CHAPTER 2

What to Expect from a Yorkie

TOY BREEDS ARE STILL BONA FIDE DOGS, and in the case of Yorkies, they're still terriers as well. Don't expect your Yorkie to be a silent decoration in your home or wear little clothes to match your outfits—this dog's size does not dictate her attitude. Yorkies may look like fussy little lapdogs, but even an encounter with a Doberman or Labrador may not convince them of their true stature. However, Yorkies can be well-mannered family pets and retain their inquisitive personalities at the same time.

Defining Characteristics

When you look at a Yorkshire terrier, you should see a small, compact dog covered in a silky coat of long, straight hair. The ears should stand up straight and not be rounded at the tips. The eyes should be attractive and not seem to pop out of the head. Weight should be less than seven pounds. No height is specified, but approximately seven inches is a good average. Size and coat are the two hallmarks of the breed.

The only other breed with which you might confuse a Yorkie is the silky terrier. Though similar in coloring and size, the silky displays far less coat than the Yorkie—the silky's coat never reaches the floor. There are other differences as well, but this is the obvious one.

The All-Important Coat

Everything about the coat is crucial—texture, length, straightness, and color. The main part of the body is a rich, dark steel-blue, and the markings on the head and legs are a deep golden tan. The hair on the head is often pulled up into a topknot or two side knots. For show, only the feet and ears are generally trimmed. Though the breed is heavily coated, it is not a major shedder. To keep it in order, however, the coat should be groomed daily.

Essential

Yorkshire terriers bred and trained for sport or show are generally the only dogs that display the full floor-sweeping coat. Pet dogs are often trimmed every so often so that the hair does not become dirty, matted, or tangled. If a Yorkie's long coat is not meticulously maintained, it can become a health and/or safety hazard for the dog.

When you see Yorkshire terriers outside the show ring, you may see anything from a dog cut down like a schnauzer, to a dog with a moderate-length coat, to a floor-sweeping full show coat. If you are not planning to show your dog, the full glory of the coat becomes less important. You can accept a dog with a slight wave to the hair (a fault in the show ring) or some tan hairs mixed into the black (another fault). Neither of these imperfections will keep a Yorkie from looking or behaving as a member of the breed should—except under the sharp eye of a judge.

The Head

The top of the head should be flat rather than rounded. There is a definite drop from the head to the muzzle, and the eyes are not set too close together in this space. The eye shape isn't specified, but most appear round. The muzzle is fairly square, and the nose is black. Both the eyes and the eye rims are dark. The nose and eyes contrast nicely with the golden tan of the head.

The standard allows for either a level bite (with the bottom edge of the top teeth meeting the upper edge of the bottom teeth) or a scissors bite (meaning the front teeth of the lower jaw align just behind the front teeth of the upper jaw when the mouth is closed). A scissors bite is actually preferable because it tends to help keep teeth a little cleaner.

The ears will not look like Yorkie ears unless they're trimmed. For a Yorkie with untrimmed ears, the weight of the hair could drag the ear tips down into a lop position. For the correct look, the top third should be trimmed so the ears can stand upright. If you were to extend the lines formed by the inside edges of the ears, they should meet in a V approximately at the muzzle. Hair hangs plentifully from the ears, both sides of the head, and the chin.

The Body and Tail

Though the standard describes the body as "very compact" and the back as "rather short," most Yorkies are rectangular rather than square. The measure from shoulders to tail is slightly longer than the measure from floor to tops of shoulders. The top of the dog should be very straight, neither dipping nor rising. Looking at a Yorkie, you should get the impression of a strong, sturdy build. The coat should shine as well.

Alert!

Don't expect to see the adult coloring of steel-blue and tan when you go to look at puppies. Puppies are born black and tan, and their coats continue changing for up to two years before they reach the final adult coloring. For this reason, many people who plan to show their dogs prefer to buy adults instead of puppies. This way they already know how the dog's coat will look.

The tail is docked while puppies are very young. Generally a couple of inches are left. The tail can be held anywhere from pointing straight up to just above the line of the body. The hair on the tail is darker and falls to the floor. If you keep your dog in full coat, you must be careful to keep this tail hair clean.

The Legs and Feet

With a dog in full coat, you won't see the legs and feet unless you really look for them. As with many of the terriers, the front legs should be straight and swing freely from the shoulder. The back legs, viewed from the side, should reach back behind the body and then angle so that the lower leg is perpendicular to the floor. Viewed from behind, the back legs should be straight.

The feet are round and compact, but they are covered with and surrounded by hair. Trim the hair around the feet, on the bottoms, and between the pads to avoid matting.

Attitude

Though the breed standard doesn't mention temperament, show dogs are expected to "sparkle." This word is used often with regard to show dogs. The Yorkshire terrier should carry herself with self-assurance and attitude. However, too much attitude can be a big turn-off for a judge. If a dog tries to assert authority over her handler, the judge, or another show dog, this will reveal that the dog is neither well trained nor well mannered. These displays could result in a penalty or even disqualification, depending upon the offense.

The Yorkshire Terrier Official Standard

The official breed standard is written to describe the ideal dog. In the case of the Yorkshire terrier, it describes physical qualities only. The standard has not changed since 1966, so one would expect dogs to be meeting it easily by now. However, the details of coat are hard to obtain, and puppies can still grow to be oversized. And even though no mention of temperament is made in the breed standard, you should always make sure that any breeder you are considering takes temperament into account. A spectacularly beautiful dog that is irritable and snappish will not be a joy to live with. Also, though standards don't customarily mention health, you certainly want your Yorkie to enjoy good health and a long life.

Where Standards Come From

A breed's parent club writes the standard for the breed; in this case, it was written by the Yorkshire Terrier Club of America. The American Kennel Club does not play a part in writing the standard. It publishes the standard it receives from the breed club.

The breeders and other devotees of the breed can from time to time bring up points they feel need some change or clarification. However, it's difficult to amend a standard, as everyone might not agree on the fine points. Standards do not change frequently; the Yorkshire terrier standard was last amended in 1966.

Breed Standard

General Appearance

That of a long-haired toy terrier whose blue-and-tan coat is parted on the face and from the base of the skull to the end of the tail and hangs evenly and quite straight down each side of the body. The body is neat, compact, and well proportioned. The dog's high head carriage and confident manner should give the appearance of vigor and self-importance.

Head

Small and rather flat on top, the skull not too prominent or round, the muzzle not too long, with the bite neither under-shot nor overshot and teeth sound. Either scissors bite or level bite is acceptable. The nose is black. Eyes are medium in size and not too prominent; dark in color and sparkling with a sharp, intelligent expression. Eye rims are dark. Ears are small, V-shaped, carried erect and set not too far apart.

Body

Well proportioned and very compact. The back is rather short, the back line level, with height at the shoulder the same as at the rump.

Legs and Feet

Forelegs should be straight, elbows neither in nor out. Hind legs straight when viewed from behind, but stifles are moderately bent when viewed from the sides. Feet are round with black toenails. Dewclaws, if any, are generally removed from the hind legs. Dewclaws on the forelegs may be removed.

Tail

Docked to a medium length and carried slightly higher than the level of the back.

Coat

Quality, texture, and quantity of coat are of prime impor-tance. Hair is glossy, fine, and silky in texture. Coat on the body is moderately long and perfectly straight (not wavy). It may be trimmed to floor length to give ease of movement and a neater appearance, if desired. The fall on the head is long, tied with one bow in center of head or parted in the middle and tied with two bows. Hair muzzles is very long. Hair should be trimmed short on tips of ears and may be trimmed on feet to give them a neat appearance.

Colors

Puppies are born black and tan and are normally darker in body color, showing an intermingling of black hair in the tan until they are matured. Color of hair on body and richness of tan on head and legs are of prime importance in adult dogs, to which the following color requirements apply:

Blue

Is a dark steel-blue, not a silver-blue and not mingled with fawn, bronzy, or black hairs.

Tan

All tan hair is darker at the roots than in the middle, shading to still lighter tan at the tips. There should be no sooty or black hair intermingled with any of the tan.

Color on Body

The blue extends over the body from back of neck to root of tail. Hair on tail is a darker blue, especially at end of tail.

Headfall

A rich golden tan, deeper in color at sides of head, at ear roots and on the muzzle, with ears a deep rich tan. Tan color should not extend down on back of neck.

Chest and Legs

A bright, rich tan, not extending above the elbow on the forelegs nor above the stifle on the hind legs.

Weight

Must not exceed seven pounds.

Approved April 12, 1966.

Terrier Temperament

Quite frankly, Yorkies are pretty full of themselves. They see no disadvantage in their small size and will stand up to far larger animals in most situations. After all, the rats they once hunted were not a lot smaller than the Yorkies themselves. This is not to say that Yorkies can't get along with others—they can. However, a certain amount of socialization and training is required.

Interaction with Others

If well socialized, Yorkies can get along with any other animals you have in the home. They have been known to become close friends with cats, though this depends on the cat perhaps more than the dog. Yorkies can be friendly with any other dogs, but they might be accidentally injured if roughhousing with larger individuals.

Yorkies make great pets for people living alone because they are such constant companions. It's difficult to be lonely with a Yorkie in the house! Yorkies can do equally well in larger households, but every member must make an effort to befriend the dog or else risk being treated as an outsider.

Yorkies make excellent watchdogs, as they're eager to bark at any item of note. Of course, you may not agree with what the dog considers noteworthy. But with some training, the Yorkie can fulfill the main function of a watchdog—alerting you to intruders—better than many larger breeds. The downside of this skill is that they tend to bond to one person, and may even bark at other family members. Again, training can help curb these annoying tendencies.

Alert!

A Yorkshire terrier is not a good choice for families with young children. These dogs do not stand for indignities, such as having ears pulled, and they can be injured easily by rough play. Yorkies make better pets for single adults, families with school-age children, and older people.

If you find that your Yorkie is overstimulated by action going on outside your home, you may have to block off access to windows. After all, you can't have the dog barking every time a neighbor walks by. In the car, Yorkies can be kept a bit calmer by riding in a crate. This will limit their view of the world passing by and lessen the urge to overreact.

Busybodies

The Yorkshire terrier's activity level tends to be high for the dog's size. Because they have to take many steps to go a short distance, they don't require miles of walking or running as a larger active dog would. But you will still find them by your side through your daily activities. They want to be part of the action. If you are looking for a dog that will lie quietly on a mat in a corner, look elsewhere—the Yorkshire terrier is not the breed for you.

You can get a variety of toys to keep a Yorkie occupied. They like to shake and "kill," so toys they can pick up and shake will be favored. Some toys are made with tails that flap wildly and make the game more exciting. Yorkies are also good candidates for the various food puzzle toys. The Buster Cube comes in a small size for toy dogs and is a particularly good choice because it holds kibble rather than treats that have more calories or a higher fat content. This toy consists of a maze of tunnels inside a cube. As the dog knocks the cube around, the food works its way through the maze and gets deposited piece by piece.

Pet Dog Versus Show Dog

The most obvious difference you're likely to see between dogs destined for the show ring and those that will become family pets is in their coats. After all, half the breed standard is devoted to details about the Yorkie's coat. Since this feature is largely out of the dog's (and trainer's) control, a future as a show dog or a pet dog is often predetermined from birth. Imperfections in a dog's coat may bar him from the show ring, but they won't keep him from becoming a lovable member of the family.

⌖ Essential

Dogs designated for pet homes should still be fairly temperamentally and physically sound. Being slightly oversized or having a wave to the coat doesn't impact a Yorkie's health. But having a bad bite or being snappish around people can be seriously detrimental.

A Perfect Pet

If all you're looking for is a sweet little dog to share your life, it won't matter if the dog you choose has technically imperfect coloring or some waves in her hair. These details are only of importance in the show ring; in your house, she will still be a beautiful and fun little pet. These dogs can offer all the love and companionship of any show dog—they just shouldn't be bred. (For information on spaying and neutering, see Chapter 10.) Details that matter only in the show ring include the following:

- Coat not reaching the floor
- Waves in the coat
- Tan hair on the back of the neck
- Tan hairs mixed into black areas or vice versa
- Oversized ears
- Rounded ears
- Weight exceeding seven pounds, even if dog is not considered fat

Other show faults, such as crooked legs, a tilting topline, or an undershot bite, could indicate health problems and should be avoided in pets as well as in show specimens.

Even if you're not looking to show your dog, you should still expect health clearances and good temperament. In fact, temperament is even more important in a Yorkie intended to spend all her time as a family member rather than a competitor. "Pet home" Yorkies may be excellent physical specimens but just lack the constant self-assured, in-your-face attitude championed in the show ring.

For Show

If you think you want a show dog, you must consider all the implications—especially if you've never shown dogs before. Your Yorkie will have to be kept in full show coat, which will reach the floor and tangle easily. Your breeder may expect you to attend a certain number of shows and may select the shows she wants you to enter. You will spend many weekends traveling to show sites rather than tending your yard, fishing, golfing, or pursuing other leisure activities. There are entry fees, hotel bills, restaurant meal prices, gas prices, and grooming fees (unless you plan on doing your own) to consider. While dog showing is a fine hobby that will provide you with a whole new circle of friends, you do have to consider the time and money involved.

To be successful in the show ring, you have to spend substantial time (if you're doing it yourself) or money (if you're hiring a professional) to keep the dog's coat in show condition. Your dog will have to be intact (not spayed or neutered), so you'll be dealing with twice-annual heats for females and temperament changes related to surging hormones in both males and females. You will be competing against many dogs from established kennels, often shown by professional handlers. Even if you're a first-time owner, you still have a chance of raising a champion dog; however, your losses will likely outnumber your wins. You must be prepared for this. Though you'll see a champion in your dog, the judge may see too little coat and ears set too far apart. You must learn to take losses in stride and only show your dog while it remains fun and pleasurable for *both* of you.

Essential

Don't ever punish your dog in any way for a show loss. A punishment given during a show will reflect badly on you as a handler, and it will also teach your dog to fear or dislike the show ring. Shows should offer your Yorkie an opportunity to shine and have fun, and they're meant to be fun for you as well.

Another thing to consider when deciding whether or not to show your dog is temperament. While all Yorkies are bright, lively, inquisitive dogs, success in the show ring requires an outgoing attitude that reaches beyond the average personality. If your dog has this type of attitude, great! This could help you win shows. However, indulging the dog's attitude too much could leave you with a controlling little canine that doesn't know his place. Lots of careful training will teach the dog when and where it is appropriate to assert himself.

Alert!

Do not succumb to ads for "teacup" or "dollface" Yorkies. These diminutive individuals, some weighing only two or three pounds, will be more susceptible to chills, falls, and side effects from anesthesia (often needed for teeth cleaning). They are also even more likely to harbor genetic defects. Responsible breeders consider females of less than five pounds unsuitable for breeding.

Lifespan

Small and active, Yorkshire terriers commonly live to fourteen years of age and are often in good health for nearly all that time. However, their small size can make them more susceptible to injury—they are often tripped over, knocked down, and even forgotten. Hereditary illnesses (described in Chapter 12) can also shorten their lifespan or bring large veterinary bills.

Photograph by Cheryl A. Ertelt

▲ **This dog is a perfect model for the Yorkshire terrier breed standard.**

Yorkies do age well, and they generally avoid many of the musculoskeletal disorders common among some larger breeds. They can stay spry and active far into old age, slowing down only a little toward the end of their lives. They are most likely to suffer dental problems in their later years and may require changes in their diet to keep them eating well.

As with most dogs (and humans, for that matter), Yorkies can become hard of hearing as they age. You need to be aware of this, as they won't be as quick to scuttle out of your way as you approach. The loss of hearing can also cause irritability or paranoia, as they will feel as though they are being snuck up on. As long as you understand the problem, you can make certain changes to accommodate your aging Yorkie. For instance, make a little more noise when you approach him, try to approach him only when he's facing you, and generally be more mindful of where you step.

 **fact**

> There are several signs that mean your dog is suffering certain aspects of old age. If the dog starts bumping into table legs or walls or becomes hesitant about moving freely around the house, she may be going blind. If your dog does not respond when called or does not react as excitedly to certain stimuli as she used to, she may be going deaf. There isn't much you can do for her in these cases except be understanding, give her plenty of space and time to move around, and comfort her when she becomes frightened.

Never Ignore a Yorkie

If you want a dog that will snooze in front of the fire while you go about your household activities, don't choose a Yorkie. This dog will be right there with you, constantly underfoot, whether you're making dinner, doing laundry, or weeding the flowerbeds. Yorkies truly want to be part of every facet of your life.

If you are a busy person with little time to spare, a Yorkshire terrier may demand too much of you. These dogs want your attention, and if you won't give it to them voluntarily, they'll force you to pay attention by misbehaving. You might be better off choosing a more independent breed if you have a busy lifestyle. On the other hand, if you crave companionship, the Yorkshire terrier could be your ideal dog. They'll play, cuddle, and exercise with you as much as you could want.

Essential

Often, a Yorkie goes to a "pet home" because she has exceeded the breed standard weight of seven pounds. While weight is a concern for show dogs, it doesn't matter so much if your dog is just a pet. As long as the individual is healthy and not overweight for her height, exceeding seven pounds is fine. In fact, larger Yorkies tend to be sturdier than the very petite specimens.

Though the Yorkie is still decidedly terrier in attitude, Yorkies are more playful than the bigger terriers. Their small size allows them to receive their daily exercise even in the confines of an apartment, making them adaptable to almost any indoor living conditions. They are not suitable for outdoor living, however, both because they demand to be where their family is and because they have no thick undercoat to keep them warm in cold weather.

Where to Find Your Yorkshire Terrier

YOU'VE NOW THOUGHT ABOUT YOUR LIFESTYLE and daily routine and have come to the conclusion that a Yorkie would fit right in. You'll have the time for daily brushing, and if you have children, they're old enough and responsible enough to handle such a small dog carefully. Everyone in the household is in agreement with the idea of a fuzzy new addition to the family. So where do you find your ideal dog?

Organizing Your Search

When you consider all the places you might find a Yorkie—breeders, rescue organizations, shelters, humane societies, and pet shops—some are definitely better options than others. This chapter will teach you where to look and how to differentiate between the great and not-so-good potential sources. You also need to know your own plans for your dog. Do you want a family pet or hope to get involved in the world of dog showing?

For Home

If you want your Yorkie to simply be a companion, you can still consult a show breeder, but you'll be looking for a pet quality dog. You can also consider rescue groups and humane organizations because it doesn't matter if you have your dog's registration papers. It is only important that the dog be healthy, amicable, and a seemingly good match for your family. You won't be able to get health guarantees from sources other than a breeder, but these guarantees aren't actually assurances of good health. These are only promises of some sort of compensation if the dog turns out to have certain problems.

For Show

If you want to compete in the show ring with your Yorkshire terrier, then you'll definitely want to seek out a show breeder. These professionals know the breed standard inside and out and have been working to improve the breed, and their particular line, for years. If you have never shown a dog before, you may have to work to convince the breeder to sell you a show prospect.

Alert!

Yorkshire terriers generally have only one or two puppies per litter, and good breeders often have long waiting lists of people interested in their dogs. Therefore, it may take some time to find a breeder with puppies available. However, don't let this frustrate you. A healthy puppy from a reputable breeder is well worth the wait.

If you have little or no experience showing dogs, you should do all you can to learn more. Attend dog shows in your area. Buy a show catalog and find the Yorkshire terriers. Look for the time and the ring where they'll be shown. Go and watch, and talk to handlers as they come out of the ring. Don't be surprised if they can't talk just then—they may have another dog to show in another class. If their dog won, they'll go back in the ring for group judging and may need time to prepare. Just introduce yourself, and if they're busy at the moment, ask to talk to them later. Most dog owners and handlers travel in RVs or vans; they may ask that you meet them at their vehicle somewhere on the show grounds at a later time.

You can also watch the bigger dog shows on television to learn more about the process. At these shows, they will usually announce the dog's name, and the name will usually include the kennel name. You can search for these kennels on the Yorkshire Terrier Club of America Web site (at ✑*www.ytca.org*). If the kennel is geographically distant from you, the breeder may be hesitant to sell you a dog without meeting you in person, or he may question you extensively before deciding. Even if one of these breeders is unable to sell you a dog, he may still be glad to recommend a good breeder closer to your area.

Show Breeders

Also known as hobby breeders, or reputable breeders, these people are in Yorkshire terriers because they adore the breed. These professionals are great sources for Yorkshire terriers, but they don't let their dogs go to just anyone. Expect to be questioned extensively before you take home a dog. Some questions you might encounter include:

- Why do you want a Yorkshire terrier?
- Where will your Yorkshire terrier live?
- Do you plan to do your own grooming?
- Have you owned small dogs before?
- Do you have a secure, fenced-in yard?
- Is someone home during the day?

The breeder will be looking for someone who has the time and interest to deal with a Yorkshire terrier and who exhibits a responsible attitude toward taking on the breed. She will want to be sure you understand what you are getting yourself into—that you are prepared for the ups and downs of owning a Yorkie. Depending on the breeder, she may insist someone be home during the day to spend time with the dog.

Questions You Should Ask

Though the breeder will be doing the majority of the questioning, you should also have questions of your own to ask her. You want your breeder to be working for the betterment of the breed and to have an intimate knowledge of the breed. Responsible breeders should be eager to answer your questions and provide information. Some of your questions for the breeder might include:

- How long have you been involved with Yorkshire terriers?
- What got you interested in the breed?
- What are the goals of your breeding program?
- What breed organizations are you a member of?
- What sports do you compete in with your dogs?
- What titles have your dogs earned?
- May I see health certificates for the puppy's parents and grandparents?
- May I meet the puppy's parents? (Note that the mother should be on the premises, but the father may not be.)
- Do you provide health guarantees?

Photograph by Cheryl A. Ertelt

▲ If you're looking for a puppy, there are many options available.

Why Ask Questions?

It is important that you ask potential breeders questions to discover their experience and goals in breeding Yorkshire terriers. If a breeder is new to the breed, he should be showing dogs—not breeding them—while he learns the pluses and minuses of the various breeding lines. You want a breeder who has spent some time learning about the breed and who is in the business to try to make improvements. Anyone breeding Yorkshire terriers should have definite goals in mind, such as reducing the incidence of patellar luxation, improving the bite, or solidifying good temperament.

Membership in breed organizations both shows a measure of dedication and provides a venue for a breeder to converse with other breeders. Competition in the show ring is a given for serious breeders, but some also compete in one or more of the many performance sports to demonstrate their dogs' versatility and soundness. More competition is preferable to less. Titles earned on close relatives of the puppies is a good indication of the pups' physical and mental proclivities.

Essential

AKC papers offer no guarantee of good health or good temperament. These documents simply indicate that a male and a female of the same breed, both registered with the AKC, have been mated to produce the litter. Beware of breeders who try to pass these documents off as more than they are.

If possible, you should try to see both parents of the puppy, or at least the mother. Other relatives have less influence on the puppies; however, the more health information you can get, the better. Fewer genetic problems in the puppy's line mean increased chances of a healthy puppy. And always look for a health guarantee that doesn't require you to return your pup;

breeders know this is unlikely to happen once you've bonded with the puppy.

A Mentor

Your breeder will primarily be your source for your new dog, but this person can also serve as a mentor throughout the life of your Yorkie. A good breeder will be happy to answer questions as they arise, teach you about the process of showing your dog (if you choose that route), and generally be a source of support as you endure the ups and downs of being a Yorkie owner. It may be difficult to find such a reputable and caring breeder, but they do exist!

If a breeder simply wants to sell you a puppy and then cut ties, don't buy a dog from this person. Responsible breeders will be interested to know how their pups are doing in their new homes. You shouldn't abuse this person by calling him every time you have a minor mishap, but this person should make himself available to you when you have big problems. If you are purchasing a pup for show, the breeder should be even more involved with your progress. In fact, you may be offered a show pup *only* under a co-ownership agreement, in which the breeder retains partial ownership of the pup and some say in where and how often you show the dog. This agreement could also limit your ability to breed the dog. While this is a reasonable step for the breeder to take in entrusting a show-quality pup to someone new to the breed, you should read the agreement carefully to be sure it is something you can live with.

Backyard Breeders

Some people breed popular dogs solely in order to make money. Some dog owners think their dogs are so wonderful that they should perpetuate them. Others want their children to see the miracle of birth. And some have accidental litters. None of these instances constitute responsible breeding. Those who sell puppies to pet shops without asking any questions, who don't do health clearances or show their dogs, and who haven't studied the good and bad points of the breed are backyard breeders. Getting a mentally and physically sound pup from these people is simply a matter of chance—with questionable odds.

Identifying a Backyard Breeder

Yorkies advertised in the classified section are almost certainly coming from one sort of backyard breeder or another. Reputable breeders generally have homes for their puppies before they're even whelped, and they don't advertise in the want ads. Another term you might see in the newspaper is "stud dog." People seeking stud dogs are owners of female dogs that have come into heat, and they're looking to breed them with any male that's available. These people do not have the dog's best interests at heart, and they're giving no thought to the consequences for the offspring. Beware of these people.

Strategy

Once you've set eyes on a puppy, it's nearly impossible to turn away; this is precisely the thing a disreputable breeder will rely on to pass off his puppies. Therefore, one good strategy is to first interview a breeder over the phone. This way, a fuzzy little face won't sway you to make a decision that will cause you heartache in the long run. Ask the breeder your list of questions, and pay attention to what he asks you in return. If the breeder asks you an equal number of questions, and if you are satisfied with the answers to your questions, then arrange to meet the breeder's dogs.

Alert!

Be extremely skeptical of any breeder who seems overly eager for you to take one of her puppies. If a breeder doesn't seem to care about where her pup is going and is only concerned that the pups be taken off her hands, this isn't the breeder for you.

Rescue Organizations

Most purebred dogs have their own rescue organizations these days, and Yorkshire terriers are no exception. Dogs may become rescue animals when puppy mills are shut down, when owners die, when kennel owners face sudden catastrophic circumstances, or when they're taken out of animal shelters by rescue groups.

 **Fact**

The Yorkshire Terrier Club of America has a rescue coordinator who may be able to put you in touch with a rescue in your area. Most urban areas also have rescue groups, For example, in Washington, the Seattle Purebred Dog Rescue has local rescue coordinators for most of the AKC-recognized breeds.

Unfortunately, these pups or adult dogs come from circumstances with significantly fewer assurances than a show kennel. A rescue dog may have a higher chance of developing genetic disease or another problem due to irresponsible breeding. However, if the dog is already an adult, many of the worst diseases and conditions will already have shown themselves. A rescue dog can be a more challenging pet, but these animals are often the most in need of secure and loving homes.

Drawbacks

One potential disadvantage of a rescue is that you will rarely have any background on the dog. There will likely be no health guarantees and no chance to meet the parents or interview the breeder. Some dogs in rescue end up there due to behavior problems, and these may not be immediately apparent. In toy breeds, such as the Yorkie, housetraining issues may be one of these problems.

Depending on the quality of the rescue organization, your rescue Yorkie will almost certainly be spayed or neutered, vaccinated, checked for parasites both inside and out, and microchipped before being released to a new home. All of these services are figured into the adoption fee.

For puppy seekers, another downside to the rescue is that you're not likely to find Yorkie puppies there. Most dogs in rescue are adolescents or older. There's absolutely nothing wrong with having an older dog as a pet, but many people have their hearts set on a puppy. However, if the age of your new dog doesn't really matter to you, consider getting a rescue dog instead of a puppy. Puppies have their adorable looks to ensure that they get homes. Older rescue dogs can make perfectly wonderful pets, and they need good homes just as much.

Positives

Rescue groups will do their best to match dogs with appropriate owners. Many groups keep dogs in foster care (living with individual families) for a certain period of time in order to learn about their temperaments. Once their personalities are known, it is easier to then place them in homes and advise the new owners of what to expect.

Question?

Where else can you look for a Yorkie in rescue?
Both rescue groups and animal shelters/humane societies may post their dogs at *www.petfinder.com*. You can search for dogs on this Web site by breed, geographic area, or a number of other parameters.

Rescue groups will be nearly as particular as the best breeders in placing their dogs. They want a lifetime placement, not an owner who is going to reject the dog and force him back into rescue status again. Be prepared to answer plenty of questions. Different groups may require fenced yards, frown on owners of pickup trucks (for fear the dogs will be relegated to riding in the bed), or insist on someone being home with the dog during the day. They will ask for (and check) references, and some may even insist on a home visit before giving you the dog. They will also take the dog back if some unforeseen problem arises.

Animal Shelters and Humane Societies

The first thing you should know is that there is no national organization of animal shelters. The Humane Society of the United States is a stand-alone nonprofit organization not affiliated in any way with humane societies around the country. The specific groups known as SPCAs (Society for the Prevention of Cruelty to Animals) are individual organizations, each serving their own locales.

 **fact**

There are two distinct kinds of shelters. Municipal shelters, or what used to be called the pound, serve as law enforcement for animal issues and jails for strays or dogs that have committed canine crimes, such as biting someone. Privately funded animal shelters, often proclaiming themselves as no-kill facilities, can choose the animals they take and hold them as long as necessary.

Drawbacks

As with rescue dogs, you are unlikely to know any history of shelter dogs. Expertise among shelter staff can vary even more widely than in rescue groups; some shelters will be little more than warehouses for unfortunate canines, while others will conduct health checks, provide training, and be quite strict about who can adopt their dogs.

The odds of finding a Yorkshire terrier in a shelter are not particularly good. Stray Yorkies often meet their deaths before finding their way to a shelter, and the few who do arrive in shelters are invariably adopted quickly. While shelters may be a good heart-warming choice for finding larger-breed dogs or lovable mutts, they aren't very helpful in your quest for a purebred Yorkie.

Positives

The most obvious plus side to adopting a Yorkie from one of these sources is that you will likely be saving the dog's life. Dogs left in shelters for too long are often euthanized, and in a place with so many dogs from so many different places, canine diseases are bound to spread. In general, Yorkshire terriers do not do well in boarding kennels, and they do even less well in chaotic shelters. If you adopt a Yorkie from a shelter, you will be performing an enormous act of kindness. In fact, many dogs will even exhibit a level of gratefulness to an adoptive owner—as though they recognize the tremendous luck they've had. Adopted adult dogs are often the most loyal and devoted of all pets.

Another small benefit to adopting a dog as opposed to buying one from a breeder is that a dog from a shelter will not cost as much as a purebred puppy. If you're not looking to show your Yorkie, and you're interested in giving a rescue adult a much deserved home, a dog from a shelter will give you just as much (if not more) love and loyalty for a much more reasonable price.

Pet Shops

Unfortunately, the majority of toy breeds sold in pet shops likely come from puppy mill operations, which are, in effect, mass canine-production machines. The conditions in these places are not always sanitary for the dogs. Puppies are generally separated from their mothers at too early an age, and canine diseases often run rampant where lots of dogs are kept. Breed rescues regularly try to keep their breeds out of the hands of puppy mill operators, but it's frequently a losing battle.

 **Question?**

How much should you expect to pay for a Yorkshire terrier?
The price can vary depending on whether you're looking at a pet-quality or show-quality individual, and on what part of the country you live in. However, whether you get your dog from a show kennel, a backyard breeder, or a pet shop, the price will likely run between $550 and $1,600.

Drawbacks

Dogs in puppy mills are bred for profit, not for the betterment of the breed. Most of the dogs used for breeding live out their lives in small cages, and their puppies do not receive the early socialization every pup needs to thrive. The pups are often taken from their mothers quite young (the tinier the puppies, the quicker they sell), and this shortens their socialization time even further. These pups can be extremely difficult to housetrain, as they have been forced to soil their living quarters by being kept in small cages.

Some of the dogs in pet shops also come from local backyard breeders. Because many of these individuals house more than one breed, and they are less than conscientious about breeding their dogs, pups sold as purebred Yorkies may in fact be crosses between Yorkies and some other toy dog breed. Even though you'll be paying exorbitant pet-shop prices, you might be bringing home a mixed-breed pup with no health guarantees.

Positives

The only time you should consider buying a puppy or adult dog at a pet shop is when the store hosts adoption events for rescue groups or local shelters. You still won't be able to obtain health guarantees or a solid background on the dog, but at least you'll be contributing to an effort to help dogs in need instead of boosting a pet shop's (and perhaps a puppy mill's) profits.

Important Information

Before you go out in search of your ideal Yorkie, you should familiarize yourself with the common genetic health problems of the breed (described in Chapter 12). Armed with this knowledge, you can discuss with the breeder how prevalent these problems are in her dogs. Don't believe a breeder who says that her pups never experience genetic problems—these conditions are prevalent enough that they will show up in any breeder's program from time to time, and you want a breeder who will be honest with you. But don't let the incidence of genetic problems scare you away from the breed, either. All breeds, and even mixed breeds, have their own set of genetic health conditions. If the Yorkie is your dream dog, there's no reason to let genetic problems dissuade you.

 Essential

If the prevalence of certain genetic problems among Yorkshire terriers is unsettling for you, do some research about the problems that affect other breeds. Yorkies are not alone; nearly every other pure-bred dog suffers from certain maladies, from hip dysplasia to heart disease. The best things you can do to avoid these problems is to get your dog from a reputable source and obtain the health history of the dog's parents and grandparents.

Finally, many breeders will insist that Yorkie puppies don't leave home until they're twelve weeks old. Friends or neighbors may tell you that this is too old—that the pup won't bond with you, or you can't shape her personality. Don't listen to them. You'll have plenty of time to bond and teach your pup good social manners with humans, but her mother and littermates can start her off right by teaching good dog-to-dog manners. A responsible breeder will also be seeing to socialization. So learn as much as you can about the breed, find a responsible source for your dog, and give your new pet—whether a purebred puppy or a rescue adult—all the love and attention he deserves.

CHAPTER 4

How to Choose Your Yorkie

ONCE YOU DECIDE a Yorkshire terrier is the dog for you, you still have a lot of decisions to make. Do you have your heart set on a puppy, or would an older dog better fit your lifestyle? Are you interested in showing, or is a pet-quality individual all you need? Do you have a strong preference as far as gender? Are there other pets already in your household? What do you expect from your Yorkie? These are only some of the questions you must address *before* bringing a new Yorkie into your home.

Know What You Want Before You Look

Once you're sitting on the floor with a litter of puppies climbing all over you, it will be nearly impossible to make a rational decision. If you haven't thought about all the important implications of getting a new puppy by this time, you probably never will. You'll end up choosing the one sucking on your fingers or the one with the brightest eyes instead of focusing on how well the breeder answers your questions or how clean the premises are. Before you even go to look at possible dogs, you should have your parameters firmly in mind or, better yet, written down. Seeing these guidelines in writing may help you stick to your plans and resist the temptation of an adorable little face.

For Show

If you want to show your dog but don't have experience in the show ring, make sure you do your research. Life with a show dog is completely different from life with a family pet. All Yorkies should have the basic terrier attitude, but those bred for the show ring generally have a bit more flash and fire. They have to dazzle judges with personality as well as looks, and you can expect them to be "in your face" sorts of dogs. Buying a show dog may also commit you to doing a certain amount of showing, if specified by the breeder. You'll have to devote a lot of time to the dog; he'll need training, exercise, and plenty of socialization. If your weekends are already full of activities, you'll have to adjust your lifestyle or decide that a pet-quality dog is the better choice for you.

For Other Dog Activities

If you're not interested in showing your dog but you do want him to do more than lie by the fireside, there are several options available to you. Both show and pet dogs should be physically and temperamentally sound enough to do any sports activities that catch your interest, such as agility and freestyle. You could also perform a public service with your dog, such as pet therapy. Luckily, these dogs don't have to have the perfect head or stunning coat that's required of show dogs. Any healthy, well-socialized Yorkie can make a great sports competitor, a helpful social volunteer, or just a loving companion.

 Fact

Yorkies can do a lot more than trot around a show ring and hang out at home. MACH3 Desmond Aloysius Shelby, CD, competes in agility with his owner, Pamela Shelby. The MACH3 designation stands for Master Agility Champion third level, and Desi is closing in on the fourth level.

Puppy or Older

Most people start looking for a dog with the assumption that they will get a puppy. But there are several other choices that still make great pets, including adolescents, adults, and even retired show dogs. Before you fall in love with a tiny bundle of fur, be sure you can accept the time-consuming responsibilities a puppy will bring.

Problems with Puppies

It's tough to imagine anything cuter than a Yorkshire terrier puppy. Their tiny size and surprising spunk are irresistible. But what many people forget is that owning a puppy is not as easy as visiting with one for a few hours. The playful biting you thought adorable at first becomes an annoying habit, and the crying in the middle of the night grows impossible to ignore. A puppy requires at least as much supervision as a toddler who has just learned to run, and once the pup has reached a few months of age, her energy will seem boundless.

 Question?

If all the breeders you contact have waiting lists for their puppies, why shouldn't you just buy a pup from the pet store down the street?

The Yorkshire terrier, like most other breeds, is prone to a host of genetic diseases that are prevalent among pet-store pups. Additionally, you may be supporting irresponsible puppy mills by buying an overpriced, premature puppy from a pet shop.

Raising a puppy is a full-time job. If no one is home during the day, it's not a good idea to bring a puppy into the household. Puppies that are left to their own devices, even if secure in a safe area, often learn to occupy themselves in unacceptable ways, such as barking constantly or chewing on whatever's available.

Also, toy-breed puppies need to be fed four times a day, which means they will need to go to the bathroom quite often. Someone needs to be there to accomplish housetraining early on, or it just won't happen.

Even if someone is home with the puppy—which is certainly preferable—this person still won't be free to go about his daily business as usual. The puppy must be supervised during every waking moment, and she must be fed, taken outside, exercised, and played with.

There may be moments when you wish you'd never thought about getting a puppy. However, puppyhood is short—especially for toy dogs—and the worst is over by the time the pup reaches six months of age. Some people gladly endure all the inconveniences for the chance to bond and mold the youngster into their ideal dog. You can start training almost immediately and continue on a consistent basis throughout your pup's life.

Older Dogs

If you don't want to endure the trials and tribulations of raising a puppy, an older dog may suit you better. When you meet an adult Yorkie, you can see exactly what you're getting—the final adult size, coat, and temperament will be fully evident.

Alert!

Don't be swayed by a puppy's cuteness! Assess your time and tolerance level realistically, and if these limits won't accommodate a puppy, search for an adult dog instead. It's far better to have slightly less time to spend with your dog than to have your relationship ruined in the early days because of standard puppy misbehavior.

Breeders may keep some Yorkies to see how they develop and then decide that the dogs don't fit into their showing or breeding program. These dogs may become available for sale when they are adolescents or young adults. They are still young and have nearly their whole lives ahead of them, but the worst of the puppy problems are in the past. Another benefit of these dogs is that they might already have undergone basic training, including housetraining.

You can also occasionally find a dog that is not part of the breeding program and that was shown to her championship, but then not considered good enough to "special" (continue showing as a champion). Such dogs may be only one or two years old, used to all the hubbub of a dog show, and able to transition smoothly into a new household. Similarly, there are sometimes retired show dogs that breeders will place so that they can receive more attention in a private home than in a busy show kennel. These are older dogs with lower energy, and while you won't have quite as many years together, if your own energy is lower too, this pet may suit you perfectly.

Adolescent Yorkies may find themselves in rescue or shelters because their families didn't plan for all the time and energy they'd require. These dogs may have acquired some bad behaviors, or they may simply be caught in an unsuitable situation. Luckily, these dogs are usually snatched up fairly quickly. Adult Yorkies often find themselves in need of homes when they outlive their owners or their owners choose a new lifestyle that doesn't include a dog. Though these dogs may grieve for a while, they will come to love and trust their new owners in due time.

Male or Female

Many people have definite, set viewpoints about which sex is better when it comes to dogs. Some will accept only males, while others swear by females. Many of these biases come from experience; for example, you might've grown up with male dogs. Other biases are based on unsubstantiated myths, such as female dogs living longer than males. If you don't have a gender preference, you'll have more choices. However, there are some important differences to consider.

Males

One aspect that many people deem a problem with male dogs is that they mark their territory by lifting one leg and relieving themselves. Neutering can lessen this tendency to a degree, as well as protect your dog from testicular cancer and prostate disease. However, the instinct to mark territory is natural in dogs and cannot generally be stifled by any means. Contrary to popular opinion, though, males tend to be slightly mellower than females.

If you intend to show your dog, it's important to know that males are slightly easier to keep in coat. They don't endure the hormonal stress of going into heat twice a year. But you will have to work a little harder to keep the long flowing coat clean, especially on the underside of the dog, because of the male urination method.

Females

Females often show more leadership qualities than males and a more independent nature. This may be the gender more likely to sound the alarm when an intruder—even one as harmless as the UPS man or the neighbor's cat—approaches the house.

 Essential

Unspayed female Yorkshire terriers must be kept safe while they are in heat. Male dogs will be able to tell that a female is in heat from a mile (sometimes several miles) away. Much larger dogs will have no qualms about mating with toy breeds, and this can cause serious problems for the Yorkie.

Unspayed females will go into heat twice a year, each occurrence lasting about three weeks. They will become moody, messy, and highly attractive to the opposite sex during this time. Spaying takes care of these problems, however, as well as decreases the chances of breast cancer to nearly zero.

One, Two, or More

Since Yorkies are so small it may seem like a good idea to bring home more than one. After all, they can play with each other and burn off some of that terrier energy. They can keep each other company when you have to go out. And two will be twice as amusing for you, right? Not necessarily.

The Downside to Multiple Dogs

The main problem with bringing two puppies home together is that they will bond strongly with each other, perhaps to the detriment of the canine-human bond. You will have to spend extra time with each pup separately to ensure that they become comfortable around humans and learn to be apart from one another.

While two pups can entertain each other, they can also encourage each other in bad behavior. If one pup is in a very active, playful mood, the other one will likely join him in racing around in circles, even if it's the middle of the night. If one is whining to be let out of his crate, the other will likely whine along; the squeaky symphony of puppy voices is too much for even the heaviest sleeper to ignore. Also, unless you are supervising them constantly, you won't know which puppy left the puddle on the living-room carpet or chewed the leg of the kitchen table. You need to be able to identify which puppy exhibits which misbehavior so that you can rectify the problems with more training.

Another issue to keep in mind is cost. Obviously, two dogs mean double the expenses, double the time, double the grooming, etc. Two dogs is a lot for a family to take on, and it's an especially big challenge for a single person or a working couple. Be sure that you can handle the cost and time commitments before you bring home two (or more) new pets.

The Plus Side to Lots of Pups

Clearly, the biggest benefit to twice the dogs is twice the fun! And if you get three or more dogs, they will be an adorable group of friends that can play together, sleep together, and take walks together. You'll certainly never be lonely with multiple Yorkies in the house. Additionally, sleeping in groups will remind the pups of when they were with their mother and littermates and will comfort them at night; this will hopefully mean less whining and more sleep for you. And one person can certainly walk two or three Yorkies, given their small size. So, even with multiple dogs you will only have to take them on one group walk.

 **Alert!**

Unless you have a reputable breeder as a mentor, don't buy two Yorkies with the idea of breeding them and recouping your investment. Yorkshire terrier litters are generally small, and veterinary bills can be large. You may find yourself losing more money in the venture than you originally spent on the dogs in the first place.

Yorkies with Others

Yorkies may be small in size, but they're large in spirit. If not taught otherwise, they may think they rule the world, including everyone and everything in your household. From other pets to small children, no one is exempt from enduring a haughty Yorkie's mood swings. However, if you politely but firmly lay down some rules, Yorkies can learn the ropes while still retaining their spunky personalities.

 **Fact**

Where dogs are concerned, household cats are pretty much in charge of their own destiny. If the cat runs, the dog will give chase. If the cat stands up for herself, perhaps delivering a swipe to the dog's nose, the dog will learn not to bother her. Once an understanding is reached between the two animals, they will usually coexist peacefully.

Other Pets

Yorkshire terriers are every bit as willing to chase the family cat as any larger dog would be. You'll need to take some time introducing the cat and dog, because the cat is well equipped to defend herself. One swipe of the cat's claws across the Yorkie's face could cause a serious injury. (See Chapter 6 for more information on introducing the two animals.)

Pocket pets such as hamsters, gerbils, and guinea pigs could arouse the dog's ratting instincts. To avoid tragedy, these small pets should be kept safe in their own cages—not roaming loose in the vicinity of a Yorkie. Cages should also be elevated on secure platforms so that the dog isn't tempted by the sight of the animals.

Larger dogs in the home may pose a greater danger to the Yorkie. Sighthounds may be excited by the rapid movement of a small Yorkie and attack the dog as a predator would prey. Other large dogs may unintentionally injure a Yorkie with rough play. So to keep your Yorkie safe, a smaller companion is preferable.

Yorkies and Children

Because they are so small and so intent on being near their families, you'll often find Yorkies underfoot. This is not a very safe place for them to be, especially when there are small children around. Being inadvertently kicked or hit with a swinging door and other such misadventures can result in serious injuries to the Yorkie. Children may not mean any harm, but they move quickly and don't always look where they're going. Children also have the desire to pick up and carry around small dogs. A drop, even from only a few feet up, can cause a Yorkie significant pain.

Aside from children's clumsiness, another danger exists when it comes to Yorkies and children. Due to their in-charge attitude, Yorkies may have limited tolerance for children. They don't appreciate rough handling and may be overstimulated by the quick, jerky movements of younger children. An adult household, or one with older, more responsible children, is a more appropriate place for a new Yorkshire terrier.

Personality Testing

If you've decided you want a puppy, you need to choose one that will suit you and your family. While a breed is a breed because all the dogs share similarities in looks and temperament, dogs within each breed are still individuals with plenty of differences. One way to get an indication of a puppy's personality is to look at the mother (and father, if possible). Much of the parents' personalities will be reflected in their offspring. Your chosen breeder can advise you as to what type of individual would suit you best, and you can perform some simple tests to make locating those ideal pups a bit easier.

Alert!

You may find some rigorous temperament tests in other books or on the Internet, but you should avoid performing any tests that may be frightening for the puppies. Any temperament test is only a rough indication of a pup's personality, so there's no point in going overboard and scaring puppies.

Shy or Bold

To test whether puppies are shy or bold, sit on the floor and see what the puppies do. The one that rushes right up and starts chewing on your shirt will likely grow to be a bold, self-confident adult. The one that hangs back in the corner of the room and won't approach willingly will likely remain shy as an adult. Your heart may go out to this timid little one, but if you want a Yorkie that will accompany you everywhere, this isn't the dog for you. A pup that approaches but keeps a watchful eye on you and is a bit cautious is simply using good sense. This behavior may indicate a pup that will grow into a sensible adult—neither too bashful nor too brazen.

Touching and Carrying

You will be grooming your Yorkie daily, so you don't want a dog that's reluctant to be touched. And since Yorkies are so small, they often need to be carried. If your dog shrinks back from your outstretched hands, you will likely have some problems. To be sure you choose a dog that is comfortable with human contact, perform a simple touch test on prospective pets.

◄ **Yorkshire terrier pups are adorable and energetic.**

Photograph by Cheryl A. Ertelt

After the pups have had a few minutes to get used to you, start touching them—gently, but all over the body. Pick up their feet; look in their ears and mouths. Then choose a puppy and pick her up. It can be pretty frightening to be lifted up five feet off the ground when you're only a few inches tall, so don't be surprised if the puppy struggles. What you're looking for is a pup that settles down pretty quickly and relaxes into your arms. When you set the puppy down, watch to see if she stays close to you or runs away to watch from a distance. The pup that stays close by shows more confidence and less distress from the experience.

Willingness to Submit and Follow

The easiest way to test a puppy's willingness to submit is to see how she reacts when overpowered. To perform this test, gently roll the puppy onto her back on the ground and hold the pup in that position. It's fine for the puppy to squirm and struggle for a few seconds; however, what you're looking for is a pup that settles down quickly after the initial struggle. One that insists on trying to win the battle will always be a handful.

You can also test a puppy's willingness to follow. After the puppies have had a chance to get to know you a bit, walk a short distance away from them. You can talk encouragingly to them in a high-pitched voice or make clucking noises with your tongue. Take note of which puppies follow you. You don't want one that is attacking your shoes as you walk or one that is lagging far behind with a frightened look on his face. One that follows close behind may grow to be a more relaxed, companionable adult.

Advice from the Breeder

Once you have located a responsible breeder, you should feel free to ask this person for advice in choosing your puppy. The breeder has been with the pups nearly twenty-four hours a day, has spent time socializing them, has taken them for their health checks and vaccinations, and has observed their eating habits. Give the breeder a detailed description of what you want from your new dog, and listen to the advice you receive in return. Breeders want their pups to fit in with their new families and will do their best to match the pups with the right people.

In addition to being your source for a new pup, your breeder can also be a continuing source of advice as your pup grows. You can call this individual with occasional questions, difficult situations, and even exciting accomplishments. A good breeder will always be interested to hear how her pups are faring in their new homes.

 **Essential**

Be sure to honestly explain to your breeder your expectations for your new dog. If two or more breeders end up telling you that the Yorkshire terrier is not the breed for you, heed this guidance. While you may love the look of a Yorkie, if the breed's personality doesn't fit your lifestyle, you'll likely be unhappy with your choice.

Pedigrees, Contracts, and Health Guarantees

Whenever you get a dog from a breeder, you should always receive some paperwork as well. Even a few dogs in rescue or from shelters will come with their papers. However, don't worry if you don't have papers for your pup. These are only really necessary if you want to show your dog. If you do have your dog's papers, you will need to know how to decipher them. They will likely include several different abbreviations and acronyms that describe your dog's genealogic history, temperament, health, and so on.

Pedigrees

A pedigree is basically a dog's family tree; it can trace back any number of generations. Any titles earned by the pup's forebears and recognized by the registering kennel club (most commonly, the AKC) will be included in the pedigree. If you are seeking a show dog, you will want to see the designation "Ch." (champion) before the names of numerous dogs in the pedigree, particularly those close to the pup, such as parents and grandparents. Other abbreviations, found both before and after the name, may indicate titles in obedience, agility, tracking, and other dog sports.

If your research has left you impressed with a particular kennel, you can look for that kennel's name in the names of the dogs in the pedigree. Read the pedigree from left (where your dog's name or litter should appear) to right, going back through generations as you move to the right.

Contracts and Health Guarantees

If you are buying a dog from a breeder, there should be a contract between you. While different breeders may choose to include somewhat personalized points, any good contract should specify:

- Names of the seller and buyer
- Name and registration number of the dog being bought
- Statement of the dog's sex, and whether it is being sold as a pet or show specimen
- A health guarantee of some sort
- Requirement for a pet specimen to be spayed or neutered by some specified age (usually six months)
- Requirement for a show specimen to be titled and checked for inheritable diseases before being bred
- A statement that if the new owner cannot keep the dog, for whatever reason, it will be returned to the breeder

Even rescue organizations and shelters may have you sign a contract when you are adopting a dog. These contracts usually specify that the dog must be spayed or neutered (unless the surgery is done before the dog is released to you) and must be returned to the organization if you choose not to keep the dog.

The health guarantee should specify what testing has already been done on the pup. Some genetic disorders can be seen very early, such as patellar luxation. This document should also guarantee good health for some specific time span—the longer the better. Of course, no one can truly guarantee good health. The guarantee means that the breeder will provide a replacement if genetic problems show up in your pup within the specified timeframe. Some breeders will require that you return the original pup when a replacement is offered. However, they know that by the time problems arise, you will already be hopelessly in love with the pup and won't return it for a new animal.

Alert!

No health guarantee can truly guarantee good health. The best you can do is make sure that as much testing as possible has been done on the dog's forebears and the dog herself. Of course, the pedigree does not include brothers and sisters of the pup's parents and grand-parents, so you have no indication of their health. A good breeder will discuss this with you.

Choosing an Adult Yorkshire Terrier

Though they're cute, puppies aren't the only choice for potential dog owners. If you're looking in shelters or through a rescue group, any Yorkies you find will likely be older. For those people who can't be home all day every day with a pup, older is definitely better. An older dog will exhibit at least the beginnings of the breed's astonishing coat, as well as a more mature personality. Even so, when choosing an older dog, you can still use the personality tests recommended for puppies.

From Shelters or Rescue

When you're looking at Yorkies in shelters or rescues, be sure to get each dog out of the cage and into closer contact with you before making any decisions. Many shelters have designated areas or private rooms where you can visit with a dog away from all the other dogs and staff. Some will even let you take a prospective dog on a little walk. Shelter surroundings can be quite stressful, and the dog's true personality may not be apparent in this environment. Dogs in shelter runs will often go ballistic when visitors walk down the aisles. Some may be depressed and unable to show you their sparkling personalities. Take some time to get to know them a bit in a quiet area.

Rescue groups generally keep dogs in foster care in private homes. The foster owners will be able to give you good information on the dog's personality, interactions with other animals, and activity level. Also, while visiting a dog at a home, you may have more opportunity to play with the dog, take the dog for a walk, and even watch the dog eat a meal. Observing even small movements and behaviors will enlighten you as to the dog's true personality.

From Breeders

In addition to having a selection of puppies, breeders also occasionally have older dogs available. A breeder may have kept an individual for show, but the coat didn't develop correctly. Or there may be a dog that has retired from the show ring and isn't getting the attention he deserves. A wave in the coat or an incorrect coat color has no bearing on how good a pet a dog will make. These dogs are older, but they will still make excellent pets and probably be very grateful to have new, loving homes. As a bonus, these dogs will likely already be housetrained and perhaps obedience trained.

Preparing for Your New Pet

YOU WANT TO BE ABLE TO ENJOY THAT MAGICAL first day with your new dog, so you need to do some work in advance. You'll need to purchase all the basic supplies, puppy-proof your house by hiding valuables and storing poisons, and choose a veterinarian—among other things. Don't bring a new dog into the house until you're fully prepared to handle almost any surprise situation.

Family Members

Before you even consider bringing a new dog home, you must have the approval of everyone in the family. If anyone seems less than enthusiastic about the idea, this issue needs to be resolved before the dog arrives. If one or more members are against the addition of a pet, you may find yourself caring for the dog alone. The entire family must be involved in order for the dog chores to be distributed evenly and for the dog to feel comfortable, loved, and accepted.

Children in Particular

While you will hopefully have promises from the other members of the family to help take care of the dog, don't rely too heavily on the promises of children (older, responsible children who can safely coexist with a Yorkshire terrier) to take care of every canine need. Even if they are miraculously conscientious about feeding, walking, and grooming the dog, you will still need to handle visits to the veterinarian, drives to the training center, and trips to the pet-supply store.

If you truly want children to be involved, perhaps you can assign some aspects of the dog's care as weekly chores, for which they will be given an allowance or a treat. Children are always more tempted to help out around the house if there is some kind of reward involved. This way, you can remind them that if their dedication comes to a halt, the reward will be discontinued as well.

 Essential

Children's interests often shift rapidly, and the desire to have a dog may be a passing fancy, quickly replaced by an interest in soccer or camping. To ensure that you're not left to deal with the dog alone, don't get a dog just for the kids. If you don't want the dog as well, this probably isn't the right pet for your family.

Chart of Responsibilities

To make having a dog a real family affair, make a chart of responsibilities and divvy them up. Post the chart somewhere prominent, such as the refrigerator, so no one can say, "I forgot." Have caregivers check off their tasks each day as they're accomplished. Your chart might include these duties:

- **Meals:** Yorkies can't eat much at one sitting, so four daily meals for puppies and at least two for adults are recommended. Set out a specific schedule for feeding breakfast, lunch, a snack, and dinner.
- **Housetraining:** Puppies will need to go out when they wake up, after they eat or drink, and after a play session. In

between, they will have to be supervised. Break up the day into supervision periods for each family member.

- **Playtime:** Yorkies conveniently can get all the exercise they need indoors, so bad weather doesn't present much of a problem. However, they appreciate getting outdoors on nice days, too. Children should spend time with them outside, without playing roughly.

- **Socialization:** Puppies need a constant flow of new experiences to help them grow into well-rounded, confident adults. They need to meet new people and encounter new challenges, in a careful, controlled manner, every day.

- **Grooming:** Yorkies will require daily grooming throughout their lives. They need to become accustomed to it early so that it isn't a lifelong struggle. (See Chapter 8 for details on grooming.) One person can be in charge of grooming, or several people can take turns.

- **Training:** Just because a Yorkie is small doesn't mean you can neglect training. Group classes usually occur weekly for periods of anywhere from six to ten weeks. In between, someone must practice with the dog daily. Sessions should be short and occur several times a day.

- **Health care:** Keep track of veterinary appointments on your chart. You can also make veterinary visits easier for everyone by making additional nonmedical visits to the vet clinic and having the staff give your dog treats and pats.

Puppy-Proofing the Home

Yorkies are small, but don't make the mistake of thinking they can't be destructive. They will leave smaller tooth marks, dig smaller holes, and have more trouble reaching tall objects such as the garbage can, but they'll still do plenty to disrupt and destroy your surroundings if you don't train, plan, and supervise effectively. Before your puppy comes home, take the time to move items you cherish and anything that could be dangerous out of the reach of those paws and jaws. Lie down on the floor to develop a Yorkie's-eye view of all rooms and their contents.

🐕 Essential

If you truly want to understand how the world looks and feels to a toy dog, lie down with your head on the floor in a busy area of the house and let your family go about their business as usual for a half-hour. You will quickly learn what frightens, excites, and even harms a Yorkie.

Kitchen and Bathroom

Either the kitchen or a bathroom is often chosen as the puppy's safe room because the floors (commonly tile or linoleum) are impervious to liquids and easily cleaned. However, these rooms also contain several items that are certainly not safe for a Yorkshire terrier. Cleaning products, certain foods, and sharp utensils should be kept high off the ground or secured in locked cabinets. Childproof locks are a good way to keep a dog away from these items.

It is also important to know that despite their size, Yorkies can jump. Counter height is actually attainable by many of these dogs. Rolls of toilet paper can be considered chew toys, and an especially spry pup could leap and land in the toilet if the lid isn't kept down. A Yorkie might even use a covered toilet seat as a ladder rung on his way to the vanity, so don't leave any hazards there either. Put away hair dryers, curling irons, razors, deodorant, and other potentially harmful items when not in use.

In the kitchen, Yorkies may not have enough heft to tip over a garbage can, but they can chew through the bottom. Dangling dishtowels will also be fair game. Be careful not to provide any objects that could serve as stepping stones to climbing to the counters or the top of the refrigerator. A Yorkie may not be able to gauge his height off the ground, and a jump or a fall could result in serious injury.

🐶 Alert!

Getting into the garbage is particularly hazardous for a Yorkshire terrier. They're small, inclined to pancreatitis, and tenacious once they decide on some course of action (such as chewing up a bone). Lock the garbage can under the kitchen sink, put it up in a closet, or find some other way to hide it from your Yorkie.

Main Living Areas

The main living areas of the home often contain prized personal possessions; toys, if there are children in the house; plenty of electrical cords; and perhaps houseplants or even other pets. If this is the case in your home, explain to everyone (children aren't the only ones who need reminders) that items left on the floor, whether homework, toys, or the remote control, may be destroyed by the dog. Also, reiterate that the dog will not be held responsible if this happens—the person will.

Block electrical outlets and cords with furniture, if possible. Do not attempt to hide cords by running them under rugs—this creates an electrical fire hazard. For any cords that can't be blocked, you can use a taste deterrent such as one with bitter apple flavor. If the dog attempts to chew on the cord, he should be repelled by the bitter taste. This does not deter all dogs, however, so you'll still need to supervise. Also be mindful not to leave heavy or breakable objects on wobbly tables. Even a little Yorkie can knock over a small pedestal table, and falling objects that a Labrador would hardly notice could kill a Yorkshire terrier.

Birdcages, fish tanks, and hamster or gerbil cages might also be found somewhere in your home. As long as the birdcage or fish tank can't be knocked over, there should be no problems there. The small furry pocket pets, on the other hand, should be kept well out of the Yorkie's reach. True to their ratting heritage, Yorkies may have the instinct to harass these small pets.

Question?

At what age is a Yorkie old enough not to be supervised all the time?
Fortunately for you, toy dogs tend to mature more quickly than their larger counterparts. While an eighteen-month-old Labrador should still be considered an adolescent that must be kept out of trouble, a six-month-old Yorkie will often start to show fewer puppy foibles and a more responsible attitude.

Plants offer a variety of risks as well. Yorkies may deem a mid-sized pot just the right area to serve as a digging pit or a potty box. They might chew on the plants themselves, which can have potential dire consequences. Some popular houseplants are noxious and others are downright toxic. You can find various lists of plants that are dangerous to dogs on the Web. Still, it's wise not to take any chances—put all plants out of reach of the dog.

Home Office

Look under any computer desk or behind any home entertainment center, and you're likely to find a tangled mess of wires. The entertainment center can be shoved up tight to the wall, with the wires safely captured behind it. The computer desk, however, will require a bit more care. You can get hooks that attach under the desk and hold the cables up out of the way. This still leaves you with all the electrical cords, usually plugged into an outlet strip. The simplest solution is to keep the pup out of the office, but if this is where you spend a lot of your time, you may want to invest in an exercise pen—a wire puppy playpen—to keep your pup close by but out of harm's way.

Bedroom and Laundry Room

These two areas are related in this discussion because many puppy transgressions will involve clothes and shoes. Your Yorkie may be small enough to fit inside your running shoe, but that doesn't mean he can't chew sizable holes in it. Your clothes are equally vulnerable to a puppy chewing attack (socks are particular favorites). To avoid damage to these items, keep all clothes picked up, shoes put away, and closet doors closed. Put laundry baskets inside closets or elevated on tables. Also, don't leave dresser drawers hanging open; a dangling scarf is never safe from a curious Yorkie.

Alert!

You may think the image of a Yorkie chewing on a shoelace is cute. Let's face it—a Yorkie doing almost anything is cute. But swallowing pieces of shoelaces can lead to an impaction in the digestive system and emergency surgery. Give your pup only safe, approved chew toys.

Garage, Basement, and Attic

Frankly, you don't live in these areas and neither should your dog. Dogs are pack animals, and your family is now your dog's pack. Leaving a dog alone in a garage, basement, or attic can cause a myriad of problems. These places generally hold many hazards, from antifreeze and herbicides to rat poison and cleaning products. If the dog were to ingest any of these toxic substances, it could cause serious internal problems or even death. Aside from harmful substances, these areas often contain heavy tools, sharp implements, and dirty or rusty equipment. Contact with these items could injure the dog in a number of ways. Simply put, it's safest to keep your pup away from these areas.

The Great Outdoors

No matter how much they're trying your nerves, puppies should not be put outside unattended, even in a fenced yard. Too many things can go wrong.

◀ Keep your Yorkie safe by puppy-proofing your home and yard.

Photograph by Jean Fogle

If your yard sprouts poisonous mushrooms or any mushrooms at all—most people aren't very adept at mushroom identification—it won't take much more than a nibble to put your Yorkie in serious jeopardy. Landscape plants can also be toxic, and danger lists often mingle plants that may only produce digestive upset with those that can be deadly. These lists also don't explain that it may only be the bulbs or the berries that cause problems. On the "better safe than sorry" premise, do not leave your Yorkie alone with plants of any sort. Certainly don't use pesticides, herbicides, or toxic snail baits in areas where your Yorkie will be allowed— choose safe alternatives instead.

 **Esseñtial**

Do not use an electronic fence to keep your Yorkie in your yard. Puppies should not have to suffer the shocks the collar provides if they venture too near the boundary. Also, the buried wire does nothing to prevent any roaming animal from entering your yard, and your Yorkie may fall prey to larger dogs, raccoons, coyotes, or other threats.

Fences must be extremely secure to thwart the escape of a dog as small as a Yorkshire terrier. Any hole could be an invitation to explore the wider world, and don't think a Yorkie can't dig under your fencing. Also be sure there are no sharp points of wood or wire to injure your Yorkie.

Choosing Your Safe Areas

Your Yorkshire terrier will want to be close to you at all times, so don't expect to use a bathroom on the other side of your house as your safe area for the dog. Instead, choose a location near the area that the family inhabits most of the time, or at least a spot that's in sight. You should be watching your Yorkie to see that she doesn't get into any mischief and to notice when she might need to go out. This room, or a crate, will also be where you leave your pup when you can't supervise.

You can use baby gates to block the door of the safe room. Of course, with a Yorkie you need a gate with a finer mesh than some have. Be sure your pup can't get her head caught in the negative spaces. If you're worried about chewing on your baseboards or through the baby gate, you can use an exercise pen to corral the pup in the middle of the room, away from any chewable surfaces. A crate can also be a useful piece of equipment throughout your Yorkie's life. See Chapter 7 for details on crate training.

A garage, basement, or other unheated area probably isn't suitable for your Yorkshire terrier's safe area. Yorkies chill easily, and a cold room will not be healthy for them.

 **Fact**

An exercise pen consists of wire panels that can fold flat or pull out to form a square or rough circle. This can serve as a puppy playpen, keeping your Yorkie safely away from hazards of any kind. Just be sure the Yorkie can't push body parts through the spaces and then get stuck.

Sleeping Arrangements

Sleeping arrangements can have a significant impact on both you and your Yorkie. If you get a puppy, you will endure quite a few sleepless nights due to shrill puppy cries. Conversely, until your pup is housetrained, she may not know to alert you when she has to go the bathroom, or you may not hear her cries if she is too far away. You will need to work out sleeping arrangements to fit your particular situation.

As a general rule, you can bring your Yorkie into your bedroom, but not into your bed. You could roll over at night and injure your sleeping pup, or she could have accidents in your bedding. Instead, bring your pup's crate into your bedroom and keep it close to your bed. This way, you can do a little bonding even while you sleep—without the risk of injury.

Do not, however, give in to the temptation to comfort your pup if she cries in the night. By responding to your pup's fussing, you only teach him that it's a good way to get attention. You can create a noisy, manipulative little dog this way. Instead, ignore whining and barking. Only talk quietly to your pup when he's being quiet, and only let him out of his crate when he's waiting patiently.

Supplies You'll Need or Want

Before you bring a Yorkshire terrier home, be sure to have several basic supplies in the house. You can certainly add more toys and treats later, but start out with at least a collar or harness, ID tag, and leash; food and water bowls; nutritious food; a crate and/or exercise pen or baby gates; and a few grooming supplies.

Collar or Harness

Because Yorkshire terriers are prone to problems with collapsing tracheas, many breeders recommend the use of harnesses rather than collars to avoid pressure on the windpipe. On the other hand, a Yorkie in full show coat is not going to be fastened into a harness that could ruin the coat. The choice really depends on your circumstances.

Whichever you choose, just be sure it's made of soft, nonirritating material with no sharp edges. The harness or collar must fit well, and if your Yorkshire terrier is a pup, check the fit at least every week, as your puppy will grow quickly. If you choose a collar, buckle and quick-release snap-ons are both good choices. Harnesses and collars come in a dazzling array of colors and prints, but always check that they meet your dog's comfort needs first, before worrying about fashion.

Identification

Have an ID tag engraved for your dog to wear on her collar or harness. You can find tags at veterinary offices, pet-supply stores, and trophy shops. Consider exactly what information you want to appear on the tag. Common choices are dog's name, owner's name, address, and phone number. But if you're wary of providing any personal information, a phone number alone will suffice if your dog is ever lost.

Trainers disagree on whether dogs should wear collars (or har-nesses) at all times or only when going out with their owners. Those who don't support constant wearing of collars and harnesses might advocate the microchip method. Both sides have merit. Though microchips offer identification that's always with the dog, as the chip is implanted between the dog's shoulder blades, an ID tag is immediately accessible to anyone who finds a lost dog.

Fact

A microchip is a small chip that contains a unique identification number. It is injected between the dog's shoulders, and the own-er's information is submitted to the chip registry. When a scanner is passed over the dog, it reads the ID number and, in turn, identi-fies the owner. The downside to this method is that not everyone knows that it exists. A microchipped dog with no ID tag could easily be taken as a stray.

Those who argue against leaving collars on dogs worry about the dangling tags getting caught in crates, fences, or decks, or dogs playing together getting their teeth caught in collars. To make your own decision, simply think about your lifestyle and the life you have prepared for your dog. A breeder might also be able to offer guidance in this area.

Leash

Leashes come in at least as many colors and styles as collars. It's nice to have something pretty, but again, consider utility first. When choosing a material, be sure it's kind to your hands. Even the pulling of a five-pound Yorkie can quickly become annoying if the leash is cutting into your hand. Next, make sure the clip is securely sewn onto the leash and the handle will not fall apart. The weight shouldn't be too heavy for a Yorkie to drag around. Then think about what length you need. Most training classes recommend a six-foot leash. Some cities specify the length of leash on which you can walk a dog within their limits.

Once you've taken care of all those considerations, you can think about appearance. You can have leashes embroidered with your dog's name. You can find patterns from floral to wild animal print. You can even find leashes with reflective material that are highly visible at twilight or after dark in car headlights. This is definitely a great safety idea if you walk your dog along roads after sunset or before sunrise.

Alert!

Because the dog has to apply pressure to pull out a retractable leash, attaching the leash to a harness rather than a collar may be a wise method for Yorkshire terrier owners. Keep this in mind when you purchase your basic supplies before the dog comes home.

Retractable leashes provide an added degree of freedom while still keeping your dog safely attached to you. Most of the leash coils inside a molded plastic housing with a handhold. The dog can pull out line to a maximum of sixteen to twenty-four feet. As the dog comes closer, the line automatically retracts back into the handle. There's also a brake to stop line from playing out. Retractable leashes may make walks in the country or around parks more fun, but they won't be welcome in training classes, and they may be longer than some cities allow.

Bowls and Food

Buy bowls the appropriate size for your Yorkshire terrier. After all, you don't want her walking through her food or taking a bath in her water. You can find aluminum, stainless steel, plastic, or ceramic bowls. If you have a dishwasher, check that the bowls are dishwasher safe, so you can thoroughly clean them once a week. On a daily basis you can wash them by hand.

In general, the material you choose for a bowl depends on preference. Metal may be a little noisier if your pup likes to push the bowl around. Ceramic bowls are breakable, but they're also heavier and not as easy to push. Lightweight plastic can be easily chewed, and heavier plastic can develop scratches that are difficult to clean.

If you bought your puppy from a breeder, find out from this person what food the puppy has been eating. With a pup from other sources, you may or may not be able to learn this information. If you do know the food to which your dog is accustomed, continue to feed it for at least two weeks, while your pup settles in. Then if you want to change foods, do so gradually, mixing a little more of the new food and a little less of the old food every day.

When choosing a food for your Yorkie, keep the size of that small mouth in mind. You don't want kibble so large that one piece will fill your Yorkie's mouth. Many manufacturers now make foods specifically for toy dogs, with small pieces and optimum nutrition. Read ingredients panels and information from manufacturers, and talk to your breeder or veterinarian when choosing a food for your dog.

Crate

Dogs as small as Yorkshire terriers have more choices when it comes to crates. Because people love to carry their Yorkies around, there are travel bags of all sorts in addition to the more usual molded plastic or hard-sided wire crates. Of course, puppies may chew the various cloth varieties if left in them and unattended.

Your dog's crate should only be large enough for the dog to stand up, lie down, and turn around comfortably. This size crate can be difficult to find for such a small dog. But don't give up until you've found the perfect one; your crate will assist with housetraining (as described in Chapter 7), serve as sleeping quarters, be a safe place when you can't supervise your Yorkie, and perhaps serve in the car as well. If you plan on flying with your Yorkie, you'll need a crate that fits under the seat. Sherpa bags and other soft variations serve this need well.

Grooming Supplies

You'll be having plenty of grooming sessions with your Yorkshire terrier, so be ready. You'll want a pin brush with metal—not nylon—bristles, a long-toothed metal comb, and perhaps a fine-toothed flea comb. For baths you need a good dog shampoo (a tearless one may make bathtime less stressful for both of you) and a conditioner. You might also want to pick up a hair dryer meant specifically for dogs.

For tooth care, buy a canine toothpaste and a child's toothbrush or a finger brush, which slides over your finger like a thimble. Canine toothpastes come in a variety of flavors that your dog will like, such as chicken, liver, and beef. Brushing your dog's teeth regularly will keep them free of plaque and decrease the need for professional cleanings.

Whatever you do, don't take the easy way out and use human products on your dog. Human shampoos have the wrong pH balance for dogs. Human toothpaste foams up, since dogs don't rinse and spit, and doesn't taste good to dogs. Human hair dryers can only be used if they have a good low-heat setting. (See Chapter 8 for details on grooming.)

Choosing a Veterinarian

If this is your first dog, or some time has passed since your last dog departed, you'll need to find a veterinarian. You should plan to take your Yorkie for a health check soon after you bring him home, and you want to have someone to call if problems should arise during the often-rocky adjustment period.

Finding Veterinary Possibilities

If your breeder lives in your area, she can provide a reference for the veterinarian the kennel uses. The bonus here is that you can be sure the veterinarian has some experience with toy dogs. However, many people travel for hours to pick up their new Yorkie, or even have the pup shipped by air. If this is your situation, you'll have to find another way to choose a vet. As with any service you may need, the Yellow Pages provide a good starting point. You can find veterinary clinics in your area by listing, and some will have display ads with their hours, any special services, and so forth.

One of the details you may see in a display ad is the AAHA logo, for the American Animal Hospital Association. This group certifies veterinary clinics that pass their standards regarding sterilization, twenty-four-hour care, isolation facilities, and more. They can provide a list of AAHA-certified clinics in your area

Of course, personal referrals may be the best route. If you have friends with dogs, especially friends with small dogs, ask who their veterinarians are and what they like (or don't like) about them. You may even choose to accompany a friend and his dog on a visit to the vet to meet the individual. This will give you the chance to observe the vet's office environment and her interaction with dogs and to ask any questions you might have.

Choosing the Right Veterinarian for You

Once you've developed a list of possibilities, take the time to visit each of them, tour their facilities, and meet the veterinarians. Make an appointment or else be prepared to wait—good practices are always busy.

While touring the clinic, note how clean everything is, how noisy or quiet the kennel area is, and the demeanor of vet techs and office staff as they go about their jobs. There should be no bad smells or dirty corners, and while dogs confined away from their owners may bark and whine, it shouldn't be bedlam. If you notice any staff members who look disgruntled, overworked, or unhappy with their jobs, take that into account as well.

Of course, have a list of questions prepared. You may have specifics of your own, but people often want to know these basics:

- A schedule of fees for office visits, annual exams, vaccinations, spay/neuter, and pest preventives

- Acceptable methods of payment, including payment plans for large expenses
- Office hours and procedures for emergencies outside of office hours
- Facilities for recovery, and if they are staffed around the clock
- Percentage of the practice devoted to dogs, and specifically to toy dogs

Fact

Veterinarians schooled in the United States generally have the title DVM, Doctor of Veterinary Medicine. The exceptions are graduates of the University of Pennsylvania School of Veterinary Medicine, who are VMDs, Veterinary Medical Doctors. Veterinarians can also be board certified, the same as human MDs, in various specialties. If a clinic is approved by AAHA, it will usually sport a decal to that effect.

Depending on your own philosophy, you may also want to ask if the clinic is open to alternative medicine (acupuncture, massage, herbs, and so on), has a specialty in veterinary nutrition, or offers boarding or training. If you are visiting several different places, take notes about your visits—you won't remember everything, and you want to be able to compare your choices. Rank your options, and keep your notes in case you make a mistake in your first choice.

CHAPTER  6

Bringing Your Yorkie Home

WHEN YOU BRING YOUR YORKIE HOME for the first time, you'll want to spend the day bonding and playing with him. You'll want to be able to enjoy the event, without worrying about what you've forgotten. You should already have a veterinary visit scheduled for the next day or so. Your supply closet should be stocked with dog food, grooming supplies, and other basics. All family members should agree that a new dog is a great idea. And if there are any other pets in the home, you should have a plan as to how to introduce them. Once these bases are covered, you can relax and enjoy yourself!

Planning Ahead

One of the most important things to remember is that Yorkshire terrier puppies need to have someone home with them all day. They need to be fed four meals, taken out every two hours, and exercised regularly. Housetraining can be a difficult enough proposition without leaving the pup on his own all day. In order to meet all your pup's requirements you'll have to make certain arrangements.

Take Time Off

There should absolutely be someone home with the dog for at least the first few weeks. Perhaps a family member can take vacation time from work or work from home temporarily. Maybe you're lucky enough to work in a dog-friendly office and can bring the pup to work with you. But if you do this, beware: adorable pups can be pretty disruptive to office routine, not to mention the potty breaks. Perhaps all family members, older children included, can combine their schedules to take turns with puppy care. Everyone might have to give up some other activity—willingness to compromise in this way is a good indication that everyone's ready to take responsibility for this new addition to the family.

Hire Help

If you can't be with the puppy at all times, your other option is to hire an in-home pet sitter. Some parents hire nannies for their children, and there's no reason you can't have one for your dog. Look for someone who is insured—they'll have free use of your home, after all—and ask for references, specifically those that indicate experience with small dogs. Be honest with the pet sitter about the pup's needs, and be sure that this person continues whatever training, food regimen, and exercise schedule you have initiated. Additionally, be prepared to spend the time you *are* home with the pup. You don't want your dog to have a stronger bond with his pet sitter than he has with you.

 **Fact**

Pet Sitters International is the largest professional pet-sitter organization in the United States. On the organization's Web site, *www. petsit.com*, you can read recommended quality standards for pet sitters, check out pet-sitter FAQs, and locate a pet sitter in your area.

Avoid the Holidays

It's a classic image: a new puppy beneath the Christmas tree with a big red bow tied around her neck. You may decide it makes perfect sense to bring a new dog home around the holidays; after all, you'll likely have some time off from work. But if you give it some more thought, you'll realize this is precisely the wrong time to add a time-intensive new pet to the household. You'll already have more to do than seems possible, from shopping to cooking, from decorating to visiting relatives. Not only will you not have time for the pup, all the excitement can overstimulate a puppy and make her more difficult to train.

Maybe your spouse has always wanted a Yorkshire terrier and you think it's the perfect holiday gift. Still, it's best to wait until some of the hubbub has died down. Instead, give your loved one some puppy accoutrements—a leash, dog bowls, even a crate—and a list of breeders or contact information for a rescue group. In addition, you can promise to help in the search for a new pup as soon as the holidays are over. You could even put down a deposit on a pup, and just wait for calmer times to bring the pup home. This may also give the recipient a chance to meet the prospective pup before the deal is finalized.

Picking Up Your Pup from the Breeder

If the breeder is at all within driving distance, go and get your pup yourself. The safest place for your new pup to ride in the car is inside a crate. However, most people want to hold a new puppy in their laps on the drive home. This is okay, as long as the person holding the dog is not the driver. And if the pup will be on a lap instead of in a crate, the driver must take extra precautions not to stop suddenly or take sharp turns. A tiny puppy can easily be flung around if the ride gets too rough.

 Essential

On your ride home from the breeder's facility, be sure to have the car windows closed or open only a crack, if necessary. An excited or nervous Yorkie could try to leap out an open window, and even hanging her head out the window could cause significant eye injuries.

Before You Head Home

While you're with the breeder, get some final information on your puppy. How often and how much is the pup being fed? What are her sleeping habits? Has any housetraining or basic manners training been done? This knowledge will give you a good starting point for raising your new pup, and it will also help ease the transition for the dog.

If you have any remaining questions, this is a good time to ask them. If you have not yet decided whether to use a collar or a harness with your pup, ask for the breeder's advice. If you'd like some pointers on how to initiate or continue housetraining, the breeder can likely provide some insight. You may not be able to think of all the questions you have; after all, you will be a bit distracted by your new pup's adorable face. So, at the very least, make sure you leave with the breeder's contact information and his preferred times to be reached. This way, even if you think of some more questions when you get home, you can simply call him up and get quick answers.

Don't Forget the Paperwork

Along with your pup, you want to remember to bring home all the appropriate paperwork. Bring a list of documents you expect to receive, and check them off before you go. Some of these documents might include the following:

- AKC individual registration (blue slip)
- Pedigree
- Vaccination and general health records
- Parents' health certificates and results of any tests done on puppies
- Sales contract

The breeder may give you much more than this, but these are the basics. Many breeders offer extensive puppy packages, including a breed book, information on breed clubs, articles they think might be of interest, information on dog sports, and brochures on pet health insurance. The breeder might even give you an old towel with the scent of the mother and littermates on it, a bag of food the puppy has been eating, or a favorite toy to help the puppy make a smooth transition into your family.

If Your Puppy Must Be Shipped

Waiting for the plane carrying your new puppy to arrive is a nerve-wracking experience. The optimal situation is for a person to travel with the pup in the cabin, but this often isn't feasible unless you can fly out to collect your pup personally. In most cases, the pup will likely be shipped as air cargo.

🐕 **Fact**

If you're hesitant to spend the money to fly to pick up your pup, check the various online discount sites for booking air travel for low fares. Sometimes you can find a cheaper flight during the week as opposed to the weekend, or you can take an overnight flight to save money. If at all possible, picking up your pup in person will make the trip easier for both of you.

Some Safety Tips

Most breeders are experienced with shipping puppies, but you should still confirm a few points for your own peace of mind. The puppy should not be given tranquilizers for the trip. Drugs work differently at high altitudes, and these can actually endanger your pup. Also, direct flights are best, so there's no chance of the pup being misplaced in some distant city during a flight change.

While air travel is more relaxing and convenient than driving, there are some rules and restrictions you should know about before planning to ship or fly with your new puppy. Airlines have toughened their own rules on shipping live animals, including dogs. Many refuse shipments during the heat of summer. Others will only allow overnight flights so temperatures are cooler. Be sure to check with your chosen airline well in advance of your flight to learn these important regulations.

If your breeder will be shipping your puppy, ask him to fill the crate's water cup and freeze it, putting it in the crate at the last moment so that the puppy will have water as it melts. It's also advisable to have something taped to the top of the crate (a bag of dog food or a rolled blanket) so that airline staff members are less likely to pile heavy luggage or other cargo on top of your pup's crate. Items will certainly shift, even during a smooth flight, and falling luggage can frighten and even injure your little pup.

Meeting the Flight

Once you know when your puppy is being shipped, call your airport and find out where you should meet the flight to collect your pup as quickly as possible. The pup will certainly be hungry and thirsty and will need to go out as soon as the plane lands. Once you have the dog in your possession, leave him in the crate, carry the crate to the car, and drive to the nearest available patch of green. With all car doors and windows closed, open the crate and fasten the new collar or harness and leash to the dog. Once everything is securely attached, let him out to stretch his legs and go to the bath-room. This brief time out of the crate will relax the puppy for the ride home. And unless there is someone else riding in the car with you who can hold the puppy during the drive, the pup will need to go back in the crate until you arrive safely at home.

Once You Arrive Home

As soon as you arrive home with your new puppy, reattach the col-lar or harness and leash and walk him around the yard. This will be his first contact with the smells of his new home. Give him time to sniff and investigate, to relieve himself, and to play a little. After he has sufficiently stretched his legs, you can take him inside.

Supervision

Once you enter the house with your pup, your biggest responsibility begins. Your pup should be either under the watchful eye of a responsible person or secure in his safe area or crate at all times. One good way to keep the puppy close is to tether him to you with a leash. This way, as you move from room to room, the puppy automatically comes with you. This arrangement doesn't mean you can otherwise ignore the pup—he could be chewing the leash or the corner of the couch if you aren't watching. You must also watch where you're walking when the pup is attached to you. He will be tiny enough to easily crawl underfoot. If you trip over him, one or both of you could get hurt.

Spend a lot of time interacting with your new puppy rather than just sitting passively and watching him. He'll be missing the company of his mother and littermates, so you need to fill that gap. Get down on the floor and cuddle with him. Play with toys together—even puppies can fetch. Or hold your pup on your lap and practice gently brushing him. This will help him get accustomed to grooming early on.

 Essential

It's never too early to start training. Your puppy can begin learning the commands "Sit," "Down," "Come," and more as soon as he's had a chance to settle in. (See Chapter 15 for details.) Don't believe anyone who tells you that a dog has to be six months old, or any other age, before you can start training. With positive methods, training can begin before a pup even leaves his mother.

While young, your puppy will alternate between being a vivacious ball of fun and a tuckered-out little tike. He will become so excited during playtime that he will quickly wear himself out. When you see him start to slow down during playtime, take him out for a potty break and then put him in his crate to nap. While he's asleep, you're off duty—but this break won't last long. As the puppy grows older, these restful naptimes will decrease, and your pup will have a more constant supply of energy. Brace yourself!

Choosing a Name

If your pup is from a breeder, she will already have a "paper" name. This is her official name registered with the AKC or other kennel club. This name likely includes the breeder's kennel name and is rather long and involved, something like Preston Bay Sparkling Sensation n' Sass. Chances are, you're not going to spit this out every time you want to call your dog. Some people choose a part of the paper name—Sass—or some variation on the name—Sparkle—as the dog's name for everyday use. Others choose an entirely original name that has nothing to do with the paper name. Whatever you choose to do, be sure to have a name picked out before you pick up your pup.

 **Alert!**

Choose a name for your dog that's short—one or two syllables—and that won't be confused with any other names in your household. If you have a spouse called Charlie, don't name your pup Harley, or they'll never be certain which one you're calling. Likewise, if you plan to use the word "no" in the dog's training, a name like Snow might confuse the dog.

If your pup is from a rescue group or a shelter, you may or may not know any prior name given to the dog. Even if you do know the name previously used, unless you know the history of the dog (it is the pet of a now-deceased owner or a retired show dog, for example), you may want to choose a new name anyway.

Making Introductions

The first few days of owning a new puppy will be hectic enough for both of you without the added pressure of entertaining guests. Your pup will likely be tired out from her journey to your home, and too much excitement in the first few days of a new situation can make her very anxious. Aside from spacing out visits from friends and family, you may also want to create a buffer period for the pup to get used to her new home before she meets any other pets.

Meeting Family and Friends

Don't overwhelm your pup the first day. Of course, everyone in the family will want to make her acquaintance, but hold off on introducing friends and neighbors for a while. Everything is new to the pup right now, and too much too soon will be upsetting. Let your Yorkie settle in for a few days before starting to schedule visits. Even then, you should space out meetings so the pup realizes that her new home will not be a three-ring circus at all times.

Meetings should be kept low-key. Even adults may be inclined to squeal over how cute your new addition is. Coach them on cooing instead. Loud noises could make your pup fearful of greetings. Even if you don't have children in your household, there are bound to be some in the neighborhood. Remind them to be quiet and to move carefully around the puppy. Don't let them pick her up. Instead, suggest they sit on the floor to meet the puppy on her own terms.

Meeting Another Dog

Yorkies are terriers that seem to imagine themselves as bigger than they are. They won't necessarily be submissive to bigger dogs. If you have another, larger dog, your first step is to arrange a meeting on neutral ground. Walk the dogs, separately, to a nearby park or a neighbor's yard. With them both on leash, but taking care to keep the leashes slack, let the dogs circle and sniff each other. Canine greetings can involve a certain amount of posturing, but keep an eye out for any bristling hair or lifted lips. Give them as much time as they want to make each other's acquaintance.

Don't be alarmed if your puppy throws himself on his back. This is just a proper way of submitting to the older, bigger dog, and this move shows good sense on your pup's part.

 **Essential**

Because puppies are so irresistible and so needy, people often spend all their time fussing over them and forget the faithful dog already in residence. This isn't fair to your older friend. Be sure to make time just for the older dog every day—a special walk, riding with you on errands, or playing fetch.

When they're either no longer interested in each other or have started offering to play, walk them home together. Check for any reactions when you reach home territory—some dogs-in-residence may be less gracious on their own turf. If any tensions arise, crate the puppy and let the older dog have free run of the premises. Pet and play with the older dog, and praise any positive interest in the pup. Then put the older dog on leash and bring the pup out of his crate, also on leash, and let them meet again.

If you take some time doing this, and remember to reserve time for your older dog so she doesn't feel usurped by the newcomer, you'll probably be fine. Keeping the pup on leash or baby-gated in a room will allow the older dog to make contact or stay away, as she chooses.

Meeting a Housecat

Before bringing your puppy home, be sure your cat has access to and is accustomed to using some high places. Any opening, such as a cat door, big enough for a cat will also let a Yorkie through, so only the heights are safe zones.

Because your puppy will be on a leash or otherwise confined, the introductions will be up to your cat. She may stay out of sight for a time, sit safely out of reach of the pup and observe, or boldly walk right past your pup. Don't fear for the cat—she's well equipped to fend for herself. Just keep your puppy from charging at the cat or barking up a storm. If you're going to turn the puppy loose in your safe room, be sure the cat is not in the room. Let them get used to each other at a safe, restrained distance.

Even if the two get off to a rocky start, chances are that they will soon become friends or at least learn to live with each other. Because a Yorkie is so small, most cats will not feel very threatened by the dog and won't try to assert dominance. You may even catch the two snuggled up together for a nap before long.

Visiting the Vet

If you have done sufficient planning, you will already have an appointment with the veterinarian set up for a few days after your pup comes home. This first visit is for a general health check. There will be no vaccinations. Whether or not your pup has had experience with veterinary clinics already, he may react by shaking and whining. Do not fuss over the shaking dog—you will only encourage the behavior. Just go calmly about your business, rewarding any signs of settling down.

Your Yorkie's Medical History

When you take your pup to the vet for the first time, bring with you any vaccination or other health records given to you by the breeder. These documents will go into your pup's medical record. The clinic may have you fill out a form, or the veterinarian may ask you questions. Provide as much information as possible—you want as complete a record as you can get. If your Yorkie came from a rescue group or shelter, be sure to make that known, but don't exaggerate or make unsubstantiated claims. For example, don't tell the vet that the dog must have been abused just because he now shrinks away from rolled newspapers. Only report details that you know are facts.

Photograph by Cheryl A. Ertelt

▲ **Your Yorkie needs regular veterinary visits to keep him healthy and active.**

The Exam

Watch your veterinarian as she examines your Yorkie. This is your first chance to see your chosen vet interact with your dog. The pup should be kept from sliding off the table, but handled gently. If you notice any rough contact or signs of serious distress from your dog, point this out to the vet. If you are unhappy with the service you and your dog receive, consider visiting another vet to compare practices.

 fact

Keep in mind that most veterinarians are generalists, treating not just dozens of breeds of dogs, but cats and perhaps other species as well. Don't be dismayed if their knowledge of Yorkshire terriers in particular is not as deep as the breeder's. The breeder has devoted herself to a single breed.

The veterinarian should listen to your pup's heart and lungs with a stethoscope, look in his eyes and ears, and gently manipulate each leg. This contact should be gentle and slow, so as not to startle your pup. Feel free to ask any questions you may have while the vet is examining your dog in this way.

The First Few Nights

When it's time for bed, take your pup outside one last time, and then put her in her crate in your bedroom. This may be the first big test of your resolve. You may get lucky, and have a pup that sleeps through the night. Or you may have a pup that cries and howls, bites or bangs at the crate door, and carries on for what seems like hours. If you go to the pup to soothe her, or let her out of the crate, you are teaching her that noise will be rewarded with attention and human contact (which is what she wants), and you'll create a lifetime of problems for yourself.

 Essential

A SnugglePet may help your puppy feel comforted at night—she's used to snuggling with littermates, after all. This floppy plush dog contains a battery-driven "heartbeat" and a microwaveable insert for warmth. You can take out the inserts and wash the SnugglePet if your pup relieves herself at night.

Ignoring the dog's fussing may cause you to lose sleep for a few nights, but this is better than ending up with a dog that throws tantrums to get her way. Some say you should tell the pup to hush. Others suggest you bang on the top of the crate. But it's best to just endure the noise in silence and let the pup see that it doesn't work. Once she learns that there's no benefit to her whining, she will eventually stop.

CHAPTER 7

Housetraining

PROBABLY THE SINGLE MOST IMPORTANT THING you need to teach your pup is where it's appropriate to relieve himself. Dogs are regularly returned to shelters and rescues over the issue of puddles or piles on rugs. In order to be successful with housetraining, you must realize that while this is intensive work for a time, it only seems like it takes forever. Once you've accomplished this challenging task, you and your dog can enjoy years of mess-free companionship.

Concerning Crates

Confining your pup when you can't actively supervise him is essential. For confinement, you can use a crate or a safe room. While your desire might be to let the pup prance feely around your house, the confinement method serves for his own good. Left to his own devices, your Yorkie could end up in a dangerous spot.

Crates Are Not Cruel

Crates are not inherently cruel devices. You can use them cruelly by confining your dog for hours and hours, but any good owner knows not to do this. Instead, you should keep use of the crate positive and upbeat. Be cheerful when you crate your pup. Put a treat and a toy in there with her. And don't make a big fuss when you take her out, as if you're freeing her from bondage.

Additionally, never use the crate as punishment. Don't throw your pup in it in anger over some misdeed. Don't use it to keep the pup out of your way for hours because you're tired or don't want to be interrupted while you watch television. Only overnight should you use it for more than a couple of hours at a time.

If you're still doubtful about using a crate, consider this. The crate protects the pup from harm (chewing an electrical cord while unsupervised) and from mistakes (which you may then be tempted to punish). It's up to you how much you want to use it, but it's better than leaving a pup on his own to get into mischief.

Good Use of the Crate

For short-term confinement, such as while you're making dinner, put the pup in his crate. Put a treat or two in there, pop the pup in, and go about your business. Give the pup a chance to relieve himself first, and you should find the crate clean and dry when you return.

 Alert!

Most dogs are reluctant to soil their beds, and at least for the first few weeks, the crate will function like a bed for your pup. Unfortunately, dogs that were raised in the wire pens of puppy mills and pet shops had no choice but to urinate and defecate where they slept. They may have lost their natural desire to keep the bed clean.

Use a cue word or phrase when you put your pup in her crate, such as "Crate up" or "Go to bed." If you use the same word or phrase consistently, and keep creating a positive experience, you'll soon have a pup that will run into her crate on her own when you say the cue. In fact, many adult dogs that have been crate-trained as puppies will retire to their crates when they want to take a nap or get away from too much hubbub. They see their crates as safe havens.

Paper and Litter Box Training

With a dog as small as a Yorkshire terrier, many people, especially those living in areas with severe winter weather, choose to train their dogs to go to the bathroom indoors. If you're considering this, you have several options to consider.

Paper Training

The most common and reliable surface of choice for paper training is newspaper. The advantage here is that if you read the paper anyway, you already have the material. You can start by papering an entire room and gradually decrease the papered area. The disadvantage is that wet newsprint can leave ink behind, and this can be unpleasant to clean up.

 Question?

Isn't it best to paper train a puppy, then later train her to go outdoors?

This method seems to make sense except it involves you going through the rigors of housetraining twice. The best thing to do is choose one method and stick to it. If you ultimately want to train your dog to relieve herself outdoors, be vigilant, take her out often, and skip the paper.

Piddle pads, or wee-wee pads, are another option, but these are generally used only for training puppies because of their high cost. However, these options might be useful to someone who can afford the cost, as they eliminate the mess of paper and litter.

Litter Box Training

You can now find litter and litter boxes specifically designed for small dogs. Breeders warn that Yorkies in full coat will be likely to drag the litter material onto the floor and you may find it sticking to their hair. For this reason, a litter box might be a better choice for Yorkies with their coats cut down for easier maintenance. Beyond the coat issue, this method does work well, and it makes for easy cleanup. There's no need to scrub the floor as there is with the newspaper method.

A less common but still feasible method is to buy a little patch of indoor lawn for your pup. The unit includes a rectangular holder for a piece of live, growing turf, a small picket fence, and a miniature fire hydrant. The lawn does require sunlight and water, so it may be more feasible to keep it just outside your back door rather than in your kitchen. The company that makes this product even offers replacement turf. The idea is that once your pup is used to relieving himself on the small patch of grass, transitioning to the lawn outside will go more smoothly.

No matter which of the options you may choose, the training procedure is the same as for training outdoors. The only difference is that the dog always relieves himself in the designated area rather than outside.

Outdoor Training

Your responsibility is to keep the pup from having accidents. You do this through careful supervision and frequent potty trips. This is especially critical with a dog as small as a Yorkie. Puddles are so small and easy to miss that if you don't see them as they're happening, they may go unnoticed, and the pup may get the idea that such behavior is perfectly acceptable.

Consistency Is Key

Set up a schedule, and stick to it. You can depend on your pup needing to go out first thing in the morning, after eating or drinking, and after vigorous play. If none of these things happen in the span of a few hours (which would be unusual), take your pup out anyway. Don't ever postpone a potty trip to make your schedule more convenient. Don't make your pup wait until your television show ends or your freshly painted nails are dry. Forcing a pup to hold it for too long can be harmful to her health and set you back in your training.

Your pup's age offers a rough estimate of how long she can hold it. If your pup is three months old, she can wait approximately three hours between potty breaks. Four months of age indicates four hours. Of course, this is only a generalization, but it can give you an idea of a starting point.

Watch your pup for signs of impending urination or defecation—sniffing, walking in circles, and certainly the beginnings of a squat. After the first few days you should see a pattern emerging and be able to schedule potty trips to meet your pup's needs.

You Go Out, Too

One of the most important parts of housetraining your dog is accompanying her outside. Even though she will likely have to go to the bathroom pretty early in the morning, you still need to throw on some shoes, put her on the leash, and take her out. If you've trained the pup to go potty on cue, you shouldn't have to wait long for results. Praise the pup once she goes, give her a treat, and go back inside. Your presence during this event is highly preferable to just letting the dog out alone. You need to be out there to observe, to praise when puppy does the right thing, and to keep your puppy out of trouble. The leash also helps keep your pup with you and on task.

On at least half of your trips outdoors, once the pup has performed her duty, take the leash off and let her run around the yard for a few minutes. If you always come in as soon as business is done, your pup may try to hold out longer to extend the trip outdoors. Conversely, in bad weather, you may find the dog beats you to the door as soon you take off the leash.

If you go out and don't get any positive results within five or ten minutes, come back in, put the puppy in her crate, and try again in a half-hour. As you get to know your pup's schedule better, you should have fewer and fewer of these "dry runs."

Alert!

Choose your potty cue carefully. If you're going to be too embarrassed to say "Go potty" in front of friends, neighbors, or strangers, then choose something more neutral, such as "Do your duty" or "Hurry up." Just be sure that your cue is not too long or too similar to other commands.

Make It Routine

Feeding your pup at the same times every day will help make potty times more predictable. Additionally, dogs appreciate a regular routine. Try to space meals four or five hours apart, depending on your schedule. For instance, if you feed breakfast at 8 A.M., then lunch will be at 12 P.M., a snack will come at 4 P.M., and dinner will be at 8 P.M. If you factor in potty breaks after each of these meals, plus one first thing in the morning and one just before bedtime, you'll be taking the dog out roughly six times a day. In fact, another potty break with some added playtime around midday would round things out perfectly.

Details

If you're going to train your dog to potty indoors, you can carry your litter box or piddle pads with you if you travel with your dog. But if you're going to train your dog to potty outdoors, you may find yourself someday in a situation you haven't faced before.

Most people train their dogs to potty in their yards, on grass. These dogs, when suddenly confronted with city sidewalks and streets, may search frantically for a patch of grass on which to do their business. You may have thought you were teaching outside as the *place* to go, when what the dog actually learned was grass is the *surface* on which to go. So, if you plan to travel, you may want to teach your pup to use different surfaces.

Photograph by Cheryl A. Ertelt

▲ **Housetraining your new dog benefits not only your Yorkie, but you as well.**

Some people want their dog to ring a bell to indicate that they want to go out. This is easily accomplished, though you have to choose a bell light enough for a Yorkie to ring easily, without getting hit in the head by it. Hang the bell off the doorknob of the door you're using to access the yard. Ring it yourself each time before going out. Most dogs make the connection and learn to ring the bell themselves. If they need a little more help, you can entice them to raise a paw and swipe at the bell—but not while they're so young they still have to hurry to make it out in time. Be aware that clever dogs may learn to ring the bell not just when they need to potty, but when they'd like a breath of fresh air. If you're not careful, you may find yourself serving as full-time door-man to your Yorkie!

Long-Term Confinement

Occasionally your pup may have to be left for several hours without supervision. This is where your safe room and/or exercise pen comes in. The kitchen, a bathroom, or an exercise pen securely placed on a washable floor will all provide space where your pup can nap, enter-tain himself, and potty if necessary without having problems. The pup might shred the newspaper you put down, but that shouldn't be considered a major transgression. The main idea is to keep the pup safe and help him learn to be alone from time to time.

Alert!

If your pup won't eat treats or play with toys when you are out of sight, he might be suffering from separation anxiety. For more on leaving dogs alone and dealing with separation anxiety see Chapter 18, page 262.

Put your pup in his long-term confinement area for a few min-utes when you're home to get him used to the idea. Only let him out when he's being quiet. If he's whining and carrying on, wait for him to settle down; then rush to let him out when he's behaving. Gradually extend the time you leave the pup in his confinement area, and spend some of that time out of sight to observe what happens when the pup can't see you. Take your time doing this, and you shouldn't experience any major upsets.

Keep an eye on your pup the first few times to see if he can find any mischief to get into. Did you leave a dishtowel hanging where puppy teeth could reach it, or forget to latch a cabinet door? Can your pup push through the negative spaces in the baby gate and get caught? Could his collar tags get hung up on something? Before you ever really leave him alone, you want to be sure it actually is a safe place.

Dealing with Accidents

No matter how careful you are, accidents are bound to happen. They're simply part of the learning process. If you catch your puppy in the act, clap to interrupt the behavior, then hurry the pup outside or to the indoor potty area. If the pup resumes relieving himself once outside, you still have to praise him—even though you know you'll have to go inside and clean up. The pup will only learn that outside is the right place to go if you praise while he's going potty there.

 **Fact**

There's absolutely no point in rubbing your pup's nose in it or swatting the pup if you find a puddle or a pile. You'll only convince the pup that you're a dangerously aggressive human, and that maybe it's better not to relieve himself in your presence. This effect will set back your housetraining and possibly damage your relationship with the dog.

Cleanup Supplies and Strategies

There are several basic supplies you'll want to have in the house during the housetraining phase of dog ownership. Some items you might purchase include these:

- Several rolls of paper towels
- Some rags or old terrycloth towels
- An enzymatic cleanser, such as Nature's Miracle, Resolve, or OdorMute
- Spray can or plug-in air freshener

You do not want to use ammonia products to clean up after your pup. Urine contains ammonia, and the scent will only encourage your pup to go potty in that spot again.

As far as how you approach the situation, you should deal with the puppy first—cleanup can wait. If you've interrupted an accident, escort your pup outside. Once that's taken care of, put your pup in her crate while you clean up. If the accident took place on a rug, and it's a puddle, first soak up most of the liquid—put down a towel, or layers of paper towels, and press them into the carpet. If it's a pile, use a plastic bag to pick it up as cleanly as you can. Then, in either case, saturate the spot with your cleanser, place a towel or stack of paper towels over it, and put something heavy on top of the towels. Leave it there to remove the moisture from the rug.

Of course, cleanup is much easier on hard surfaces such as linoleum, wood, or tile. You can still use the enzymatic cleanser, after testing in an inconspicuous spot, to eliminate any odors that might lure the puppy back.

Housetraining Setbacks

Some people will tell you that toy dogs simply can't be housetrained. That's silly. These people just haven't taken the time and care to get the job done. Dogs cooperate best when rules are clear and enforced; ineffective supervision that allows accidents to go undiscovered confuses the dog about what's right and what's wrong. So, be fanatically dedicated to supervising your dog, and you shouldn't experience any housetraining setbacks.

Training an Adult Dog

The main difference in housetraining an adult rather than a puppy is that the adult will not have to go as often, making your task easier. However, already developed bad habits could make your job harder and lead to setbacks in training. To learn what your adult dog knows, keep him tethered to you and watch carefully for any signs that the dog needs to go. If he looks at you and whines, or tries to take you to the door or potty area, you may have a dog that already has some housetraining experience. All that's left for you to do is be sure the dog understands how to access the potty area and generally keep an eye on things.

If the dog hasn't been previously housetrained, or if in the past he was simply left to potty where he lived (as is the case for dogs housed full-time in wire cages), treat him as you would a puppy. Supervise carefully, and reward correct behavior enthusiastically.

Sudden Problems

If your housetraining has been going well and all of a sudden you start seeing more mistakes, you've probably become overconfident and let up too much on your supervision. If you rededicate yourself to supervising, you should get right back on track in no time.

If you thought you had the training finished, and your dog has been reliable for months, then suddenly starts having accidents, look for a reason. Schedule a checkup with your veterinarian. A bladder infection can make urination more urgent, and maybe the dog just couldn't get outside in time. Changes in circumstances, such as a family member leaving the household, can upset the dog and cause housetraining lapses. To remedy the situation, go back to supervising and pay more attention to the dog.

Dog Doors

If you want your dog to eventually use a dog door, ignore the door while you are working on basic housetraining. You have to accompany your dog out anyway, and you don't want to waste any time trying to get the dog through a dog door. The door comes into play later, once housetraining seems to be reliable.

Teaching a dog to understand the concept of a dog door when he constantly observes people going in and out of a normal door can be quite a challenge. You'll have to use a specific method. Have a family member on each side of the door, hold it open, and encourage the dog through. Send the dog back and forth several times, making a fun game out of it. Then hold the door only part-way open, and let the dog push it all the way open as you call him through. Gradually hold the door open less and less.

 **fact**

The term "dog door" generally brings to mind one particular style with a flap that hangs down. However, there are plenty of other varieties. A rigid plastic door that's hinged on the side and pushes open like a regular door may make more sense for your little Yorkie. You can find a wide selection at *www.petdoors.com*.

After you've played this game a few times, go to the door and encourage the dog to go through the door on his own. If it doesn't work at first, try standing on the other side of the door and urging him through with your voice. Keep working at it until he consis-tently gets it right.

Something to keep in mind when selecting a dog door is exactly what functions you'd like the door to have. For instance, there may be times when you don't want the dog to use the dog door, such as if the lawn is being chemically treated, the driveway is being repaved, or it's just too hot or cold for the dog to be out-side. To be prepared for all possible situations, choose a model with a locking function that also provides a visual indication to the dog that the door can't be used when locked.

CHAPTER

Grooming

GROOMING NOT ONLY KEEPS your Yorkie's magnificent coat in order, it also gives you valuable bonding time with your dog. This is also a good time for you to do a daily check for minor problems. Because Yorkshire terriers must be groomed often, getting them accustomed to the process while young will result in a much easier, more enjoyable relationship throughout life.

Basic Supplies

You read a bit about grooming supplies in Chapter 5, but there's a lot more to the grooming process than buying a brush. The details will depend on whether you will do all the grooming yourself or hire a professional to do the tough stuff. If you plan to take on the grooming challenge, you'll need several brushes, shampoo, plenty of towels, nail clippers, dog toothpaste, and a toothbrush. You can groom your Yorkie sitting in your lap, use the kitchen counter, or even invest in a grooming table.

Brushes and Combs

You will need at least a couple of brushes, even if they are exactly the same. This is because when you brush your pup out after a bath, the brush will be getting wetter as the dog is getting drier, and you will want to be able to change to a dry brush.

Recommended brushes are stiff rather than soft, with bristles of a material other than nylon, which breaks the coat. If you choose a pin brush, choose one without the small balls on the ends of the pins, as these tend to pull at and break the coat.

 **Alert!**

When it comes to grooming tools, you get what you pay for. Bargain combs and brushes may turn out to be uncomfortable to use, may lose teeth faster than your dog sheds hair, and will generally prove disappointing. If you pay for high-quality supplies, you'll be rewarded with years of high-quality performance.

A comb will also be needed. Select a metal one with long teeth, with a handle comfortable to hold in your hand. You may also want a fine-toothed flea comb. This can be used both as a finish comb, to be sure no small mats are hiding in your Yorkie's coat, and on the face to clear away eye mucus.

Scissors and Nail Clippers

A good pair of blunt-tipped scissors will make trimming your Yorkie's ears and paws slightly less frightening for you. Be sure the scissors cut easily, without pulling on the hair. If you're left-handed, search for a pair made specifically for lefties; otherwise you will find yourself pulling the Yorkie's hair while you are trying to cut it.

As far as nails are concerned, your dog will be more comfortable with his nails kept short. Of the several styles of nail clippers available, those that operate the same as scissors are a bit sturdier and easier to use than the guillotine type. Some people prefer to grind nails with a Dremel tool rather than cut them, but many dogs become frightened by the sound and appearance of this tool. If your dog is very frightened of having his nails trimmed or you are worried about hurting him, you might prefer just to have your vet or a professional groomer do the job for you. These professionals are used to dogs squealing and squirming, and they have special equipment to help the task go more smoothly. If you do decide to trim your dog's nails yourself, be sure to have some styptic powder on hand. Occasional nail bleeds are to be expected, and this product will help you manage the problem.

Fact

Yorkies that are carried around by their owners have little opportunity to wear their nails down and will need frequent nail trimming. Yorkies that frequently go for walks on hard surfaces will wear their nails down more effectively.

Shampoos and Rinses

Any good dog shampoo will do just fine for your pup. However, because you have to shampoo your Yorkie's head, you may want to look for a tearless shampoo in case any should drip into his eyes. Just don't use shampoos meant for human hair. These products do not have the proper pH balance for canine hair.

To make brushing easier and to keep the coat gleaming, you'll also want to choose a conditioner. Some products are conditioner/ detangler combinations. You can find them as sprays or pour-on liquids.

Dental Care

One common problem among Yorkshire terriers is crooked teeth. In particular, Yorkies often have overlapping, somewhat jumbled incisors, which can be prone to plaque buildup. For this reason, it is important that you pay attention to your dog's tooth care.

Toothpaste for dogs does not foam up as toothpaste for humans does; this is because dogs can't rinse and spit. Dog toothpaste is also flavored to make it palatable for them, chicken flavor being the most common choice. You do have a couple of options for getting the toothpaste onto the teeth. A child's toothbrush is a good size to use on a Yorkshire terrier. You can also buy a device that slides over your finger like a thimble, so you can reach more areas of the mouth. Finger brushes can be purchased from many pet-supply stores and veterinarians.

Essential

Dirty teeth can actually impact a Yorkie's total health adversely. Unhealthy teeth lead to offensively bad breath and gum infections. The solution to these problems is costly veterinary dental cleanings. To avoid danger to your Yorkie (and your wallet), take the time to clean your dog's teeth on a regular basis.

Grooming Your Yorkie

If you got your pup from a breeder, chances are good that the pup has already experienced some hair trimming, nail trimming, brushing, and maybe a bath. Whether or not this has happened with pups from other sources is unknown. Positive experience with grooming can make your life easier, but if the dog ever had a painful or frightening grooming experience, you will be faced with a bigger challenge.

Brushing Up

Brush your Yorkie daily. While Yorkshire terriers have no undercoat, their hair does tend to tangle and mat. The longer it goes without being brushed, the worse the tangles are likely to be. You can sit on the floor with your dog, put the dog up on a table, or hold the dog in your lap—whatever suits both of you. If you're going to use a table, be sure to keep one hand on the dog to steady him and keep him from jumping or falling off the table.

If you begin a brushing routine when your pup is young, there won't be all that much coat, and brushing will be quick and easy. This experience will help prepare you for the more serious grooming you'll have to do as your Yorkie's coat matures.

Before you brush, either spray the coat with water or conditioner or wet the brush. Brushing a Yorkie coat while it is dry tends to break the ends and impede its growth. Brush from the part in the middle of the back to the end of the coat. Brush all sides of each leg, especially the breeches behind the rear legs. Then turn your attention to the head.

Photograph by Cheryl A. Ertelt

▲ **One essential for a healthy Yorkshire terrier is good grooming habits.**

Hair cascades from everywhere on the head, so take your time. Brush the topknot from above the eyes, between the ears, and down the back of the neck. Brush each set of side whiskers down the side of the head. Then brush the chin whiskers down the chest. If you find any tangles, be sure you wet them down, then hold the hair behind the tangle so your fingers are against the skin as you use the other hand and the brush to work out the tangle. This technique keeps you from pulling on the dog's skin.

 **Question?**

There's so much hair! Where do you begin?
This chapter provides basic grooming instruction, but if you think a tutorial would help, ask your breeder or a groomer to show you how to bathe and brush your Yorkie. Once you've seen the correct way to do it, you'll pick up the skill quickly. And since Yorkies need to be groomed every day, you'll get lots of practice.

Trimming Hair

Yorkshire terriers are not extensively trimmed, as are some other breeds such as poodles or Kerry blue terriers. Generally, the hair on their ears and feet is trimmed, and the body coat may be shortened to keep it from dragging on the ground. If you do not plan to show your Yorkie, however, you can cut the coat down more considerably.

 **Essential**

Look closely at photos of Yorkshire terriers. Examine how the ears look, where they are trimmed and where hair starts to flow. Try to follow these examples. Just remember that hair grows back. As long as you're careful and don't cut your dog, you won't do any permanent harm.

Even with puppies, the hair growing on the ears can become so heavy that it pulls the ears down. Yorkshire terrier ears should stand upright, so the hair must be trimmed to allow this. Start about two-thirds of the way up the ear from the base (one-third down from the tip) and scissor the hair from the inner and outer surface. You could also use clippers for this part of the task. Then trim the edge of the ear, following the curve of the ear and being careful not to cut the ear leather itself. Take your time with this, especially if working on a squirmy puppy.

Also keep in mind that clippers make noise and vibrate. You can't expect to just put them in a pup's ear and have the pup stand calmly. Let the pup get used to the sound, with the clippers lying nearby, while you play with him or feed him some treats. Then clip some less-threatening body part, like the stomach. Finally, hold the clippers closer to the head. Work up to your final goal gradually.

The hair on the feet also has to be trimmed. Feet should be kept compact and rounded, so follow the circle of the foot and trim away excess hair. Also trim hair under the foot from between the pads.

Bathing

While some breeds require relatively few baths in a lifetime, Yorkshire terriers need regular bathing to keep them looking and smelling good. A bath once a week is a common recommendation, but if you're not showing your dog, twice a month should be sufficient.

Lathering Up

Bathing a Yorkie is a bit different from bathing a lot of other breeds. The hair should not be rubbed in circles, as you might do with your own scalp or with shorthaired dogs. After brushing to remove any tangles, put the Yorkie in the sink and wet the coat. If your faucet includes a sprayer, use it for more thorough cleaning.

You have to be careful when lathering up your Yorkie. Instead of rubbing the hair in circles, use your fingertips to clean down to the skin, then hold a section of hair between your hands and slide out from the body to the end of the hair, bringing the shampoo along the hair. Take your time to cover the entire dog this way.

Rinsing

Once you've accomplished soaping up, you need to rinse. The sprayer in your sink will be useful here as well. Start at the head, being careful not to spray into eyes or ears. Then work from the part down one side of the body, then the other side. Work until you're sure all the soap is gone. Any soap left on the dog will dry the skin and coat and cause irritation. Be sure you thoroughly rinse the belly and between the legs.

Alert!

Only use lukewarm water when washing your Yorkie. Water too hot will be uncomfortable for the dog and dry out his skin, and water too cold can result in chills. Check the temperature before you direct any water onto the dog. Additionally, be sure the water pressure isn't too high.

If the rinse you've chosen should be applied while the coat is wet, apply this product as soon as you've rinsed the shampoo out of the hair. Then use your hands to run water away from the body and off the end of the hair. Where hair hangs clear of the body, you can squeeze it between your fingers to remove water.

Drying

Wrap your Yorkie in a towel, and pat him lightly to draw water out of the coat. When one towel is saturated, change to a dry one. Remember that rubbing could tangle and break the hair. Patting is a better idea.

Once you've gotten out all the water you can with towels, stand the Yorkie on a dry towel for good footing and brush and dry the coat. You can use a regular hair dryer if it has a low-heat setting. Having a stand for it will leave your hands free for brushing. If you need a dryer, there is a model made for dogs, known as "the duck," that is relatively inexpensive and that comes with a stand.

Take your time, and be sure your pup is dry everywhere, including under the body and inside the legs. Do not let a Yorkie outside for several hours after a bath, until you are positive the dog is absolutely dry.

Tooth and Nail Care

As already mentioned, you should brush your Yorkshire terrier's teeth regularly to avoid tartar and plaque buildup and the need for frequent veterinary cleanings. Brushing every day is ideal, but if you can't manage that, try for at least two or three times a week. Nails need to be kept short enough not to interfere with walking.

Chews for Teeth

In addition to brushing your dog's teeth, you can give him chew treats that help to remove plaque and tartar. A product called Greenies comes in a size specifically for toy dogs and does a good job of removing tartar. Be sure your dog chews the Greenie into bits—the dog should not gulp it down whole. Some dogs need a little encouragement to eat a Greenie the first time, but most eventually come to enjoy the treat.

Tooth Scaling

Some groomers also scale (clean) dogs' teeth. Before you give the go-ahead for such a service, ask for and check references. Opinion is divided on how safe a procedure this is, so you want to be sure that the professional you choose is highly trained and experienced. Also, be sure no tranquilizers are used. While this procedure may be thorough, it will likely be expensive. If your veterinarian has to clean your dog's teeth, the dog will almost always be anesthetized—anesthesia can cost quite a bit as well. Clearly, the best option is to brush the dog's teeth yourself.

Trimming Nails

The Yorkshire terrier standard calls for black nails, meaning you can't see the blood vessel inside the nail. Black nails can be difficult to trim, especially for an owner who is nervous about hurting her dog. However, with enough practice, this challenge can be overcome.

Ask the breeder or your veterinarian to show you how to trim nails, pointing out where the nail narrows and starts to curve, and what the inside of the nail looks like as you get close to the quick. You can always cut a little at a time, examine the inside, and then cut a little more. If your dog has dewclaws, don't forget to trim them. These don't have as much opportunity to be filed down with walking.

 **Fact**

You shouldn't hear your dog click when she walks across an uncarpeted floor—that's a sign the nails are too long. Overlong nails push the toes out of position and can create sore feet. Always keep nails trimmed to avoid any damage to your dog—and your hardwood floors.

Get your pup used to nail trimming gradually, if the breeder hasn't already done this. Trim one nail and give a treat. If your pup is still calm, trim another nail and give another treat. Don't be in a hurry to get the job done. Instead, concentrate on keeping it as positive as possible, with plenty of patience and lots of treats.

Nail-Trimming Tips

Have some styptic powder on hand in case you make a mistake. Qwik Stop is a popular, widely available brand. If you cut a little too much and get a drop of blood, put a pinch of the powder directly on the cut and pat it in a little. The bleeding should quickly stop.

Hold your pup's foot gently for nail clipping, not in a tight grip, and use your trimmers to cut the tip off one nail. Those who use a Dremel tool to grind the nails rather than cut them say it's easier to avoid mistakes this way because nail is removed gradually. However, you must be sure that no hair gets tangled in the tool. You'll also need to let the tool run nearby without using it first, so the dog can get used to the sound it makes before you bring it close to him.

Cleaning Eyes and Ears

Like many toy dogs, Yorkshire terriers tend to collect dirt at the corners of their eyes. This mucus can form hard little balls in the hair there and be difficult to clean if not taken care of regularly. If you check your Yorkie's eyes every morning, you can easily scrape away the dirt with a fingernail.

Yorkies' upright ears do not usually suffer problems that require attention. The only problem that might arise is mats in the ear hair if you let it grow too long. Always keep your Yorkie's ear hair trimmed and tidy so that no obstructions form and muffle his hearing. Also check the ears for foxtails or other weed seeds and ticks if your pup runs around in tall grass. Some dogs are wary of letting a person touching their ears, so be gentle at all times.

Using a Professional Groomer

Though you should brush your Yorkie every day, you may want to hire a professional to do the bathing and trimming. Or maybe you will do your regular maintenance grooming, but you'd like a professional to do the job before a show. If your time is limited, perhaps you'd rather spend it on training your Yorkie and taking walks together, and leave the grooming to a professional. That's fine—just put some time into choosing a reliable groomer.

Finding a Groomer

If you know any other Yorkshire terrier owners in your area, get groomer recommendations from them, or ask your veterinarian. If you can't get recommendations, ask groomers about their experience with toy dogs and with Yorkshire terriers in particular. Ask to watch them groom a toy dog, to see how they handle the dog. Take a look around their facility. While there may be hair on the floor, and dogs in holding pens may bark a bit, it shouldn't be dirty or overwhelmingly noisy.

If you're not showing and you'd like your Yorkie clipped down for easier care, be sure you agree on exactly what's going to be done. If you are showing, make sure that your groomer understands exactly how a Yorkie should be groomed for show.

Questions to Ask

First and foremost, you should ascertain that the groomer you've chosen doesn't use tranquilizers on dogs. Some groomers, when faced with a dog that objects to being groomed, customarily administer some sort of tranquilizer. This is risky, and you don't want it happening to your dog.

Also, make sure the groomer won't just put your Yorkie in a crate with a cage dryer after a bath. The Yorkie needs to be brushed out. In winter, be sure the facility is adequately heated. Yorkies chill easily when wet and must be thoroughly dried in a well-heated environment.

Another good idea is to request that you stay and observe as your dog is groomed. This way, you can be sure everything is done according to your wishes. If you notice any unprofessional behavior or unsanitary areas, you can remove your dog from the facility and find a new groomer right away.

Yorkies for Show

Yorkshire terriers destined for the conformation show ring must be kept in full coat. Because this means the coat will reach the floor or beyond, if the hair is left to drag, it will get dirty and break. To avoid this, the coat is wrapped—tied up in little bundles all over the dog. This takes some practice, but you can ask your breeder to show you how to do it.

 **Essential**

Keep in mind that although much of the judging in the show ring is focused on the dog's physical appearance, judges will probably also be touching the dog's body. A long, flowing coat is all well and good, but if it feels a bit dry to the touch, the judge will notice. Be sure that you or your groomer uses a canine conditioner when bathing the dog to keep the coat soft and shining.

Yorkies are shown with the hair on top of their head done up in a topknot. This also requires some practice. If you are planning to show but your breeder is not nearby, do your best to meet other Yorkie enthusiasts and handlers. Your veterinarian may be able to refer you to the owners of his other Yorkie patients. Any of these people will likely be able (and very willing) to help you.

If the coat grows too long, it should be trimmed to allow the Yorkie to show good movement. The full show coat is a beautiful quality, but this image can be quickly spoiled by a dog tripping over his coat in the show ring. Coat trimming for show dogs should only be done by an experienced professional.

Yorkies at Home

Yorkies that are meant simply as pets can have their coats clipped down to make upkeep less work. Some breeders are offended by this, as the coat is the breed's signature glory, but it's a matter of practicality. A full show coat would turn into a tangled mess if the dog was playing outside and being touched by children on a daily basis.

For pet dogs, you can choose among several popular clips. The puppy cut just shortens the coat all over. The modified Schnauzer cut, or Snorkie, clips the body close and leaves the hair on the head and legs longer. The hair can be layered, so it still looks long and glamorous, but isn't as thick. And the head can be trimmed in a modified Westie cut.

 **Fact**

In large part, the success of a home trimming is in the tools. If you're using old scissors or clippers with dull blades, you're probably not going to be happy with the results. Always invest in high-quality equipment recommended by breeders to receive the best possible outcome.

Whatever you do, don't become anxious or upset about a bad haircut. Hair always grows back. If a groomer makes a mistake, simply take it in stride and find a different groomer for next time. If you do it yourself and make a mistake, the problem will grow out, and you'll be able to start over in a couple of months. Your Yorkie won't know the difference.

CHAPTER 9

Basic Nutrition

O BVIOUSLY, ONE OF YOUR DAILY CHORES is to feed your dog. But how do you choose the type and flavor of the food, and how much do you give the dog? Does it matter when and where you feed? And what about treats and table scraps? The breeder may have told you one thing and your veterinarian another. Read on to learn how to differentiate between dog foods, how much to feed, and when to do it.

What a Dog Needs

Dogs require proteins, fats, vitamins, minerals, and water. While they have no absolute need for carbohydrates, they can burn them for energy. Carbs are included in dry foods to create the correct consistency for forming them into shapes; plus, they help maintain good gastrointestinal tract health.

Proteins and Fats

Proteins are actually composed of amino acids. There are twenty-two amino acids, ten of which must be provided in the dog's daily diet. It's not enough to just provide protein—it has to be the correct protein or blend of proteins. Dog foods that have passed the Association of American Feed Control Officials (AAFCO) feeding trials will have the correct amino acids included.

A certain amount of fat is necessary to make food palatable and to allow fat-soluble vitamins to be absorbed. Fat is also a high-calorie dietary component of great concern in the feeding of Yorkshire terriers, with their predisposition to pancreatitis. Do not buy a high-performance food for your Yorkie, as these generally have higher levels of fat than are necessary or even safe for a Yorkshire terrier.

 **Fact**

Canines are scientifically classed as carnivores, but they are more properly called "opportunistic scavengers." While wild canines certainly bring down big game such as moose, they also hunt mice, scavenge garbage dumps, and steal from other predators. They also eat ripe fruit and berries along with meat.

Vitamins and Minerals

Vitamins can be divided into two categories: fat soluble and water soluble. The water-soluble vitamins can't be stored in the body and must be consumed every day. Vitamin C and the B complex vitamins are all water soluble.

Alert!

Many home-prepared diets fail when it comes to providing all the minerals dogs need. This can lead to a large variety of health problems. On the other hand, supplementing balanced diets with extra calcium or other minerals can also result in health problems.

Minerals also fall into two categories: macrominerals and trace minerals. Trace minerals, or microminerals, are needed in only very small amounts and can become toxic if provided at larger levels. Minerals interact with each other in myriad ways, and an excess of one can lead to a deficiency of another. Fresh, cool water should always be available to the dog as well—this will help the dog process these minerals.

Commercial Foods

Today, there's more choice than ever in packaged dog foods, with some foods certified organic, others flash-frozen, and every shape, size, and color of pieces. Canned foods seem to target toy dogs specifically, with their small serving size.

You can learn a lot about a dog food if you understand the information provided on the label. The main display panel, ingredients list, guaranteed analysis, and method used to substantiate the life stage statement all provide facts about the food. Further information can be obtained from manufacturers' literature, Web sites, and phone calls to manufacturers' toll-free numbers.

Ingredients Panel

Every package of dog food includes an ingredients list. Just like people foods, ingredients are listed by weight, with the component weighing the most listed first. Of course, you have to consider that an ingredient such as chicken includes a lot of water weight, whereas chicken meal is a dry ingredient.

Ingredients may be listed more than once in various forms, such as ground yellow corn, cornmeal, and corn syrup. While all these forms of corn may be listed individually below the main meat ingredient, if you added them together, corn might move up to second, or even first on this list.

The quality of an ingredient may not be apparent simply from its name. An ingredient list cannot distinguish highly nutritious poultry by-product meal from nearly indigestible, nutritionally useless poultry by-product meal. The name does not tell you which is which, and no reference to the quality of ingredients is permitted on packaging. Because ingredients listings, such as "by-products," offer no easy way to discern quality, some dog owners avoid foods that contain them at all, opting instead for whole ingredients such as turkey or cottage cheese.

The AAFCO is the Association of American Feed Control Officials. They are an advisory body whose main focus is feed animals such as cattle and hogs. But they also write the definitions for dog food ingredients, as well as the guidelines for conducting feeding trials of those foods.

Guaranteed Analysis

This small box looks very reassuring and scientific with its list of nutrients and percentages or quantities of each included in the food. However, this information can be confusing. When you are comparing different foods, it's important to notice the moisture content in each. A food with 23 percent protein and 10 percent moisture has the same amount of protein per serving as a food with 23 percent protein and only 7 percent moisture. This distinction means that with the former food, you are buying water instead of food. The AAFCO guidelines for nutrients are given on a dry-matter basis, so foods can be compared on an equal plane. A dry-matter analysis can usually be found in the manufacturer's literature, which pet-supply stores sometimes stock near the foods. You may also find the food's digestibility in the literature (it should be at least 75 percent).

Main Display Panel

The front of the bag, box, or can is the main display panel. Here you'll find the net weight of the package ingredients, the flavor of the food, and a nutrition statement regarding what life stage the food is meant to satisfy. The latter designation could be for growth (puppies), maintenance (adults), reproduction (pregnant or nursing females), senior, or possibly performance. Another designation is "meets or exceeds the nutritional requirements for all life stages of your dog." This means the food is calorie-dense enough for puppies and may contribute to obesity in adults.

Promotional statements may appear in banners or balloons, saying such things as "100% nutritionally complete" or "Reduces tartar." These claims are pretty reliable. General claims must be verifiable, and the Food and Drug Administration must review health claims.

Other Information

Somewhere on the packaging you will find the method used to substantiate the life-stage statement. Look for the statement "Animal feeding tests using AAFCO procedures substantiate that [product name] provides complete and balanced nutrition for [life stage]." This is preferable to a statement that the product was "formulated" or "calculated."

Feeding guidelines will be included on the label. These are exactly as their name states—guidelines. Individual dogs vary depending on age, size, activity level, environment, and their own metabolism, so these specifications should only be used as a starting point.

🐕 Alert!

Obesity is a very serious problem for pet dogs. The most severe consequence of obesity is a shortened lifespan—and you want to have as much time as possible together, don't you? Always consider how much you are feeding your dog in order to preserve his health and extend his life as long as possible.

Calorie content of the food is generally included as well. It's stated as "Metabolizable energy: kilocalories per kilogram (kcal/kg)," or may also be given as kilocalories per cup. You can compare calorie counts across different foods to find differences.

The manufacturer's or distributor's name and address must also be on the label. Look for the notation "Manufactured by." This means the named company makes its own food and is responsible for quality control. Any questions or problems with the food can be directed to this company using the toll-free number usually given on the packaging.

Product Freshness Dating

Four methods are generally used to date packages. The international date code consists of two numbers for the day of the month, two numbers for the month, and two numbers for the year. So, 270605 means the twenty-seventh day of the sixth month in 2005, or June 27, 2005. Julian calendar dating counts the days of the year from start to finish—1 to 365 or 366—and the last one or two numbers of the year. So the code 0485 or 04805 means the forty-eighth day of the year 2005, or February 17, 2005.

"Best before" uses the month/day/year format to indicate the date by which the product should be eaten. So, 08/2%5 means you should use up this food by mid-August 2005. The manufacturer calculates the shelf life, including a margin of safety. The food may have been manufactured anywhere from a month to a year prior to that date.

Canned, Kibble, or Other

By far, the majority of dog food sold in the United States is dry, accounting for 80 to 90 percent of sales. Canned foods are slightly more popular among owners of toy breeds, such as the Yorkshire terrier, than in the general dog population. Semimoist packaged products have nearly disappeared from shelves, while frozen foods have not yet gained much of the market share.

Dry Food

Dry food is easy to store and available in a wide variety of package sizes. Packaging adds little to the cost. With its low moisture content, dry food is energy dense. A smaller quantity meets the dog's daily energy requirements. Dry food may be left down for the dog to eat free choice, or can be fed in meals. Something called "mouth feel" factors into how attractive a food is to a dog, and some dogs prefer the crunch of dry. Additionally, dry food may help remove tartar from teeth.

Stool quantity depends to a large extent on the food's digestibility. If the piles in your yard would lead people to think you have a Great Dane rather than a Yorkshire terrier, you may want to consider switching brands. Though the price of your current brand may seem like a bargain, you're paying for a lot of ingredients your dog can't use.

 **Fact**

A food with higher digestibility will mean you feed less, so though the price per pound may be higher, the same-size bag will last longer. Your dog will also produce less excrement when eating this food.

Dry food is generally extruded—the dough is pushed through a die to form shapes. A coating of fat is sprayed on, and the shapes are dried to nugget hardness. A few dry foods are still made as kibbles, baked in sheets and then broken into pieces, rather than pressure-cooked like extruded foods.

Canned Food

Most advertising of canned foods is aimed at toy dogs because it's an uneconomical way to feed. You're buying a lot of water content, and a large-breed dog would likely need several cans per meal. Canned food can't be fed free choice because it spoils if left out. Additionally, because they contain little or no carbohydrates, canned foods can create softer stools. Dogs switched abruptly from dry to canned may suffer diarrhea.

Canned food is generally higher in fat than dry food. Also, the increased palatability may encourage dogs to overeat. Canned food also tends to stick to teeth and gums, and it can hasten dental problems if not cleaned away. It can also lead to more pungent doggy breath.

Essential

Given the Yorkie's predisposition to problems with teeth, canned may not be a good choice unless you are dedicated to frequent brushings. Dry foods will help to clear away plaque from the teeth and will not get stuck in spaces between teeth as easily as canned food.

Owners using canned foods have a tendency to overfeed because the dog shows more enthusiasm for freshly opened food. Owners tend to ladle out all the contents of the can, regardless of whether it's an appropriate serving amount. Canned foods are helpful, however, for anorectic dogs or those with tooth or mouth problems. The high moisture content releases both flavor and odor, encouraging dogs to eat, even through oral pain.

Food in Other Forms

Semimoist foods, most often sold in hamburger-like patties or ribbon chunks with a white strip of "fat" running across each chunk, have decreased in popularity. These products require sugars to prevent spoilage, as well as preservatives. They are the canine equivalent of fast foods.

Frozen foods have gradually increased in popularity, though they still lag far behind dry and canned. These foods do not have to be processed at high temperatures, sparing nutrients from destruction by heat. They do have to be refrigerated, and should be heated to room temperature before serving. Their fat content may be too high for a Yorkshire terrier.

Where and When to Feed

Once you've decided what to feed, you still need to determine where your dog will eat her meals and exactly how you're going to portion the food out to the dog. This decision depends upon several factors in your home, as well as the personality of the dog.

Where to Feed Your Dog

Dogs are creatures of habit, and they appreciate a set place where their food is provided. Many owners choose the kitchen for its ease in cleaning up any spills. As long as the dog can stand comfortably on the floor, without slipping, this room is a good choice. Similarly convenient areas include laundry rooms and pantries, which generally have tiled floors and easy access to water for easy cleanup.

Wherever you decide to feed your dog, she will be happier if you are within view. Dogs are communal eaters. They like to be there while you eat and like you to be there while they eat as well. You may want to keep the food and bowls somewhat hidden away, but the dog will probably be reluctant to eat in a dark closet at another end of the house. Keep the eating area close to the main living space, and be sure there is plenty of light in the room where your dog eats.

Free Choice

Also known as *ad libitum* or self-feeding, this feeding method requires the least amount of owner participation. Its popularity has decreased, however, as dogs have become more integral members of the family. The method limits the choice of food to dry. With food left out and available to the dog at all times, anything but dry would quickly spoil. Even dry should be thrown out if not consumed in a day or two, at most.

With free choice, the dog makes the decision of how much to eat. Some dogs will adjust their daily intake to match their energy requirements, but some will consistently overeat and quickly become fat. If you decide on a free-choice program, you must vigilantly monitor the dog's condition. For dogs that do limit their intake, being able to eat many small meals may both help keep them occupied and keep their metabolism ticking over at a higher rate.

A potential drawback of the free-choice method, aside from dogs that overeat, is that you won't be able to observe the dog's eating habits. Refusal of food is often the first indication that a dog is ill, and with free feeding some time may be lost before the owner realizes the dog isn't eating.

Timed Feeding

A variation on free feeding, this plan involves putting down a large amount of food at set times each day. The dog is allowed to eat for some predetermined amount of time—fifteen minutes is a common choice—and then the food is removed.

While you can see how much your dog is eating with this method, it still allows the dog to overeat. Plus, it encourages dogs to gulp their food, knowing that it will be taken away. It's equally unsuitable for those dogs that nibble their food and take a long time over their meals.

Portion Feeding

With this feeding method, the owner determines the maximum amount the dog can (and should) eat and gives this amount to the dog at specified times during the day. The tricky thing about this option is that the owner must know how much the ideal amount of food for the dog is.

Essential

You can easily use your bathroom scale to weigh your Yorkie. First weigh yourself. Then pick up your dog and weigh yourself again. The difference between the two numbers is your dog's weight. Otherwise, go and use the scale in your veterinarian's office—this gives you a chance to have a nonthreatening visit.

Remember that the feeding guidelines on the package are only guidelines and are on the high side of average to account for the widest possible variation. You can use them as a starting point, but you will probably need to make adjustments. If you combine foods—dry and canned, for example—you need to consider total calories from both foods.

To determine the correct amount of food for your dog, choose a portion of food to start with. Feed it for a week and assess. Weigh your dog to determine if he's gaining or losing weight. Adjust food accordingly.

When to Feed Your Dog

Presuming that you aren't choosing to feed free choice, you need to decide on mealtimes for your dog. Note that the word is plural: mealtimes. Even though Yorkies are small, they still need more than one meal each day. In fact, an adult Yorkshire terrier should have at least two meals a day and might prefer three. A puppy should have four or five.

If someone is home during the day, this shouldn't be a problem. You can give your dog breakfast, lunch, and dinner. Keep in mind that while you may vary your own mealtimes, dogs appreciate routine, and will like their meals at the same time each day, if possible. Your dog will likely let you know in no uncertain terms when it's time to eat!

If no one is home during the day, you have two choices. You can feed the dog breakfast and dinner and hire someone to come in and give the dog a walk and some lunch. Or you can feed the dog breakfast, feed the dog as soon as you get home, and feed the dog a snack before bedtime.

Homemade Diets

If you decide to use a homemade diet, you have to be careful to provide good nutrition and safe ingredients. You can't decide you're too tired to bother and serve your dog leftover spaghetti one night and French toast the next. You'll need to use a tested recipe and all the ingredients it calls for on a consistent basis.

Raw Food

Some breeders, even Yorkshire terrier breeders, are now promoting raw-food diets for their dogs. You should think seriously about this before following such advice. Raw foods and bones diets have been promoted largely by two veterinarians from Australia, neither of whom is a nutritionist, and are untested and unproven.

 **Question?**

If your breeder feeds raw and her dogs look great, why shouldn't you feed your Yorkie the same way?
You certainly can. First, be sure you're willing to spend the time and energy to gather the ingredients and prepare the food. Then be fanatically dedicated to cleanliness to avoid infection. Finally, realize that dogs have died from intestines punctured by bone fragments and required surgery for fractured teeth or impacted intestines.

If you choose to follow this diet, be advised that raw meat must be handled carefully to avoid exposing yourself and your family to *E. coli* and salmonella bacteria. Dogs fed the diet for the first time often react adversely, with vomiting and diarrhea. The bones can cause tooth fractures or, worse, punctured intestines from bone fragments. Yes, wolves may eat raw meat and bones. But no one knows how many wolves die young from problems with bone fragments. And Yorkshire terriers are most definitely not wolves.

Home-Cooked Diets

You can find tested recipes for home-cooked dog foods in books and on the Internet. Your veterinarian may even have one available, if you ask. Some of these recipes started as alternatives for dogs suffering from food allergies, while others were created just because owners wanted to cook for their dogs.

Be sure that any recipe you choose has been time-tested, and then follow it carefully. Some ingredients used in small quantities may seem unimportant and hard to find, but they provide essential vitamins and minerals.

Treats

More than half of dog owners admit to giving their dogs treats. Those using positive training methods use treats as rewards in training. There's nothing wrong with giving treats to your dog, as long as you don't give too many and you're sure they're the right type of treats.

 **fact**

Some treat manufacturers are responding to the popularity of positive training by making tiny morsels of treats rather than large biscuits and sausage rolls. Other treats can easily be broken into tiny bits for this purpose.

Many treats contain high proportions of fat and sugar. This can be a particular problem for Yorkshire terriers, so choose your treats wisely. Hard biscuits tend to be lower in fats and sugars (and better for teeth) than all the various soft, chewy treats.

Table Scraps

Years ago, a dog's entire diet often consisted of table scraps. Of course, years ago our own diets were less processed and less packaged, and table scraps were more likely to have good nutritional value. Today, table scraps should be kept to a bare minimum to ensure your dog's health.

Keep Them Limited

Nutritionists recommend that treats of any kind, including table scraps, should not provide more than 5 to 10 percent of the dog's daily caloric intake. However, you're unlikely to know how many calories are in that chunk of baked potato with sour cream and morsel of pork chop. So, more realistic advice may be to give only a tiny amount of table scraps, on an occasional basis.

Don't use table scraps in an effort to encourage a finicky dog to eat. Unless you're willing to actually grind the food and the scraps together, the dog will likely eat the table scraps and leave the rest of the food behind. This will only encourage the dog's pickiness to the point that he won't eat anything but scraps. A diet consisting entirely of scraps of human food will quickly lead to obesity and digestive problems.

Foods to Avoid

With Yorkies, it's not a good idea to give fat trimmings from meat. It's simply too much fat for a small dog inclined to pancreatitis. If you want to give a treat of meat, offer a piece of lean meat instead.

You've probably heard that chocolate is poisonous to dogs. While it may not cause a dog to drop dead on contact, chocolate does contain certain elements that are harmful to dogs. The theobromine in chocolate can cause serious health disorders, ranging from vomiting to irregular heartbeat and even death. The darker the chocolate, the more theobromine it contains.

Onions can cause destruction of red blood cells in dogs, though the amount consumed has to be rather large to create this effect. Raisins and grapes have also created serious problems for some dogs, though no one yet understands why. And, of course, bones can splinter and puncture vital organs.

Avoiding Obesity

Obesity has serious health consequences for dogs. These include heart disease, breathing impairment, a tendency toward diabetes, impaired liver function, and increased stress on ligaments, tendons, and bones. Heat stress becomes more likely. Skin problems may occur. Surgery is complicated because finding correct anesthesia levels is more difficult and suturing is trickier.

 **Essential**

> Dogs are accomplished actors and can use their bright pleading eyes and cocked head to convince you they can't live without a bite of whatever you're eating. Don't give in! A moment's pleasure in giving your dog a treat is nothing compared to the two or three additional years you may have together if you keep your dog lean.

Keeping an Eye on Weight

You can use the rib check test combined with the body condition scoring system to assess your dog's weight. If you are uncertain of what you are seeing and feeling at first, you can ask your veterinarian to help you get used to making a judgment.

To perform the rib check test, first place both your thumbs on your dog's backbone with your fingers extending down her sides. Run your fingers along the rib cage. If you can't easily feel the bony part of each rib, the dog may need to lose weight.

Second, stand directly over your standing dog and look down at her. You should see a clearly defined waist behind the ribs. This is more difficult with Yorkies than with some other breeds because of the profuse coat. Use your hands. If your dog does not have a definite hourglass shape, she may need to lose weight.

Third, check your dog's profile. Again, the Yorkie's coat may get in the way here. If the dog is in full coat, do this while the coat is tied up in wraps. If the dog is clipped down, you shouldn't have a problem. You should see a clearly defined tuck up, where the abdomen rises behind the rib cage. If you don't, your dog may need to lose weight.

The body condition scoring system builds on the visual and physical exam of the rib check test by rating a dog on a scale of one to nine according to the results of the rib check. Your veterinary clinic probably has a visual chart of dogs with body conditions from emaciated to obese. Ask to see this, and consider where your dog fits into the progression.

Helping Your Dog Lose Weight

If you have a dog with a weight problem, you should definitely be using portion feeding, so you control the dog's intake. Feed as many small meals as possible to keep the dog's metabolism operating at a higher rate without encouraging obesity. Be sure that all family members are in accord with the weight-loss program. One person slipping treats to the dog will sabotage all your efforts. Keep the dog out of the garbage and the cat's litter box as well.

Photograph by Cheryl A. Ertelt

▲ **A proper diet, combined with exercise, helps prevent canine obesity.**

Give your dog your time and attention in place of food treats. If you absolutely can't stop giving treats, then at least switch to low-calorie choices. You can also switch to one of the "lite" or low-calorie foods. Or you can feed less of your regular food and bulk it up with low-calorie ingredients such as carrots or pumpkin.

Of course, you can also increase your dog's daily exercise to help him lose weight. If you continue to feed the same number of calories but burn more of them with longer, faster, or more frequent walks, the dog should lose weight relatively quickly.

Basic Health Care

HUMAN MEDICINE HAS BEEN SLOW to shift its focus from treating disease to preventing disease. You can do better for your dog. Read this chapter and Chapter 12 to identify common hereditary diseases of the Yorkshire terrier, and to understand how to use veterinary checkups, vaccinations, spay or neuter surgery, and home health exams to your best advantage.

Vaccinations

Vaccinations have long been the reason to bring a dog to the veterinarian once a year. However, these yearly visits for vaccinations may not be as necessary as they once were. This may confuse you if your vet still recommends yearly boosters. To make this determination you must look at what vaccinations are, how they work, and which ones your dog needs.

What Vaccinations Do

When you give a vaccination, whether to a puppy or a human baby, you are presenting some form of a specific virus to the body's immune system. A competent immune system, thus challenged, makes antibodies against the virus. The antibodies fight to neutralize the virus, protecting the recipient against the disease.

Any of three types of vaccines might be used. Killed vaccines are exactly what the name suggests: dead viruses. They store well, and they cannot cause disease when administered. But because they are combined with adjuvants—materials to make them more effective in creating an immune response—they are the form most often associated with adverse reactions to the injection.

Modified live viruses are the actual live viruses, changed to make them less virulent. But in an animal with a weakened immune system, this form of vaccine can cause the disease. Recombinant vaccines are the newest form, currently available for rabies, distemper, and Lyme disease. They rely on gene splicing, presenting a portion of the virus or bacteria DNA to the animal. They can't cause the disease and also seem to be causing fewer reactions to vaccinations.

Which Vaccines to Give, and How Often

It was once common to deliver a whopping combination vaccine—DHLPP or some variation (standing for distemper, hepatitis, leptospirosis, parvovirus, and parainfluenza). Most veterinarians now give vaccines for fewer diseases, and they may separate the vaccines into individual injections.

The core vaccines, those essential for all dogs, are now agreed to be rabies, distemper, hepatitis (also called adenovirus 2), and parvovirus. All are serious viral diseases, potentially fatal and highly contagious. Rabies can be transmitted to humans and is invariably fatal once signs of disease occur; therefore, vaccination is regulated by state government. Some states require annual rabies vaccinations, but most mandate vaccinations every three years.

Other vaccines that might be offered to your dog include bordetella (kennel cough), Lyme disease, leptospirosis, parainfluenza, and giardia. Some boarding kennels require a bordetella vaccination because kennel cough is highly contagious among dogs housed closely together. Those with sporting dogs competing in field trials in the Northeast may choose a Lyme vaccine because the disease is common there. Those who go hiking and let their dogs drink from natural water sources may consider a giardia vaccine because the disease-causing organism is common in streams and lakes everywhere. Leptospirosis vaccines are known to cause frequent and extreme reactions in toy dogs, and these should not be given to Yorkshire terriers. If your veterinarian recommends anything beyond these core vaccines, ask why.

Advice on how often to give vaccinations has changed in recent years. Puppies still require a series of shots. They shouldn't be given too early, or the immunity received via nursing will interfere with creation of antibodies. But you also don't want to wait too long and risk exposing your pup to disease. In general, puppies should receive their first immunization at six weeks of age, their second three weeks later at nine weeks, and their third after another three weeks at twelve weeks. The rabies shot is given at sixteen weeks of age. A booster is given at one year of age.

Alert!

Some dogs have adverse reactions to vaccinations. Signs might include a lump at the vaccination site, generalized hives, swelling on the face and muzzle, lethargy, and anaphylactic shock. Careful veterinarians keep dogs in the office for a half-hour after the injection—most reactions occur in that time.

Once dogs have had their series of puppy shots and the one-year booster, vaccinations can then be renewed every three years. Some advise that all vaccinations should be stopped once dogs pass ten years of age, but this remains controversial, especially for toy breeds, with their generally longer life spans. Many Yorkshire terrier aficionados recommend that vaccinations be separated for these tiny pups. Each shot would only cover one disease, and shots for the three core diseases other than rabies could either be given the same day, but separately, or separated by a few days. This results in quite a few injections, making the veterinary visits rather unpleasant. You want to consider the pluses and minuses before committing to this course of action.

Parasite Control

Dogs fall prey to both external and internal parasites. Fleas and ticks on the outside and a variety of worms on the inside can compromise health on their own and spread secondary disease. Keeping your Yorkshire terrier parasite-free is part of good health maintenance.

 Essential

Don't fall into a false sense of security when it comes to fleas. Even if your Yorkie doesn't spend much time around other dogs, she is still at risk. These pests can be found anywhere environmental conditions allow for their existence. Denying a flea problem will only give it time to worsen.

External Parasites

Flea and tick prevention and eradication has gotten much simpler in recent years. You used to have to fog the yard, bathe and dip the dog, and bomb the house—each of those procedures using chemicals—repeatedly during flea season. Now, thanks to the newer products, you can give the dog a monthly pill or use a spot-on preventive without having to worry about hazardous chemicals. What will work best for you depends on your area of the country and your lifestyle. Consult your veterinarian for a choice of products. Also, note that some preventives are active against fleas only, while some work against fleas and ticks, and some also claim to repel mosquitoes.

Internal Parasites

Dogs can be infested with a variety of internal parasites, all called worms. Most of these worms, including roundworm, hookworm, tapeworm, and whipworm, occupy the digestive tract. They cause internal bleeding, diarrhea, and a dull-looking coat because they leach nutrients away from the dog. Routine examination of stool samples can identify worms, and deworming medications can combat them.

Heartworms are an even more serious threat, as they actually live and grow in the dog's heart. Good preventives exist, but once the dog has a heartworm, treatment becomes difficult. A dog should be tested for heartworm before being given a heartworm preventive. Dogs already suffering an infestation can be further sickened by the preventive.

Some canine worms can be transmitted to humans. This should not cause you undue alarm, as it's a rather rare occurrence. But it should provide additional motivation to see to your dog's good health.

Spay and Neuter

Spaying (for females) and neutering (for males) refer to the surgical removal of the reproductive organs. Unless a dog is part of a carefully considered breeding program, spaying or neutering is highly advised.

Benefits

For females, spaying before the first heat nearly eliminates the risk of breast cancer and does eliminate any chance of ovarian or uterine cancer (because those organs are removed). It also does away with ovarian infections and the mess and fuss of twice-yearly heats.

Spayed females don't have changes in hormones related to coming into heat, and they may be less apt to show personality changes as a result. They will not roam in search of a mate, and they are less likely to exhibit false pregnancies.

For males, neutering reduces the risk of prostate and testicular cancer. Neutered males are less likely to roam in search of attractive females, and they may even be less prone to aggressive behavior.

Drawbacks

Most of the supposed drawbacks are inaccurate. Spaying or neutering does not cause obesity. It will not make your Yorkshire terrier lazy. If it changes personality at all, it will be for the better, making a dog more affectionate and less aggressive. Dogs have no inherent need to have (sire) a litter before being spayed or neutered.

 **Fact**

Spaying and neutering does decrease or eliminate sex-related hormones, which may slow metabolism slightly. But the normal progress of the dog from adolescence to adulthood has the same effect. To keep a dog trim, the amount of food must be balanced with energy requirements throughout life. In other words, spaying and neutering do not make dogs fat—eating too much and exercising too little certainly will.

Two valid concerns are anesthesia and surgery. Both do involve some element of risk. However, anesthetics have improved, with most veterinarians now using reversible anesthetics. Surgery should utilize all the common precautions of sterilizing instruments, everyone scrubbing up, and close monitoring of the patient. Feel free to question your veterinarian about anesthetics, surgical procedures, and his or her experience doing spays and neuters on toy dogs.

When to Spay or Neuter

For those adopting from shelters or rescue, the decision will often have been made for you—the dog won't be released without first being altered (another word for spay or neuter, covering both sexes). If you are purchasing your Yorkshire terrier from a breeder, you may get advice to wait until some specified age to spay or neuter. Provided that age is no more than six months, you can abide by the breeder's wishes. You want to spay before the first heat or neuter before puberty to get the full health benefits of the surgery. And while the average age for the first heat is nine months to a year, Yorkies have been known to come into heat as young as seven months. So don't delay.

 **Essential**

Costs for spaying and neutering vary from practice to practice. The less-involved neutering procedure averages between $75 and $150. The more surgically complex spay procedure costs $100 to $250. These costs are generally included in the cost of adopting a shelter dog.

Home Health Checks and Handling

You can do a lot to maintain your Yorkshire terrier's good health by conducting regular exams, observing your dog's eating and bathroom habits, and recognizing changes in behavior. All of this can offer early clues to medical problems, often making resolution easier, quicker, and less costly.

Additionally, whether you've adopted an older Yorkie or found yourself a puppy, you need to accustom the dog to being handled. Of course you can overpower a Yorkshire terrier, but that's not fun for anyone, and you're not going to be able to examine the mouth of an agitated, snapping dog.

Puppy Handling

While your puppy is young, take some time each day to look in ears and eyes, open the mouth, examine paws, and generally feel all over. Encourage the pup to roll on his back for a belly rub. Check his hind end. Keep all of this positive and upbeat, making it a game between the two of you. If you are always calm and upbeat while doing this, most puppies will soon learn to relax and let themselves be handled.

fact

If you have a dog that's very reluctant to be handled, you may want to learn about clicker training. This positive training technique has proven particularly useful with behavior modification. Good books on the subject are available.

Adult Handling

If you've adopted an older Yorkie, you still need to accomplish all this, but may have to move more slowly. For a dog reluctant to let you examine his mouth, for example, scratch under the ear, down the side of the face, flip up the lip on that side for a quick peek, then go back to scratching or even give a treat. As the dog becomes more used to the procedure, actually stick a finger behind the canine tooth and pry the mouth open for a second. Don't insist on holding it open, or you'll encourage the dog to fight you. Remember to reward with scratching and a treat.

Photograph by Jean Fogle

▲ **Performing regular home health checks on your Yorkshire terrier ensures a better life for your pet.**

When you're able to at least open the mouth for a quick peek, start using a cue for the behavior. Use something positive and cute—"Toothies" or "Open wide"—to help keep it upbeat and remind the dog that he is not in any danger. Apply the same idea to any body part the dog is reluctant to have you handle. Move slowly and keep it positive—you'll get there eventually.

How to Examine Your Yorkie

In order to be able to spot a problem, you must be familiar with your Yorkie's normal, healthy condition. To do this, you should give your Yorkshire terrier a weekly exam. You'll come to know every curve of that little body, and will recognize any small changes. Once you've accustomed your Yorkie to the exam, it should be a happy, bonding experience for both of you. You can also combine your Yorkie's health check with regular grooming. You have to brush your dog regularly anyway.

The Mouth

If you've followed the previous directions to teach your Yorkie to open her mouth upon request, you can look in for any tooth problems and check on tartar buildup. Press lightly on the gums to see that a nice pink color returns quickly. Pale gums can be a sign of internal parasites, gastrointestinal disease, or other problems.

The Eyes

Eyes should be clear and bright. Yorkies do tend to collect some mucus at the inside corners of the eyes, but this can be easily cleared away while you're checking the eyes. Note if there's any more of it than usual—that could indicate a problem. Squinting, constant blinking, or pawing at the eyes could also mean there's something wrong.

The Ears

Look down inside the ears. They should be clean and pink. If there's substantial wax buildup or debris, clean it out with cotton balls and an ear cleaner. Also, use your nose and sniff each ear. A bad smell means an infection and necessitates a visit to the veterinarian. Also, check for any weed seeds in the ears or in the coat.

The Feet

Check each foot; this is most easily done with your Yorkie lying on her back. See that the nails are not too long, that no foreign substances or mats are lodged between the pads, and that the pads aren't cracked or cut. Trim long hair. Many dogs dislike having their feet touched, so work on handling them over time.

The Body

Run your hands down the chest, down each leg, and along the body. Feel for any mats or foreign substances in the coat. Check how much fat is over the ribs. Watch for any flinches that might indicate a sore spot. Pay special attention to the region beneath the tail. You want to be sure it's clean back there. If the dog is reluctant to have you touch the area around his anus, it may mean the anal glands are impacted. Your groomer or your veterinarian can express them, and can show you how to do it if you're interested.

Question?

How can you examine or clip a Yorkie's rear end if he's reluctant to be handled there?
Try trainer Terry Ryan's "peanut butter therapy" (or use low-fat cream cheese instead). Smear a little cream cheese on the refrigerator door at Yorkie height. Sit on the floor while you let the Yorkie lick off the cream cheese. Next time, while the Yorkie licks, part the hair at the dog's rear end and scratch a little, take a couple of swipes with the comb, or clip a few strands of hair. Add a more handling each time.

Normal Parameters

You don't customarily take blood pressure on dogs, but you do check temperature, heart rate, respiratory rate, and urination/defecation routines. Dogs have normal ranges for these measures, just as humans do, so get to know your Yorkie's regular rates.

Heart Rate

The normal heart rate for a toy dog at rest ranges from 90 to 160 beats per minute. Exercise, fear, and high temperatures all tend to elevate heart rate. Puppies' heart rates are generally higher than those of adults. To take your Yorkie's heart rate, press your fingers against the left side of the rib cage where the front leg joins the body. Count beats for fifteen seconds, and then multiply the number of beats by four.

Respiratory Rate

Average respiration ranges from ten to thirty breaths per minute. This is normal breathing, not exercise- or temperature-induced panting. Count your dog's respiration when he is in a normal, calm state—not panting.

 Fact

Dogs do not sweat through the skin as we do. They open their mouths, stick out their tongues, and pant. This evaporates water from the mouth, releasing hot air from the body and bringing cooler air into the lungs. The only place dogs can sweat is through the pads of their feet.

To determine respiratory rate, watch your Yorkie's chest rise and fall. Count the breaths for fifteen seconds, and then multiply the number of breaths by four.

Temperature

The average canine temperature ranges from 100° to 102.5°F. Don't panic if your dog's temperature is over 100—it could be normal. When her temperature rises above 103°F, however, you know there's a problem.

 **Alert!**

> Have someone help you take your dog's temperature, if possible. If the dog were to sit down suddenly, it could break the thermometer and create a veterinary emergency. Hold your Yorkie still, and keep him standing while his temperature is being taken.

To take a dog's temperature, you use a rectal thermometer. Coat it with a little petroleum jelly, lift the tail, and insert the thermometer a couple of inches into the anus. Leave it there the recommended amount of time (digital thermometers register more quickly than bulb thermometers), then take it out and read it.

Giving Medication

Sooner or later, you'll have to give your Yorkie some kind of pill or liquid medication, or put drops in his eyes or ears. Many people dread this chore, but it doesn't have to be a struggle. Your Yorkie might be wary of foreign substances and cold drops in his eyes or ears, but with lots of handling and practice you can make this process go quite smoothly.

Pills

If a pill is small and can be given with food, you can try wrapping it in a piece of luncheon meat or rolling it up in some cream cheese. But because Yorkies are small dogs, many don't gulp large hunks of food as readily as bigger dogs. If your Yorkie eats the food treat but spits out the pill, you'll have to give the pill alone. Open your dog's mouth with your nondominant hand—if you're right-handed, that would be your left hand. Have the pill ready in your dominant hand. Put the pill in the dog's mouth, as far over the back of the tongue as you can manage. Hold the dog's mouth closed and stroke down the throat to encourage swallowing. When you let go of the dog, watch to see that the pill isn't spit out.

If you have trouble with this, you may want to try a pill shooter. It looks like a syringe without a needle, and it holds a pill at the end rather than liquid. You simply put the shooter in the dog's mouth and depress the plunger to release the pill. Get advice from your veterinarian before using this, because you could damage the dog's mouth or throat if you use it incorrectly.

Liquids

You could try using a spoon to pour liquid down your Yorkie's throat, but this can often result in more liquid spattered on you and the walls than is consumed by the dog. Instead, use a syringe (without a needle). Fill it with the dose of medicine, put the end in the pouch formed by the dog's cheeks, hold the mouth closed, and slowly depress the plunger.

Eye and Ear Medications

For eye drops, use one hand to tilt your Yorkie's head back. Hold the medicine bottle above the eye and squeeze out the prescribed number of drops. Do not actually touch the eye with the bottle tip.

For eye ointment, hold the muzzle still with your nondominant hand, using your thumb or finger to pull the lower eyelid down. With your other hand, bring the applicator close and squeeze a line of ointment onto the lower lid. Release the lower eyelid and very gently rub over the eye to distribute the ointment.

The dispensing bottle of eardrops will generally have an extended applicator to reach down into the ear. Hold your dog's head, insert the applicator in an ear, and squeeze. Remove the applicator and massage the base of the ear to distribute the medicine. Don't let your dog shake his head (he'll want to) until after you've massaged the ear.

CHAPTER

Common Illnesses and Injuries

YORKSHIRE TERRIERS ARE ROBUST for their size, but their size can make them prone to several injuries and conditions. In addition to accidentally being kicked or tripped over, Yorkies commonly suffer from allergies, diarrhea and vomiting, increased vulnerability to weed seeds, chills, and eye and teeth problems.

Allergies

Dogs are susceptible to the same variety of allergy triggers as humans—foods, inhalants, and contacted substances. They can also be allergic to fleabites (as can humans). Determining the precise cause of an allergy is often difficult and time-consuming. The exact symptoms caused by the allergen may suggest one cause over another, and treatment can be based on that suspicion. Improvement indicates a correct choice.

 Essential

Your veterinarian might suggest taking skin scrapings or doing intradermal testing (injecting possible allergens under the skin) to try to pinpoint allergy causes. This is a reasonable course of action, but be aware that it doesn't always result in definitive answers.

Flea Allergies

Don't be in denial about possibly having a flea or two on your dog or in your home. These little pests haven't managed to exist through history because they're easy to kill. Instead, confront the problem using one of the good flea preventives available, and check often for signs of fleas. One good way to check for the presence of fleas is to brush your Yorkie's underside—the stomach and between the hind legs—then clean the comb out onto a moistened white paper towel. Flea dirt consists mostly of dried blood, and if it's present, you'll see red spots on the towel.

In dogs that have a flea allergy, a single fleabite could be enough to cause chewing and scratching. Most of the chewing will center on the base of the tail and between the hind legs. This condition can worsen quickly and cause hot spots, or raw, irritated patches of skin.

Fact

Spot-on flea products also kill ticks, which is certainly a bonus if you live in tick territory. Some of these products claim to take care of mosquitoes as well. Ask your veterinarian for advice on which brand and type of product to use.

The ultimate solution is to keep your dog and home flea-free. While this does take some effort, it's much easier than it used to be. Consult your veterinarian about a spot-on product for your Yorkie—the active ingredient kills fleas but has no effect on mammals—and a combination pyrethrin/IGR spray for your home. The pyrethrin is a toxin, but it kills fleas and then quickly degrades into harmless by-products. The IGR is an insect growth regulator, preventing flea eggs from hatching or larvae from developing, and is entirely safe for mammals.

While you are gaining control of the flea problem, you may need to also take action to help your Yorkie cope. Rather than using a flea shampoo, which is harsh, use a spot-on treatment and a soothing medicated or oatmeal shampoo to help calm the skin. Your veterinarian may suggest some antihistamines to make life easier and let hot spots cool down. Severe cases may even require a short course of steroids.

Food Allergies

Dogs develop food allergies over time, so a food that your Yorkie was eating quite happily at one point may cause problems a year or more later. The symptom, again, is itchy skin, but the itch from a food allergy tends to focus on the ears, face, stomach, and back of the hind legs.

If your veterinarian suspects a food allergy, he will probably want to put your dog on an elimination diet. He might recommend a commercial diet with limited novel ingredients (meaning things your dog hasn't eaten in the past), or a homemade diet, usually consisting of lamb and rice. However, there's no longer anything special about lamb. It was once used as the protein portion of a novel-ingredients diet because most dogs had never eaten lamb. Now, with all the lamb-and-rice diets available, other proteins such as duck or venison have to be used.

The dog has to eat only the prescribed diet for several weeks. That means no other treats or snacks can be given, unless they contain only the same ingredients as the prescribed diet. You may be able to find some sort of treat with the same ingredients but in a slightly different form, or you'll have to use the diet as both dinner and treats.

If the allergies improve while on the elimination diet, the proposed diagnosis of food allergies is confirmed. Ingredients are then slowly added, one at a time, in an attempt to find the specific food(s) causing the problem. Wheat, corn, beef, and milk are frequent culprits. Preservatives or artificial colors and flavors could also be to blame. Once the allergy-triggering items are identified, a permanent diet can be recommended.

Inhalant Allergies

Dogs can suffer from hay fever, the same as humans. If the itching and scratching is seasonal, suspect a pollen allergy. Use all the same strategies you would use with a human sufferer—install HEPA filters in your home, and stay indoors as much as possible when the pollen count is really high. Ask your veterinarian about giving your Yorkie antihistamines or even corticosteroids if the problem is severe.

Essential

Allergy testing in dogs is expensive, time-consuming, and often inconclusive. Details of when the allergy occurs, and observation of where biting and scratching are concentrated can be just as diagnostic.

Though a problem with inhalant allergies is usually seasonal, the biting and scratching are more generalized than with most other allergies. Hot spots often result, which then have to be treated. Dogs with pollen allergies often develop allergies to other substances, such as dust or mold.

Contact Allergies

Because the problem comes from direct contact with some material, most of the chewing is directed at the feet and underside. Carpeting is often the culprit. Upholstery could also be suspected if your Yorkie is allowed on the furniture. Many people choose to remove their rugs as a response to the problem.

Dogs can also be allergic to other substances with which they come in contact. Shampoo is one possible cause. Because Yorkies are bathed often, this is an important point to consider. Other triggers might be plastic food and water dishes, which can cause discomfort around the muzzle, or flea collars, which can cause scratching around the neck.

Hot Spots

When itching and scratching gets too frequent and is directed at a specific area, the result can be a hot spot. Much of the hair is chewed or scratched away and the skin is warm, red, and swollen. You need to clip away the rest of the hair on the spot and apply medications recommended by your veterinarian. Unfortunately, this can be a painful procedure for the dog.

To keep the dog from continuing to bite at the same or a nearby spot, you may need an Elizabethan collar—a cone-shaped plastic device that attaches around the neck and extends around the head—or the newer BiteNot collar—a rigid neckpiece that doesn't allow the dog to turn his head. To stop scratching, you may need to put socks over the dog's rear feet.

Question?

Can't you just cover the hot spot rather than use that awful Elizabethan collar?
Unfortunately, this will not work. Covering a hot spot will only keep it moist and encourage bacteria to breed. You have to leave it open to the air for it to heal, and a dog with free range of motion will not be able to resist the temptation to chew.

Diarrhea, Vomiting, and Refusal to Eat

An occasional stomach upset is to be expected and is not generally a cause for concern. As long as it lasts only a day or so, you can just ride it out. But if it continues for two or three days, you need to see your veterinarian. These conditions can worsen quickly with Yorkshire terriers.

Diarrhea

If your Yorkie's stools are looser than usual, or even liquid, she's suffering from diarrhea. There can be a large number of causes—

a little touch of an intestinal bug, internal parasites, unusual levels of excitement or anxiety, or eating something that just doesn't agree with her. Many diseases can also cause diarrhea.

On the first day you notice the diarrhea, you shouldn't feed your Yorkie. Make sure plenty of cool clean water is available, but give the digestive tract a chance to settle down. On the second day, offer bland foods such as cottage cheese or boiled chicken with the skin removed, mixed with rice. If the diarrhea hasn't resolved by the second day, see your veterinarian.

If the diarrhea is bloody or black (which indicates blood), tarry looking, or unusually yellow and fatty looking, don't wait to see your veterinarian. If it's accompanied by vomiting or a fever, that also necessitates an immediate veterinary visit.

Vomiting

Vomiting can also be caused by a variety of factors, including high levels of anxiety or excitement, eating something that doesn't agree with the dog, or eating too quickly. A number of diseases can cause vomiting as well.

 Essential

While it may be upsetting to see your dog vomit, dogs are actually quite good at bringing up offending foods or particles. If the vomiting is just a momentary upset, your dog will likely appear completely unfazed by it. In this case, try not to overreact.

Like diarrhea, if vomiting is mild, you can withhold food for a day to give matters a chance to quiet down. Then offer only a spoonful or two of bland food and wait to see if your Yorkie keeps it down. If all goes well, offer a little more. Return to regular meals gradually.

Violent vomiting and vomiting accompanied by diarrhea both require an immediate visit to the veterinarian. So does vomit containing blood or worms (which may look like grains of rice), vomit that smells like feces, and vomiting that continues even after the dog has been fasting.

Refusal to Eat

Yorkshire terriers can be fussy eaters, and you can help make them that way by catering to their whims. It's not unusual for a small dog to skip a meal or even a day's worth of meals now and then. Don't rush to offer delicacies to entice your Yorkie to eat— you'll teach your dog to hold out for better, and create a manipulative creature with an unbalanced diet. Just offer the regular meal, and if the dog doesn't eat, offer it again at the next mealtime. If you absolutely have to do something, try warming the meal slightly— dogs find warm food more appealing.

Continued refusal to eat could indicate dental problems or a viral infection of some kind. Either of these, as well as refusal to eat accompanied by weakness or depression, requires a veterinary visit.

Alert!

If you can see a foxtail in your Yorkie's ear or nose, don't try to remove it unless you're sure of your abilities. Unsuccessful removal attempts can actually drive the weed seed farther in and cause significant problems.

Foxtails and Other Weed Seeds

Lots of weeds have seeds with clever systems for latching onto the fur of passing animals and distributing themselves. Foxtails are probably the best known, but there are plenty of others. The problem is that their attachment system of little barbs is so effective that they often fail to drop off. Once they get into the fur, they tend to move forward, eventually reaching skin. Dogs have required surgery for foxtails that have burrowed tunnels under the skin or gotten stuck in ears, noses, or eyes.

Photograph by Cheryl A. Ertelt

▲ **If your dog spends a lot of time outdoors, keep an eye out for weed seeds stuck in her coat.**

The seeds dry over the summer and are at their worst in late summer and early fall. Any time you go into the great outdoors, especially when weed seeds are at their worst, give your Yorkie a good once-over once you're back inside. A thorough brushing will uproot most weed seeds. Also check in ears and carefully around eyes, nose, and mouth.

If your dog suddenly starts sneezing repeatedly, a foxtail could have become lodged in the nose. Head shaking or pawing at the ears might indicate a weed seed in the ears. Compulsive licking of a paw might mean a foxtail is hidden there. If you can't isolate the problem, a visit to your veterinarian is in order.

Hypothermia

Because of their small size and lack of a thick undercoat, Yorkshire terriers chill easily. They are not equipped to stay outside in freezing temperatures for long periods of time, nor are they equipped to be wet in an unheated environment. You may find it strange to put clothing on a dog with such a luxuriant coat, but it's necessary to keep your Yorkie warm. Go for practicality over fashion. Look for a sweater or jacket that's easy to put on and take off.

Signs of hypothermia include uncontrollable shivering, lethargy, depression, and finally, unconsciousness. If your Yorkie appears to be suffering from the cold, pick her up and put her inside your jacket to share your body warmth. Once she returns to normal, don't simply put her back on the ground. Swift changes in body temperature can cause stress to your Yorkie's body.

Also keep an eye out for frostbite. Ears, toes, and scrotums are most susceptible, and older dogs with less efficient circulation are at increased risk. Symptoms are the same as for humans—red or pale skin, pain, and itching. Warm the affected area gently, without rubbing.

Bumps and Bruises

Dogs are prone to different sorts of lumps and bumps, especially as they grow older. Some are no cause for concern, while others definitely require veterinary intervention. It can be difficult to tell which is which. Check for any new bumps every time you groom your Yorkie so you'll at least catch them early. Your Yorkie's annual exam should include an all-over body check for any lumps and bumps. Senior Yorkies should have an exam every six months.

Usually Harmless Lumps

The "old dog" bumps commonly seen are sebaceous adenomas. They often appear around the eyes or on the legs. They're smooth, pink, and healthy-looking and usually present no problems. If they develop on the eyelids, they may have to be removed to prevent irritation.

Cysts are firm lumps you can feel under the skin that develop in blocked hair follicles. There's no need to take any action unless they become infected, in which case they will need to be drained or removed.

Warts can grow anywhere on the body. Also called papillomas, they result from a virus. They only require veterinary attention if they're growing in an area that makes them uncomfortable, such as in the mouth.

More Worrisome Lumps

Abscesses are infections resulting from a puncture wound. Though they are more commonly seen in cats than dogs, they can happen to Yorkies. They will need to be drained, and the dog will be put on antibiotics.

Hematomas happen most often in the ears, maybe as a result of violent shaking of the head. A blood clot forms and creates a lump. Some hematomas resolve on their own, while others must be drained. If they recur, the veterinarian will sometimes stitch the section of the ear flap together—front to back—to keep liquid from gathering there.

Dogs can develop several kinds of skin cancer: basal cell tumors, mast cell tumors, melanomas, and squamous cell carcinomas. All require veterinary treatment, ranging from surgery to radiation and chemotherapy.

Perianal tumors develop in older dogs, nearly always male, and usually intact (not neutered). They appear as lumps around the anus, either singly or in clusters. They are surgically removed, and the dog is often neutered at the same time. Some can be malignant, in which case radiation and/or chemotherapy may be needed.

Bruises

If you have an armload of groceries or are carrying a laundry basket, it's really difficult to see the Yorkie running around at your feet. Even without a load in your arms, if you don't glance down, you might not realize the dog is there. So, unfortunately, Yorkies often are unintentionally stepped on, kicked, or knocked with opening or closing doors. To avoid such mishaps, try to know where your Yorkie is before you move, especially around doors or stairs. Be particularly careful in the kitchen. Tripping over your

Yorkie while you're carrying pans of hot water or food could result in serious burns for both of you.

 **Essential**

> You might want to teach your Yorkie to stay out of the kitchen while you are cooking. She can learn to watch from the doorway, close enough to keep an eye on things, but she won't be underfoot. Be sure to reward her for good behavior.

It's often hard to judge the extent of an injury of this sort. Many dogs are stoic and won't complain about the pain. Any misadventure that appears potentially serious—falling down the stairs or being slammed with a door—should be followed with a visit to the veterinarian. Dogs have died from unrecognized internal injuries.

Eye and Teeth Problems

Eye and teeth problems are more common among small breeds, including the Yorkshire terrier. Fortunately, eye problems are not as common among Yorkies as other toy breeds, and tooth problems can generally be prevented with a good dental care routine at home. As long as you stay on top of your Yorkie's general health, most major problems can be easily avoided.

Eye Problems

The Yorkie actually rates as quite healthy in the eye department, compared to other toy dogs. Remember that the standard calls for eyes "medium in size and not too prominent." Hence, the Yorkie avoids the problems faced by breeds with more bulging eyes. The Yorkie's eyelids don't usually cause problems with rolling inward or outward either.

Retinal dysplasia can be inherited in Yorkshire terriers; see Chapter 12 for more information on this condition. All dogs may develop cataracts as they age. You'll see a cloudy, often bluish spot in the eye. Some interfere with sight. They can be surgically removed. Finally, because a Yorkie is no bigger than a cat, a swipe from a cat's claws may connect with the Yorkie's eyes and scratch the cornea.

Teeth Problems

Dental health can be a weak point in many toy breeds. The smaller jaw still has to accommodate the same number of teeth as larger muzzles, and in order to fit, teeth often overlap or shift sideways.

Dogs don't tend to get cavities as humans do, but their teeth do build up tartar and plaque, which can inflame gums, ultimately leading to tooth loss, and may even cause disease in internal organs. Brush your Yorkie's teeth as often as you can, and have them cleaned by your veterinarian when necessary.

Yorkies can fracture teeth by chewing on bones or other hard objects. Tug is not an advisable game to play with Yorkies because it's too easy to injure their teeth and mouths. Instead, play fetch with soft, squeaky toys, and let the Yorkie "kill" the toy by shaking it.

CHAPTER 12

Congenital and Hereditary Diseases

AS WITH ALL POPULAR BREEDS these days, Yorkshire terriers can suffer from a variety of hereditary diseases. This makes screening adults essential and early health exams of puppies important. Patellar luxation and portosystemic shunt, for example, can often be identified early. Parents can be screened for retinal dysplasia, and their histories should reveal any epilepsy or collapsing trachea. Know as much as possible to avoid these disorders, but take heart that most can be corrected or managed.

Patellar Luxation

This is the scientific terminology for slipping kneecaps, a condition that occurs in the hind legs. Patellar luxation is often considered congenital in toy breeds because conditions to predispose toward it are present at birth, and it can often be seen as soon as puppies start walking. This is thought to be a hereditary condition.

The luxation can range from occasional, with the kneecap in correct position more often than not (grade 1), to permanent, with the kneecap never where it belongs (grade 4). Dogs with a kneecap out of joint may move with a skipping action or carry the affected leg so it doesn't touch the ground.

Symptoms

Puppies may show signs of patellar luxation from the time they begin walking, including failing to straighten the leg and carrying it oddly. Such early signs usually indicate a more severe problem, grade 3 or 4. Those with less severe abnormalities may show an abnormal gait from time to time, but they quickly revert to normal.

Veterinary attention usually isn't sought until the dog is older and the unusual gait is appearing more frequently. Individuals with a grade 1 condition present at birth may not show signs until their senior years, when years of minor trauma have weakened the soft tissues and caused increasing joint pain.

Watch the hind legs of a dog in movement. If it looks like the dog is skipping, the dog is probably carrying the affected limb and only putting it down every two or three steps. You could also see the hock (the prominent joint at the top of the section of leg perpendicular to the floor) flexed out while the knee turns in and the foot points in, forming a pigeon-toed position. In severe cases, the dog may not use the leg at all.

 Essential

Several organizations exist to help breeders and others track hereditary diseases in dogs. The Orthopedic Foundation of America (OFA) began with hip dysplasia, but now tracks eye disorders and a variety of skeletal disorders. CERF (Canine Eye Registration Foundation) specializes in disorders of the eye.

Diagnosis

The veterinarian will watch your dog move, checking for the symptoms previously described. She will also manipulate the joint, feeling for the patella pushing out of position and for looseness in the medial collateral ligament, which should help hold the kneecap in place. The way the patella acts when being manipulated can usually determine the grade of the condition.

In cases where a low-grade condition suddenly worsens due to overexertion or injury, the dog may suddenly be unable to stand. This can appear to be a neurological disorder, but both hind legs should be checked for patellar luxation.

Treatment and Prognosis

With grade 1 or 2 conditions, the dog may be functional and able to move about normally most of the time. It will be up to you and your veterinarian to discuss whether you should adopt a watch and wait plan, keeping vigilant for any worsening of the condition, or elect immediate surgery.

fact

Though patellar luxation is common in Yorkshire terriers, the Orthopedic Foundation of America (OFA) has no database on the breed because fewer than fifty evaluations have been submitted in the past twenty years.

The veterinary orthopedist has a variety of surgical choices. The groove in which the patella sits can be deepened, the tendons and muscles can be realigned through well-placed incisions or sutures, and bones can be somewhat rebuilt. Ligaments and meniscus should be examined for any injuries, and repaired if necessary, during surgery. Prognosis for complete recovery is good in dogs with grade 1 or 2 conditions. More severe disorders can require more extreme surgical options.

Collapsing Trachea

The trachea, which carries air from the throat to the lungs and back again, is a soft tube held in a semiround shape by a series of C-shaped rings of cartilage. The ends of the cartilage are connected by a flexible membrane. When the cartilage rings are malformed, or the cartilage degenerates over time, the trachea flattens or collapses.

No one yet understands exactly how or why this happens. Because it occurs most often in certain breeds, including Yorkshire terriers, a genetic component is suspected. An abnormality, probably inherited, in the chemical composition of the rings causes them to soften and lose their rigid shape.

Symptoms

The sign most often noted by owners is a chronic cough. It occurs because the flexible membrane, no longer held taut, droops and tickles the lining of the trachea. Coughing happens more during the day than at night, and is often described as a dry, honking cough. Pressure from a collar, excitement, and exercise can all initiate coughing. Symptoms generally worsen in hot, humid weather, when the dog needs to pant. Dogs suffering from collapsing trachea may be unable to exercise without coughing. Eating and drinking can also bring on coughing.

⌇ Essential

Dogs with a collapsing trachea should not wear a collar or even a harness that could create pressure on the trachea. If a harness is your chosen alternative, be sure it doesn't ride up the chest. You could also use a head halter to avoid pressure on the throat or chest.

Diagnosis

A breed subject to the problem and a history of coughing are enough to raise strong suspicion of the existence of the condition. Lightly pressing on the trachea during a physical exam can often induce the cough, but definitive diagnosis requires testing.

X-rays (radiographs) of the chest can show the shape of the trachea. However, this is a tricky proposition because a collapsing trachea changes its shape between inhalation and exhalation. The technician has to manage to take radiographs during both phases of respiration, which is not an easy accomplishment. Because coughing can also be an indication of heart disease, your veterinarian might also recommend a chest x-ray to be able to check the heart.

Fluoroscopy is also an x-ray procedure, but one that provides an ongoing real-time look at the trachea throughout respiration. Endoscopy (a procedure also conducted on humans) offers an entirely different option, sending a flexible tube down into the trachea for an interior look at the structure.

Alert!

Reverse sneezing is another cause of coughing common in toy breeds. It's caused by a temporary spasm in the back of the throat and does not require veterinary intervention. The cough sounds like someone with badly stuffed sinuses trying to inhale hard. Gently rubbing the throat can soothe the coughing, but it should cease on its own in under a minute.

Treatment

Nonsurgical treatment involves taking care of any concurrent conditions that worsen the problem, and avoiding environmental triggers. If the dog is overweight, weight loss will likely be the first recommendation. Overweight dogs in general have a harder time breathing, and they pant under less exertion and at lower temperatures. You should also avoid exertion hard enough to force the dog to pant, and do your best to keep the dog from becoming overexcited. Also, keep the dog away from dry, dusty locales; don't smoke around the dog; and use a cool-water humidifier in the house to keep air moist.

Medicines might be given to help with the problem. The same bronchodilators used for humans are used for dogs. Time-release formulations are used for dogs so they don't have to be given as often. Anti-inflammatory medications—corticosteroids—may also be used to ease the swelling of the trachea. Because of side effects, they should be given short-term only. Finally, cough suppressants might be recommended.

A veterinary survey showed that over 70 percent of dogs diagnosed with collapsing trachea responded to management of concurrent conditions and medication. Roughly 15 percent were found to be candidates for surgery. The chance for improvement after surgery is good if the collapsing portion of the trachea lies in the throat rather than in the chest. Dogs under six years of age fare better than older individuals. The surgery generally involves placing a prosthesis around the trachea, and it must be performed by a specialist. A new surgery option uses a stainless steel self-expanding prosthesis, placed in the trachea as a stent. While this is still a fairly rare choice, its results have been excellent.

Pancreatitis

Though pancreatitis is not actually a hereditary disease, the fact that the Yorkshire terrier, along with a few other breeds, shows a higher occurrence rate than among dogs in general indicates some as-yet undiscovered genetic predisposition. The actual problem usually crops up in middle age, more often in females than males. Overweight dogs are more susceptible.

Nutrition definitely plays a part. Dogs that are routinely fed high-fat diets or fatty people-food treats or that help themselves to garbage are placed at higher risk. Hyperlipidemia (a metabolic disorder resulting in high amounts of fats in the blood), trauma to the area of the pancreas (under the stomach), some medications, and chronic kidney disease can all contribute to pancreatitis.

Symptoms

Symptoms may be vague and mild at the beginning of an episode and worsen over time. Typical symptoms include vomiting, loss of appetite, and abdominal pain. The abdomen may appear swollen. You might see diarrhea, or a yellowish oily-looking stool. The dog may be dehydrated as well.

 **Esseñtial**

> While your dog is healthy and happy, pull a little bit of the loose skin at the back of the neck away from the body and watch how quickly it snaps back into position when you let go. When a dog is dehydrated, the skin will not be so quick to snap back into position. You do this as part of a routine health check.

Some dogs suffering from pancreatitis will seem to be depressed, not taking pleasure in the things they usually enjoy. Some might exhibit a hunched, uncomfortable-looking position. The dog might also have a fever.

An attack of pancreatitis is an emergency condition and is potentially life threatening. As it worsens, it can result in infection throughout the body, multiple hemorrhages, heart arrhythmia, and autodigestion of the stomach or intestines by enzymes being released by the damaged pancreas.

Diagnosis

The veterinarian will suspect pancreatitis based on the history given by the owner, a physical exam, and the presence of any risk factors such as obesity or recent consumption of a high-fat meal. That will be followed with some tests.

Blood will probably be drawn for a complete blood count (CBC) to evaluate the presence of the pancreatic enzymes amylase and lipase. The white blood cell count is usually elevated. A newer blood test, the serum trypsin-like immunoreactivity assay (TLI assay), is even more specific to the pancreas.

Radiographs may be taken of the abdomen. An appearance of ground glass where the pancreas should lie is fairly definitive. An ultrasound could also be done to help the veterinarian look for pancreatitis, an abscess in the pancreas, a tumor, or fluid in the abdominal cavity.

Do only enough testing to be sure of the diagnosis. Testing is expensive for you and stressful for the dog, and treatment should start as quickly as possible. Early treatment is essential to a good outcome. In larger dogs, bloat is the most-feared medical emergency of the gastrointestinal tract. In small dogs, an attack of pancreatitis is more likely, and it is just as much of an emergency.

Treatment

Pancreatitis requires several treatment goals. The pancreas must be rested, avoiding stimulation of enzyme secretion. The enzymes already circulating in the blood have to be removed. At the same time, the dog's electrolyte balance has to be maintained and dehydration avoided. Because all food and water intake is stopped for several days, the dog will have to receive fluids either under the skin or intravenously. Dogs showing signs of pain can be given painkilling medications. They may also be given drugs to stop vomiting and antibiotics to avoid infection of other body systems.

For all of this treatment, and because matters may worsen before they improve, the dog will be hospitalized. A stay of several days is common, and severe cases may require a week or more.

Individuals that don't respond to treatment could require surgery. This should be undertaken only in serious circumstances because dogs already suffering pancreatitis are at a higher risk for complications from anesthesia and surgery. However, severe inflammation, an abscess or tumor, or bile duct obstruction may mean surgery is the only option.

Prognosis and Prevention

Early recognition and treatment improve the outcome. Mild cases of pancreatitis generally resolve well, though it is a fairly unpredictable disease. Dogs with more severe cases can recover, but the odds are not as good, and more complications can arise. Some dogs experience one bout, recover, and with some changes in feeding never have another episode. Other dogs have a mild case, recover, and then have a worse occurrence. The best course of action is to avoid as many risk factors as possible.

First, keep your Yorkie lean. Overweight dogs face a far greater risk of pancreatitis. Second, do not feed high-fat foods. Dogs that have already endured an episode of pancreatitis may need to eat a special low-fat veterinary diet for a while or for the rest of their lives. Finally, have regular veterinary exams to check for any predisposing conditions or illnesses.

Portosystemic Shunt

During development of the canine fetus, blood bypasses the liver, going directly back to the heart via a shunt. In normal development, this shunt closes off just after birth, and blood from the intestines is then sent through the liver to be detoxified before being routed back to the heart. If this shunt does not close, the pup develops a congenital portosystemic shunt.

Acquired portosystemic shunts are seen much later in life, developing as a response to portal hypertension. This, in turn, results from liver diseases such as chronic hepatitis or cirrhosis. It probably isn't hereditary.

Symptoms
While the shunt is usually present at birth, it takes some time for effects to be seen. Most dogs are diagnosed between six months and two years of age. In puppies, symptoms are subtle, but a pup may be smaller than littermates and show a failure to thrive, or a general impression of less than perfect health.

Later signs can include vomiting, diarrhea, pica (eating non-food items), anorexia, and polydipsia and polyuria (drinking and urinating more than normal). Fluid can leak from the portal system into the abdominal cavity—the dog will appear pot-bellied. Because the liver plays a significant role in metabolism of drugs, a dog with a portosystemic shunt, when anesthetized for spay or neuter surgery, can take an uncommonly long time to wake up from the anesthetic.

Failure of the liver to clear toxins from the blood can result in detrimental effects on the brain. After a meal, when a large amount of by-products of digestion are circulating, the dog may stumble, walk in circles, or stand with his head pressed against the wall or the furniture. Seizures can occur.

Because the liver isn't metabolizing ammonia and urates effectively, compounds concentrate in the urine and cause stones in the urinary system. The stones result in bloody urine, straining to urinate, more frequent urination, abdominal pain, and possibly vomiting.

Diagnosis

As with many health problems, the first step is blood work. Blood work results showing elevated liver enzymes, lowered red blood cell count, low blood urea nitrogen (BUN), and low blood glucose indicate a possible portosystemic shunt. Urinalysis showing ammonium biurate crystals increases the probability.

 Question?

If other tests will have to be done after the blood tests anyway, why should you bother with the blood tests?
Blood tests are relatively easy, inexpensive, and nonspecific, so they can quickly give a strong indication of what might be happening. Certain diseases can be ruled in or out on the basis of blood tests, saving you from more stressful and expensive testing that might be unnecessary.

Two more specific blood tests can then be used. Blood ammonia levels are checked. A high result indicates possibility of a shunt. The bile acid level blood test requires two samples: the first after the dog has not eaten for twelve hours, and the second two hours after a meal. If portosystemic shunt is present, the sample after eating will show elevated levels of bile acids in the blood.

If all indications point toward a shunt, an ultrasound may be done if an experienced diagnostician is available—it can be tricky to find and see the shunt this way. Alternatively, a minor surgery called a portogram can be done. Through a small incision, dye is injected into a vein draining the small intestine, and a series of x-rays is taken. The radiographs will show either a normal circuit of blood through the liver or blood being carried past the liver in a shunt.

Treatment

Surgery is required, but some dogs may need to be medically managed first to improve their general health to prepare to undergo the surgery. The diet may be changed to a low-protein choice, antibiotics might be given to decrease bacteria in the digestive tract, and lactulose, a laxative, can help decrease absorption of ammonia and other toxins.

The aim of surgery is to close off the shunt. Unfortunately, this can't be done all at once because the underdeveloped liver can't adapt to the sudden increase in blood flow that would occur. The sudden inflow of so much blood leads to portal hypertension, and can cause death within hours. So the shunt can only be partially closed.

One option is to partially close the shunt, wait a couple of months to give the liver time to adapt, and then perform a second surgery to further (maybe completely) close the shunt. Obviously, multiple surgeries increase the risk of surgical complications. The other option is to place a device called an ameroid constrictor around the shunt vessel. An outer metal ring holds the inner dried casein material against the shunt. As the casein beings to hydrate in the body, it swells, and because of the metal ring outside, it can only swell inward. At the same time, it inflames the vessel, creating swelling. It can take anywhere from two weeks to three months for the constriction and swelling to close off the shunt. The danger is in closing too quickly and creating portal hypertension.

For several months following either surgery, the dog remains on the special diet, antibiotics, and a laxative. Exercise must be strictly limited, and the dog should stay in clean areas only.

◄ Paying close attention to your dog's health aids in the prevention of common congenital and hereditary diseases.

Photograph by Cheryl A. Ertelt

Prognosis

If the condition is a single shunt that can be completely corrected—the shunt closed off—before the dog reaches a year of age, chances are good that the dog can lead a fairly normal life. After two years of age, progressive liver atrophy can make recovery impossible, and the dog can only be medically managed during a significantly shortened lifespan.

The surgery, though absolutely necessary, carries a substantial risk, with the mortality rate given as anywhere up to 20 percent. Some dogs develop constant seizures after surgery. Some dogs with corrected congenital portosystemic shunt develop acquired multiple portosystemic shunts later in life.

This is not an easy problem to resolve. If buying from a breeder, be sure that no relatives of the pups suffer from porto-systemic shunt.

Lymphangiectasia

In a normal circulatory system, the lymph vessels collect lymphatic fluid from the body tissues and return them to the blood. With congenital lymphangiectasia, the lymph vessels are abnormally enlarged and leak fluid into the intestines. Special lymph vessels in the intestines called lacteals can burst. Because these lacteals are designed to absorb fats, fats and proteins are lost when they burst.

Fact

You may have heard in human medicine that lymphedemia is often experienced by women who have had surgery because of breast cancer. The associated lymph nodes are removed, and fluid collects in the arm. This is the same process as in dogs with lymphangiecta-sia—in canines, the fluid collects in the abdomen.

Symptoms

Symptoms include nausea, vomiting, diarrhea, and abdominal pain. There may also be swelling in the abdomen. Conversely, the dog might lose weight. These symptoms, however, can indicate a number of disorders known collectively as protein-losing enter-opathies. Tests are required to pin down a definitive cause.

Diagnosis

Blood work will show a low lymphocyte count, low cholesterol levels, and low albumin levels. While these are all suggestive of lymphangiectasia, the definitive diagnosis requires a biopsy. The biopsy may be done via surgery or endoscopy. A biopsy showing enlarged lymph vessels indicates lymphangiectasia.

Treatment and Prognosis

The first goal of treatment is to reduce inflammation. Corticosteroids are commonly given, sometimes with diuretics to reduce fluid accumulation. The second goal is to reduce the pressure in the lymph vessels while restoring normal protein levels. Dietary modification can help here, with a low-fat, high-quality protein formulation. You may have to give a supplement of fat-soluble vitamins because the dog will not absorb these well.

Lymphangiectasia cannot be cured, but it can often be well managed throughout the dog's life, with only occasional symptomatic episodes.

Other Possibly Hereditary Disorders

Though there is less definitive evidence that the following problems are inherited, they do tend to show up in certain breeds, including the Yorkshire terrier. Only retinal dysplasia might be reported to and followed by any of the disease registries.

Idiopathic Polyarthritis

Idiopathic simply means "of unknown origin." Though most common in large dogs, this disorder is also frequently seen in Chihuahuas, toy poodles, and Yorkshire terriers. Idiopathic polyarthritis is characterized by stiffness or lameness, along with fever that does not respond to antibiotics, anorexia, and a general depression. These symptoms cycle from hardly noticeable to worsening and back again. A course of glucocorticoids given for several months usually provides effective control.

Hemorrhagic Gastroenteritis

Toy dogs are said to appear predisposed to this serious disorder. Formerly normal, healthy dogs, generally two to four years old, suddenly have an acute attack of bloody diarrhea and vomiting. Though nothing may have changed in daily routine or diet, the problem is thought to result from a hypersensitivity reaction.

Supportive treatment should be started immediately. Food and water are withheld while fluid therapy and antibiotics are given. When food is reintroduced, the diet should use a protein source new to the dog, mixed with rice. Most dogs respond well, though up to 15 percent have repeated episodes.

Color Dilution Alopecia

The Yorkshire terrier's blue-black color lies at the root of this condition. The DNA portion that changes black to blue, "coat color phenotype dd," is also responsible for coat problems. Affected pups are born with normal coats, but they begin to show problems as they approach one year of age. They can develop follicular seborrhea (dandruff), folliculitis, and progressive hypotrichosis (less hair than normal) in the blue-coated areas.

Retinal Dysplasia

Several types of retinal dysplasia exist, but the one to which the Yorkshire terrier is susceptible is inherited as a recessive trait. This consists of incorrect development of the focal areas of the retina. Depending on the extent and placement of the malformation, there could be no symptoms or the dog could have impaired central vision.

Idiopathic Epilepsy

Though other breeds are more afflicted and show a more definite genetic component, the Yorkshire terrier also falls victim to epilepsy of unknown cause. Diagnosis consists of eliminating other possible causes of seizures. Treatment has improved greatly, and the prognosis is fairly good.

Socialization

DOGS ARE SOCIAL CREATURES, but they weren't born knowing how to fit into the human world of carpets, closets, cars, and cats. They need a lot of early encounters with different bits and pieces of the world around them to grow into confident adults. Anything from a tiny twig to a big boulder may be a sudden cause of alarm to a pup. Furthermore, there are vacuum cleaners, hair dryers, doorbells, and television sets to contend with. It can be a scary world for a small Yorkie.

Getting Out and About

Your daily errands and daily walks can both offer plenty of opportunities for socializing your Yorkie. You have an advantage over owners of bigger dogs because you can carry your little dog into shops where larger canines can't tread. It's a show of good manners to ask the shop owner if he or she minds, but you'll find that many banks, post offices, and stores will welcome your Yorkie.

Outdoors

On walks, let your Yorkie do just that—walk. She needs the exercise, and she needs to get used to viewing the world from toy dog level. It's a whole different world down there from the one she views when you're carrying her in your arms.

Most Yorkies are fairly self-assured and won't find much to hesitate over in the environment. In fact, you may find yourself more concerned with keeping your Yorkie from trying to rule the world! If your Yorkie proves to be a bit more timid than most, use the "jolly routine" (described on page 182) to help her get past her fears and accept new things.

If you view your walks as exercise for yourself as well, that's fine. Your Yorkie is capable of keeping up with a brisk walk. But choose one section of your walk, or a destination such as a park, where you'll slow down and let your Yorkie smell the roses. Walks are also great times to practice your training (as described in Chapter 15).

Alert!

While a Yorkie trained to use a litter box may have no physical need to venture out of your house or apartment, she certainly has a mental one. She will have to visit the veterinarian from time to time, and someday you may want to travel. Let her experience the world now so she won't be afraid of it later.

Always keep one eye open for potential hazards or problems. Ask other dog owners if their dogs are good with small dogs before you approach. Don't let them just barrel up to you, either. Insist that children ask permission before they run up to pet your dog. If you decide they can pet your Yorkie, instruct them to crouch down and gently extend their hand for your dog to sniff, then to scratch the chest or under the chin rather than patting on top of the head. Don't hesitate to tell them to stop if you think they're being too rough or you see that your Yorkie isn't enjoying it.

Indoors

When you carry your Yorkie, you automatically elevate his status. He's taller, and backed up by your presence, he may feel more daring. Don't put up with any unacceptable behavior—nip it in the bud, and you'll be a lot better off. If your Yorkie starts to bark or growl while you're carrying him, immediately put him down rather unceremoniously—don't hurt him, but don't be solicitous about it either—and then turn your back on him. If you have to go outside before you can put him down, do so as quickly as possible. This is not a behavior you can afford to ignore.

 **Question?**

Can you carry your Yorkie zipped up in her Sherpa bag?
Yes, you certainly can. Just be sure that it's well ventilated and that she can see out, and remember that you're carrying a living being, not just a package. And take time to let her out for a romp if your errands are going to take much longer than a half-hour.

If shop owners ask you to put your Yorkie down on the countertop or the floor so they can pet and play with him, that's fine, as long as you ensure he can't fall off. But don't assume that everyone is dying to fawn over your little dog. They may let you in the store as a show of good customer relations, but that doesn't mean they necessarily like dogs themselves.

In the City

City dogs have to learn to accept crowded sidewalks, traffic noise, sirens, construction noise, and perhaps police or carriage horses—all the many sights and sounds the city provides on a daily basis. The crowds on the sidewalk can present a bit of a problem for your Yorkie—it's easy to get lost amid all those quickly moving feet. You might want to try and take your walks in less crowded areas or at off-peak sidewalk travel times.

In nearly any city, you'll be expected to curb your dog and to pick up any excrement he deposits. Carry some plastic sandwich bags in your pocket or handbag so you'll always have a way to take care of this. If there are plenty of trash receptacles available, you can easily dispose of your dog's waste while walking. However, if receptacles are lacking, carry your sandwich bags plus zipper-closure bags. After you pick up, put the sandwich bag in the zipper bag, zip it shut, and at least you'll have a clean, odorless bag to carry.

Try not to react to sudden city noises as much as possible. You want your dog to learn to accept them calmly, so you should too. A momentary startle is to be expected, but recovery should be quick.

In Suburban and Rural Areas

When out and about in suburbia, your dog is likely to encounter kids playing, as well as bicycles, skateboards, scooters; other neighborhood dogs; and school buses. In true country areas, she'll probably see horses, sheep, bicycles, school buses, and loose dogs, and she may hear coyotes howling.

Loose-running dogs can be a problem. A fenced yard will keep them safely away from your Yorkie. Fencing will also discourage coyotes. Be aware that your Yorkie is small enough to attract the attention of eagles or large hawks. Yorkshire terriers have been attacked and even carried off by these creatures.

 **Essential**

What you may see as reassuring, your dog might interpret as cause for concern. The more nonchalant you can be about events going on around you, the more in charge you appear, and the less worrisome you make things appear to your dog. Cooing and coddling will only make things worse.

The "Jolly Routine"

Use this simple ploy any time your Yorkie is startled by something. Rather than trying to soothe your pup with patting and cooing be upbeat. Smile and be enthusiastic as you tell your Yorkie, "Wow, that was a big bang! We should go see what made it!" If you don't seem to be concerned about something, it helps your dog decide there's no need to worry about it.

If you've already done some training, have your dog do a few quick, simple exercises such as sit and come, and reward these actions enthusiastically. Start this little game with your pup right away, and you shouldn't have any problem with fear issues. If your pup already has some issues, see Chapter 18 for more in-depth advice on how to deal with them.

Meeting New Friends

While she's still young, you should provide your Yorkie with the opportunity to meet a large variety of people. Many dog owners who neglect this undertaking are surprised and embarrassed to find that their dog barks relentlessly at visitors of a different ethnicity than their own human family. People of different races not only look but smell different to the dog. You need to accustom her to the many differences out there.

Do everything that you can to meet a wide variety of people. Look for not just ethnicity, but size, appearance (beards, hats, glasses, devices such as walkers or wheelchairs), personality (loud and overpowering, shy and timid), and ages (from as young to as old as you can trust with your Yorkie). Visit places where you can people-watch, such as parks, shopping centers, and beaches.

You can stage the first meetings with friends and neighbors whom you can trust to follow your instructions. That way, you can be certain they're as nonthreatening as possible. But sooner rather than later you'll have to take the plunge and go out in public.

Canine Pals

A dog needs experiences with other dogs to be a well-rounded canine. You want to be cautious until your pup has completed his first series of shots, but you don't want to be a recluse. Introduce your pup to other dogs gradually, so as not to overwhelm him.

Puppy Classes

A good place for a puppy to meet other canines is in puppy class. You should be asked to show proof that your puppy has had whatever vaccinations are appropriate for her age. That indicates the other puppy owners have had to show the same proof, so you know all the pups have been seen by their veterinarians and had their shots.

Puppy classes generally only accept dogs up to a certain age— four months or six months are common cutoffs. Some may also be divided by size. This means your Yorkie might be cavorting with Maltese, Pomeranians, toy poodles, Brussels griffons, small mixed breeds, or any of a variety of small dogs. While this division by size isn't essential, it is a nice bonus. You won't have to worry about gawky Lab puppies crashing into or falling over your Yorkie.

 Fact

Puppies used to be kept at home, totally untrained, until they were six months old. This practice—supposedly to keep pups safe from disease until they finished all their shots—caused them to miss out on the best time for socialization and training.

Puppy classes should include playtime for the great dog-to-dog socialization it offers, but they shouldn't be a nonstop free-for-all. Puppies should also receive the beginning stages of training and be carefully exposed to a wide variety of sights and sounds.

Play Dates

Once your puppy has aged out of puppy classes, you'll have to take a more proactive role to keep him engaged with other dogs. If you and some other handlers from puppy class hit it off, you may want to continue meeting once a week or twice a month to let your dogs keep playing together. They already know each other. You could take it in turn to visit each others' homes, or meet at a nearby off-leash park, if you have one. (The next section provides more information on dog parks.)

If you can't attend a puppy class, or you did but haven't met anyone there you'd like to keep in touch with, ask your breeder if she knows any other Yorkie owners in your area. Post a notice at your local pet supply store that you'd like to start a playgroup. You could also join a group pet-dog manners class. The dogs won't be given play time during class, but you may meet others there who would be interested in arranging some play dates.

Dog Parks

Dog parks can be both a blessing and a curse, depending largely on their clientele. Where interested owners have had to fight hard for the privilege of a few acres where dogs can run and play, they're likely to be firmly in charge of seeing that rules are obeyed and etiquette is observed. In other places, where a dog park was suddenly added to the recreational possibilities, you may find that no one takes responsibility. Obviously, you want to find and use the former sort of dog park.

Alert!

Dogs have been attacked, injured, and even killed by other dogs in dog parks. Socialization is important, but so is safety. If you don't know the dogs and people in a dog park, always watch from outside first. If you aren't sure it's safe, don't go in.

Dog parks almost always have a posted set of rules. But these rules are not worth much if no one bothers to follow them. So, when visiting a new dog park, stand outside and observe. Ask yourself the following questions:

- Is it clean? People should be vigilant about picking up after their dogs, and there shouldn't be any litter on the ground.
- Are people watching their dogs? It's okay to socialize, and many friendships begin or blossom at dog parks, but everyone should be keeping at least one eye on his dog at all times.
- Is rowdy behavior stopped before it escalates? Dogs may be running around at top speed, chasing each other, and barking occasionally. But they shouldn't be attacking others.
- If children are present, are they staying with the adults or playing quietly in their own group, rather than running wildly with the dogs?
- Are people careful about opening and closing gates when coming and going?

If everything looks good to you, enter and hang around the outskirts of the park. Either let your own dog off-leash, or be sure to keep the leash slack if other dogs come over to greet yours. Tight leashes can interfere with appropriate dog greetings. If anything makes you uncomfortable, or if your Yorkie snaps or growls at other dogs, leave. This is not the place to work out issues.

A Baby in the House

A new baby in the family can be puzzling for a dog. It smells human but doesn't look like other humans, and it certainly doesn't sound like other humans. A baby can become a rival for attention if the Yorkie is ignored while the baby is showered with affection. Be proactive about adding a baby to your household, and everyone can get along just fine.

Pre-Baby Preparations

You can help your dog prepare to welcome the new family member by letting her meet other babies beforehand, if possible. Ask the mom to sit on the floor and cuddle her baby while you let your on-leash Yorkie approach and sniff. You don't want to hold the baby out to the Yorkie because it may appear as if you are presenting a toy.

 **Essential**

Everyone will be busy with the new arrival. You might be losing sleep. If you already have other children, they may be acting up in a bid for attention. Yet you still need to find time for the dog. View a nice long walk as a chance for both you and the dog to get away from all the fuss for a while.

You can also make or buy recordings of a baby crying. Play the recording while you go about your business at home. By doing both of these things, your Yorkie will have a chance to gain some experience with the sound and smell of babies before you actually have one in the house permanently.

Pre-Training

If you haven't yet taken your Yorkie for training, now's the time, before you find yourself trying to deal with a new baby and an untrained dog. Take a class and be sure to work extra hard on sit, down, stay, and preventing jumping up. These skills will come in handy for keeping your Yorkie out from underfoot and from jumping up while you're holding the baby.

◄ **Socialization cuts down on unpredictable Yorkie behavior.**

Photograph by Jean Fogle

You can even go so far as to practice your training while you carry a doll wrapped in a blanket. You'll learn the mechanics of trying to hold a baby and control your dog, and your Yorkie will get used to the sight of you carrying a small bundle.

Homecoming

If the new mom has been away for even a couple of days, your Yorkie will probably be eager to welcome her back. So have someone else carry the baby and leave the mom's hands free to greet the dog.

Once everyone has settled down, let the Yorkie approach the baby the same as you did when doing pre-baby preparations—have someone sit on the floor and hold the baby while someone else holds the Yorkie on-leash. Remember not to hold the baby out to the dog, but rather hold the infant close and let the dog come up to sniff.

Be sure that other family members give the mom some time to spend with the dog so your Yorkie doesn't feel pushed aside by the infant. Most Yorkies are used to being the center of attention and won't take kindly to suddenly being ignored. Keep up your usual activities with the dog, even though everyone has more to do and may be getting less sleep.

People Leaving the Home

Whether the kids are going off to camp or college, the household is splitting up due to divorce, or there's a death in the family, people are bound to leave at some point. This can be confusing for the Yorkie, and it's especially distressing if the departing one is the Yorkie's special person. Getting your Yorkshire terrier out of the house and doing the things she's always enjoyed can help stop her moping. Play her favorite games, or take her for a long walk to take her mind off a person's departure.

If People Will Return

You can accustom the Yorkie to temporary departures. If you use the same phrase every time someone leaves for a trip of overnight or longer—"See you soon," or "Long goodbye," or anything else you'll remember—your Yorkshire terrier will learn, over repeated departures and returns, that the person will be gone for a time but will eventually come back. Many dogs find this knowledge very comforting, and they continue to behave normally rather than moping or watching obsessively for the missing person.

When People Won't Be Coming Back

If the departure is permanent, there's no point in pretending it isn't. Your temporary departure cue might reassure your Yorkie for a time, but sooner or later the dog will realize the person isn't coming back. Then the dog may be even more deeply distressed, and you will have lied to your Yorkie.

In the event of a death in the family, if it all possible, let the dog go to the place of death (if it happened at home), or give the dog a personal article that belonged to the deceased to sniff and smell. Dogs do have an understanding of death as final, and their keen sense of smell communicates a great deal to them, including the fact that someone is dying or has died. While your Yorkie may miss the person and be depressed, at least he'll gain an understanding of what has taken place.

Moving to a New Home

Have you ever seen an ad for a dog for sale that read, "Moving, and can't take dog"? There are very few legitimate reasons to put your dog up for sale, and just because you're moving isn't one of them. Yes, humans have a mobile society, and families move frequently. But your Yorkie is a definite part of your family and should remain a part of your family no matter how many times you may move.

Changing Veterinarians

Once you know you're going to move out of your present area, ask your veterinarian if he is acquainted with any veterinarians in your new location. They might have gone to veterinary college together, met at veterinary conferences, or even worked together at a former place of employment. If the answer is yes, introduce yourself to the new veterinarian and mention your current vet. If your vet doesn't know anyone in your new area, you'll have to go through a search for a new suitable veterinarian.

Obtain your Yorkie's records from your present veterinarian. You'll certainly need to know when you're due for any booster vaccinations, and you should have proof of your Yorkie's spay or neuter. Also, obtain a supply of any medications your Yorkie takes regularly, so you won't have to worry about this for a while.

Help Your Yorkie Settle In

Take your Yorkie along on any preparatory visits to your new abode. This will give her a chance to at least see and smell her new surroundings before the upset of uprooting. Problems are most likely to occur in the first couple of weeks after moving. Misbehavior after a move usually results from insecurity, so punishment will only make it worse. Instead, be extra vigilant about keeping your Yorkie out of trouble.

If you are moving into a previously occupied house or apartment, especially if you know the previous owners had pets, you may want to have the new place bombed for fleas and the carpets steam-cleaned. That way, evidence of any housetraining accidents will be cleaned up, any flea problems will be eliminated, and the scent of the previous pets will be diminished. Keep an eye on your Yorkie the first few days to see that he doesn't feel compelled to mark his new territory.

Move your furniture in before you move in with your dog, if possible. This will not only keep your Yorkie safely away from movers, it will also reassure him with the sight and scent of familiar surroundings. When you bring him in, show him where his food and water bowls and old familiar dog beds are. Let him check out his new, hopefully fenced, yard. If fencing hasn't yet been installed, keep your Yorkie on-leash and accompanied by a family member until fencing is present.

As long as you keep to your accustomed routine as much as possible, your Yorkie should eventually settle into the new home without any major complications. If you move often, observe your Yorkie's behavior the first time around so you can make any modifications to the moving process in the future. Any effort you put forth to make your Yorkie more comfortable during this time will pay off when you find yourself with a calm and quickly adjusted pet.

CHAPTER 14

Choosing a Trainer and Classes

AGOOD TRAINER can be invaluable, especially if you're new to dogs. This person can help you understand and deal with the progression from puppy to adolescent to adult. You'll learn how to teach your Yorkie good manners and perhaps some useful tricks, and see if you might want to continue into competition. But trainers are not all alike, so you have to invest some time and thought into choosing the one for you and your dog. While books can teach you a lot, you can't ask them questions and they can't observe your dog. You should certainly still read books but also take at least one class.

Locating and Interviewing the Trainer

Whether you live in the city or the country, there are probably a number of people teaching dog classes in your area. Odds are their experience and techniques will vary widely. Luckily, you can do a little preliminary sorting from the comfort of your home.

Where to Find a Trainer

The first place you can obviously look is your local phone book. But understand that anyone can say he's a dog trainer and even take a large ad to that effect. There is no regulatory organization and no set test anyone has to pass to claim the title of dog trainer. A better course of action might be to note the names in your local phone book, then check them against the membership lists of the associations related to dog training. (See Appendix C for Web sites of the associations.)

The National Association of Dog Obedience Instructors, or NADOI, is the oldest group in existence, but not the largest. Members have to have been teaching dog classes for a specified period of time. They have a small annual meeting and conference.

Alert!

Few occupations are as entirely unregulated as dog training. Someone who has never even seen a dog before could take out ads as a dog trainer without encountering any legal problems. To be sure that you don't waste your money on a con artist, do sufficient research and try to speak with people who've used the trainer you're considering.

The Association of Pet Dog Trainers, or APDT, was formed specifically to promote positive methods of dog training. APDT has grown quickly, and it is the largest organization, holding a multiday conference every year. Professional members must be teaching classes. After a specified number of teaching hours, they can take a written test to qualify for the title "Certified Pet Dog Trainer" (CPDT). They have to take continuing education to maintain that designation.

The International Association of Animal Behavior Consultants (IAABC) is the newest of the bunch. Currently, they require applicants to fill out an extensive application, including essay questions, which they then assess for knowledge of learning theory and canine behavior. In the future, approved courses will be required. Members are called certified dog behavior consultants (CDBC).

If no one in your area is a member of any of these organizations, talk with local veterinarians for guidance. Some work closely with reliable trainers, referring behavior problems to them.

 **Fact**

> Actual university-certified animal behaviorists are few and far between. Anyone calling herself a behaviorist without the appropriate veterinary board certification is being dishonest. Be wary of these individuals.

What to Ask a Trainer

First, you can ask about any memberships in professional organizations. There are sometimes omissions from the Web site lists. The person may have joined recently, or another group may have organized. Second, ask what continuing education they avail themselves of. New techniques and new training devices come along regularly, new studies are released, and it's always good to hear from a variety of experts. Good trainers tend to frequent seminars, attending at least a couple every year.

Ask for the trainer's training philosophy, or basic techniques used in classes. You want someone who's using lure/reward or clicker training, the two most-common positive methods. Stay away from anyone using choke or pinch collars, electronic collars, or force training. If the person can't quickly explain how he trains, he doesn't have the foundation of understanding necessary for teaching good dog classes. Someone who's teaching others has to understand why they're doing what they're doing or they won't be able to explain procedure or adjust methods if they aren't working.

Ask how long the person has been involved in training dogs, and where he acquired knowledge related to dog training. You can also inquire specifically about experience with toy dogs or Yorkshire terriers. If you're asking about a puppy class, ask how the puppies are screened before coming to class. You want to be sure health risks are minimized. Finally, ask if you can observe some classes. Trainers should welcome the opportunity for you to watch them work. Cross off any who refuse. You should be welcome to observe, but your dog should stay at home or in the car. Dogs not registered for the class should not be allowed in the building while class is taking place.

Observing Classes

Expect to sit somewhere out of the way of the class participants, and watch quietly when you sit in on a training class. You can't interrupt the training to ask questions, but you can gain a lot of information just by observing.

While you watch a class, you should observe several details. Pay attention to the trainer's teaching methods and the students' responses. Also notice how the dogs are reacting to the training. Consider the following questions:

- Do people and their dogs seem to be enjoying the class?
- Does the instructor explain new exercises clearly?
- Does everyone have time to practice each exercise?
- Does the instructor or assistant give some one-on-one attention to each student?
- Is everyone treated courteously throughout class?
- Are students given written materials to refer back to?

If you feel so inclined, you can ask some of the class participants how satisfied they are with the training. Are they learning what they need to know to continue training their dogs? Does the instructor help them overcome any rough patches, explaining a procedure in a different way to help them gain understanding? Are they learning what they expected to learn, and would they take a class from this trainer again?

Private or Group Classes

The norm for dog training in the United States is group classes. These are less expensive than more private options, and they allow the dog to see other dogs and people in controlled circumstances.

But not every dog is suited for group classes, and some handlers prefer other choices.

 **Essential**

If you are having serious problems training your Yorkie, you need private training at the least, or perhaps a certified behaviorist. Serious problems disrupt group classes—dogs that exhibit them should be seen privately.

Private Classes

Private classes could consist of you, your Yorkie, and a trainer. The trainer's total attention is focused on the two of you. This may be the correct choice if your dog has some issues that need to be resolved, such as aggression. It could also help you if your learning style doesn't fit well with group activities.

The other major private option is board and train. In this case, the trainer takes your dog for some period of time, generally several weeks, and the trainer does the actual training. Be aware that you will not be there to see what is happening with your Yorkie, so the trainer has to be someone you trust absolutely. This type of training works only if there is time at the end of the board and train for you to receive instruction. You have to know the cues that have been used with your Yorkie, how to react if the dog doesn't respond to a cue, and how to keep the dog interested. You may also want to consider taking at least one class with your dog so you understand the theory and mechanics of training.

Group Classes

Group classes don't imply large numbers of students. The trainer/assistant to student ratio should be no more than one to four. Handlers should have space around them so that dogs have a few feet of maneuvering room without getting in each other's faces. The noise level should be kept to a minimum.

The class should have definite goals. These might be written down as part of your class materials. The trainer may also spell them out in class descriptions or just go over them verbally at the beginning of class.

Puppy Classes

As already noted, puppy classes serve as both socialization and an early learning opportunity. They are also a great place for you to bond more closely with your Yorkshire terrier. Positive reinforcement training is rewarding for both dog and handler.

Lure/reward training is commonly used with puppies, and they respond to it very well. It also has the benefit of being easy for most new trainers to master. You use a tiny piece of food as a lure—it's important your treats are small, because you will use quite a few in training and you don't want to make your Yorkie fat. Hold the treat between your fingers and put it right in front of your Yorkie's nose. Now if you move the treat, the dog's head should follow. If you can move the head where you want, you can move or position the dog where or how you want. Instructions on using lure/reward training for some basic good manners behaviors are detailed in Chapter 15.

Clicker training pairs a marker—that is, the clicker, a little plastic box with a metal strip that makes a distinctive sound when you press it and let it go—with treats so that the dog associates the clicker sound with getting a treat. The clicker can then be used to mark behavior that you want to train. Clicker training is particularly useful for more complex behaviors or tricks, such as "Limp," that have to be trained in increments. In this case, you would click for the dog lifting a front foot off the floor, then lifting it higher, then holding it up, then moving another foot forward while holding the foot up, and so on.

Photograph by Pamela Shelby

▲ **Training is not only fun, but it also further socializes your Yorkie.**

Beginning trainers often find it hard to deal with the clicker. You can achieve a similar effect by using a specific word, such as "Yes," as a marker in place of the clicker. It's not quite as precise or unique—after all, the dog hears you talk all day, but he doesn't usually hear a clicker. But it's still useful because you can say your marker faster than you can get a treat out of your pocket or bait bag, once you're not using the treat as a lure anymore. So you stand a better chance of marking something you want—say, a sit—rather than something you don't want—the dog getting up out of the sit. Chapter 15 includes detailed instructions for using a marker to train some behaviors.

Class Size and Makeup

You don't want too many puppies together in one place or they can escalate each others' excitement and get very noisy and hyperactive. Eight is probably enough, and there should certainly not be any more than ten.

Question?

Won't a tiny little Yorkie be hurt playing with bigger puppies?
The other pups won't hurt a Yorkie if they're polite individuals that
learned from their mothers and littermates how to keep play under
control. Puppy classes may even have a "class dog" that has a proven
record of playing well with others. Temperament matters at least as
much as size.

In some areas you may find a majority of toy dogs, while in others it may seem to be all hounds and Labs. Trainers can't always
put only toy dogs in a puppy class if there aren't enough around.
What trainers can do is select appropriate puppies to play with
each other during socialization sessions, rather than just having
people count off or letting puppies loose depending on where
their handlers happen to be sitting. Additionally, there need to be
definite age limits. Ten-week-old puppies shouldn't be mixed in
with ten-month-old puppies.

Class Curriculum

Classes can vary widely in terms of what puppies actually
learn. Some are given over almost entirely to puppies playing with
each other. Some are replicas of good manners classes, with a
younger canine clientele. Others aim at socialization, not only to
other dogs, but to all sorts of environmental possibilities.

The best classes combine a little bit of everything. Puppies
have play sessions, and handlers practice calling puppies back to
them, only to let them go play again. This is not a formal recall,
which should be practiced later, but it's a building of the bond
between puppy and human, and a chance for the pup to learn
that checking in with her handler doesn't mean an end to the fun.
Puppies should also be presented with a wide variety of sights and
sounds in a nonthreatening manner. Bicycles, wheelchairs, shopping carts, skateboards, vacuum cleaners, and loud people are

among the things that a pup might experience in class to prepare him for the real world. People should learn how to look in puppies' ears and mouths and pick up feet, and puppies should learn to let them. Of course, this training should always be fun and relaxing.

Good Manners Classes

Most dogs will benefit from taking a good manners class of some sort with their handlers. These classes go by various names—basic obedience, pet dog manners, or novice obedience—and teach the basics you and your dog need to get along in society. Puppy classes may or may not include some of these basics.

The Curriculum

Manners classes should be focused on making your dog a good member of the community. He should learn not just to sit, but to sit rather than jump up on people when greeting. (Many Yorkie owners ignore this because their small dogs are in no danger of knocking anyone over, but they can definitely rip stockings and get clothing dirty.) He should learn to lie down on cue and stay there, so you can make sure he'll stay out from underfoot when you're busy doing something. He should learn to walk nicely on a leash, without pulling. (Again, many Yorkie owners ignore this because their dogs are too small to pull them down the street. But pulling can still get annoying, and a Yorkie shouldn't be creating pressure on his throat.) Of course, your dog should learn to come when called. The trainer should also be willing and able to take a little time after class to help solve specific problems such as digging or barking.

Small-Dog Considerations

Group classes usually take all those interested, so you're likely to be sharing your class with large dogs. The trainer should take care to see that handlers take their positions in class without letting their dogs make contact with others. If you don't feel safe, don't hesitate to say so, or even to leave if the problem isn't resolved.

If the trainer or assistant works with you and your dog, she should not loom over your Yorkie—it's polite to approach from the side and to crouch down to the dog's level. These people should have a gentle touch with dogs, and especially small dogs.

Essential

Toy dogs may be small, but they're still dogs. You need to let them be dogs. If your Yorkie hides under your chair for the first few minutes, just ignore her. Act unconcerned yourself. She'll see that nothing bad is happening and will gradually feel more secure.

In class, resist the urge to hold your Yorkie on your lap. She should be down on the floor just like all the other dogs. If you decide she'll be worried in class and fuss over her, you'll actually create an insecure dog. As long as you have your own space, out of reach of other dogs, let her see for herself that she's safe near you.

Continuing Education

You don't have to stop taking classes once you've graduated from good manners class. There's plenty to do after basic training. Going to classes gives you a weekly outing with your Yorkie and should encourage you to spend time practicing at home. The time spent will keep your skills sharp and exercise your dog's mind.

Canine Good Citizen

Canine Good Citizen (CGC) training is sort of a formalized version of good manners training. It will build on what you've already learned, making good behavior more reliable and the situations your dog is encountering more difficult. Your dog will have to sit at your side while a stranger walks up and greets you, accept petting from a stranger, walk politely on-leash, sit, down, and come on cue, and more. This course generally ends with handlers and dogs taking the CGC test. If you pass all ten parts, you can receive the CGC certificate. Your Yorkie can do this even if you don't have registration papers—it's the only AKC activity that is open to unregistered dogs and mixed breeds.

Training for Sports

You can compete in a great variety of canine competitions with your Yorkie. Chapter 17 takes a more in-depth look at the sports themselves. Right now, you're concerned with training, so continue to seek out classes using positive reinforcement. Your trainer should have a background in competition or be actively competing to best understand all the nuances of the sport and the stress of competition. Be sure you are prepared, as well as your dog. Competing for the first time can be quite nerve wracking, and you need to learn to keep yourself calm to avoid upsetting your dog.

Tricks and Games

Another way to continue your education is by playing group games with dogs or teaching your dog tricks. Some games might be just for fun, while some will strengthen your dog's obedience skills, and others might even use your dog's phenomenal nose to play scent games.

Fact

While many dog owners find it difficult to commit time to basic dog training, everyone seems to enjoy showing off tricks. Smart trainers incorporate a trick or two even in their beginning classes.

Tricks are fun for everyone. They're usually things your dog can do anyway, such as sit up or roll over, but put on cue. Some might be a bit more involved, such as limp or salute. You can also combine behaviors to make little stories. No one can promise your dog is going to be a star, but you can take part in talent competitions, often offered at pet walks or county fairs. You may even win a prize.

Therapy Work

You might want to consider sharing your wonderful Yorkie with others while providing a public service. Groups such as the Delta Society Pet Partners program and Therapy Dogs International offer tests to check if dogs are suitable candidates. Delta also offers training for dogs and their handlers. A class would present you and your dog with situations you might be likely to encounter when visiting, such as people with walkers or wheelchairs, or someone with difficulty speaking. Chapter 17 includes more information on pet therapy.

CHAPTER 15

Basic and More Advanced Training

WHILE YOU SHOULD ATTEND A CLASS of some kind with your Yorkie, both for the face-to-face help you can get and the socialization opportunities for your dog, you can certainly also do some training at home, either while you're looking for a class or after you've graduated from one. Even the youngest puppy can learn—in fact, puppies are often better at this training than older dogs. Back when people used force methods, you couldn't train puppies because the techniques were too rough for their bodies and minds. Now, you can start early and never stop.

Keep It Positive

Training doesn't require choke collars and corrections. In fact, in the safety of your home, you don't need a collar and leash at all. Positive training is very hands-off. It works best if you can practice in brief sessions several times a day. Try to practice each behavior five to ten times in each session, and do three to five sessions a day. Practice every day if possible.

Lure and Reward

This is the form of training most commonly used in beginning classes. It's very effective in teaching whole behaviors that the dog does often, such as sit, and it's easy for most people to understand

and use. At its most basic level, you use a treat as a lure to get the behavior you want, and then give the treat as a reward. Eventually, you have to put the behavior on cue, so that it comes in response to a verbal or visual signal, and get rid of the lure. This part is sometimes neglected, but it shouldn't be. This chapter will walk you through the use of lure/reward training to teach sit, down, and come.

Clicker Training

Clicker training is also used in some beginner classes, but having to handle an additional item—the clicker—makes life difficult for some trainers. The clicker is simply a marker, a sound to mark a behavior that you like and want the dog to repeat. In place of the clicker, you can use a verbal marker such as "Yes." The verbal cue lacks a few of the advantages of the clicker, but it can work perfectly well and is easier for some people to handle.

fact

There are lots of books and videos on clicker training. If you find yourself getting hooked on this fast and fun way of training, seek out some of these resources to help you and your Yorkie further your skills.

With the clicker, you can break a behavior into smaller pieces and build up to the complete behavior. This lets you train more complex things than sit and down. This chapter will take a brief look at using clicker training to teach your dog to walk nicely on leash or to heel.

Praise

Verbal praise should have a place in your training, too. Everyone likes being told when they're doing a good job, and dogs are no exception. You can use your voice and whole attitude to assist in training. When you need your Yorkie to calm down and focus, don't get excited and shout—that only adds to the energy level. Instead, speak in a low voice, drawing out your words. Be still, and speak quietly. When you want to get your Yorkie excited, use a higher, squeaky voice and short words in rapid succession. Move around and wiggle your body as if you were wagging a tail.

Don't reserve praise just for formal training sessions. Any time you see your dog doing something you approve of, offer a few words of praise. Dogs that only get attention from their humans when they're doing something bad—barking at the door, getting in the garbage, chewing on a rug—will quickly learn that the way to get their human's attention is to misbehave. You may think you're punishing your Yorkie by shouting at him, but if you ignore him the rest of the time, then shouting can actually be a reward. Negative attention is better than no attention at all, as far as the dog is concerned. So make a continuing effort to praise and reward good behavior whenever you see it happening.

Lures and Rewards

Most training uses food rewards because they're easy to carry and use, not to mention extremely effective with most dogs. Select treats that can be broken into very tiny pieces—low-fat cheese sticks, flat strips of jerky, or little pill-sized commercial liver treats. You can mix treats in with some of your dog's daily kibble and give out various pieces at random or save the higher-valued treats for more difficult behaviors.

You can also use toys as treats, if your Yorkie finds them rewarding. Play a quick game of fetch, or let your Yorkie "kill" a favorite squeaky toy. Drag a toy on a string for your dog to chase. Any game your dog enjoys will be viewed as a reward. The more rewards you have in your arsenal, the more you'll be able to vary your training and keep things interesting for your dog. So make an effort to find toys and/or games your Yorkie enjoys.

Training "Sit"

Dogs know how to sit. They do it all the time. You're not teaching them to do the behavior; instead, you're teaching them to do it when you ask for it. A dog that is sitting can't be jumping up on anyone or chewing on table legs. Training your dog to sit on cue puts the action under your control.

Photograph by Cheryl A. Ertelt

▲ **The sit command should be mastered early.**

Using the Lure

Hold a bit of food between your fingers and hold it right in front of your Yorkie's nose. When your dog's attention is focused on the food, move it back over the dog's head, between the ears. When the nose follows the food and moves up, the rear end automatically goes down, because of the way the dog is constructed. As soon as the dog's rear end hits the ground, say your marker word—"Yes!"—and give the dog the treat.

If the Yorkie stands up or jumps up after the treat, you're holding it too high. Keep it just above the dog's head. If your Yorkie backs up instead of sitting, work with the dog in a corner.

Fading Out the Lure

Very early in your training, after no more than a week of practice, do one or two sits to warm the dog up, then make exactly the same hand motion, but without the treat in your hand. Be ready to mark—"Yes!"—and reward—have treats on a nearby counter, in a bait bag you're wearing, or in your other hand, behind your back. You'll find this most effective if you keep everything exactly the same except for removing the food from your hand. If you have any problems, go back to using your lure for a few repetitions, then try again. Once this consistently works with your dog, you have successfully converted your lure into a hand signal.

Adding the Cue

Note that in all the training thus far, you've said "Yes" to mark the behavior you want, and you've certainly praised your Yorkie for successful tries. But you haven't told the dog to do anything. You've relied on the power of the lure.

Essential

Humans tend to want to start giving the dog orders right away. But the dog can't understand English, no matter how smart you think she is, until you demonstrate what specific words mean. So try to be quiet while you train—it will let your dog concentrate on learning and make your words more important when you do use them.

When your dog is responding well to your hand signal—that means your Yorkie gets it right eight out of ten times—it's time to add your verbal cue. The sequence is very important.

Stand perfectly still and say your new cue word—"Sit"—then use your hand signal. Continue to mark and reward when your Yorkie complies. You can use your dog's name before the cue, if you like ("Angel, sit"). Note that the word comes first, and it occurs without your doing anything else. If you were to say your cue and use your hand motion at the same time, the dog would attend to the hand motion she already knows and might not pay any attention to what you are saying.

After only a couple of sessions of saying your cue word, say it and then wait to see if your Yorkie responds. Many dogs will surprise their owners by promptly sitting. Be ready to mark and reward. If your Yorkie doesn't sit after you wait a second or two, use your hand motion. Continue saying your cue word first, and try again after a few more repetitions.

Finishing Up

To make the "Sit" command really useful, you want it to happen on cue, but you also want it to *keep* happening. That is, you don't want a dog that sits and then pops right back up. You want your Yorkie to keep sitting. To do this, you need to switch from using a marker word to using a release word.

Your first step in this phase is to choose a release word. Make it one you will remember, but try to avoid words that often come up in conversation. People tend to want to use "Okay," but it occurs so much in everyday conversation that it's not really a good choice. Imagine this: Your dog is standing in your car with the door open, waiting to have her leash attached. A friend says, "See you tomorrow," and you respond "Okay." If "Okay" is your release word, your dog could jump out of the car, possibly into traffic. So, try to think of something else—"Free," "Release," "Finished"—whatever will work for you.

Once you have your release word, your training sequence changes. Now you say your cue word, and your Yorkie sits. You wait a second and give a treat while your dog is still sitting, and quickly say your release word. Praise your dog. Notice you have now dropped using your marker word and are instead using your release word at the end of the behavior. Be sure to reward while your dog is still in position—you don't want to reward him for getting up.

Gradually increase the time between having your dog sit and saying your release word. Make it unpredictable—one second, four seconds, two seconds, one second, five seconds—not just longer every time. After you've practiced for a few sessions, sometimes release the dog without giving a treat first. This is the start of phasing out the food. You never get rid of rewards—you wouldn't keep going to work if they didn't pay you anymore, would you? Instead, you just make them unpredictable, like playing a slot machine.

 **Question?**

Shouldn't you be telling your dog to stay?
Remember, dogs don't understand English. So "Stay" has no meaning for your dog. You can use it if you like, but the actual rules of the game are that the dog should continue doing what you've told him to do until you either release him or give him another cue. Always remember to release your dog, or your dog will (rightfully) begin to decide for himself when the exercise is over.

Finally, practice in different locations. Trainers call this "taking it on the road," and your training isn't complete without it. Until you show her otherwise, your Yorkie may think your cues only mean something in the room you usually use for training.

Training "Down"

Dogs know how to lie down just as well as they know how to sit. But they may be less willing to lie down when you ask them to. Lying down is a submissive position. A Yorkie that is insecure may not feel safe enough to lie down, while a Yorkie that is very self-assured may see it as a war of wills and be reluctant to give in.

Using the Lure

At the start of training, the down usually happens most easily from a sit. Cue your dog to sit. Hold the food lure in front of your dog's nose; then drop it quickly to the floor right between the dog's front feet and move it slightly away from the dog. Many dogs will follow the treat and lie down. Say your marker word, and give the dog the treat.

Some dogs will instead pop up out of the sit to follow the treat with their nose, without having to lie down. If your Yorkie does this, before moving the treat, put one finger on your dog's rump just forward of the tail. You're not trying to hold the dog forcibly in a sit but just using a gentle little reminder to keep the rear end on the ground. Now, with your finger on your dog's rump, move the lure to the ground and slightly away from the dog.

An Alternate Method

Don't despair if your first tries don't work. Instead, try this alternative. Sit on the floor. Have some treats handy. Bend one knee so that your leg forms a low bridge. Put your hand, holding a treat, under your leg. Show the treat to your Yorkie, then slowly draw the treat back under your leg, enticing the dog to follow. If your Yorkie is reluctant at first, bend your leg enough that the dog can just walk under it. As your Yorkie gets accustomed to going under your leg, gradually bend your knee less, so that the bridge gets lower. When it gets low enough, your Yorkie will have to lie down to pass under. Be sure to use your marker word as soon as your Yorkie assumes the down position.

This method will take a little longer, but it avoids the struggle of trying to physically place your Yorkie in a down. It also gives your dog a chance to learn that it's safe to lie down when you ask.

Following Through

See the detailed instructions on page 209 for fading the lure, adding the cue, and extending the behavior. These techniques work exactly the same for teaching the down as they do for sit. It's even more essential to take it on the road when you're working on down and to be careful about gradually moving to more challenging locations.

When you have both the commands "Sit" and "Down" on cue, you can practice interspersing the cues—"Sit," "Down," "Release"—mixing them up and rewarding every one, two, or three behaviors. If the dog doesn't respond to a new sequence the first time—asking for a sit from a down, say—go back to using your lure for a couple of repetitions and then try again.

Alert!

Before you add your verbal cue, give a little thought to what you want it to be. Most people use the word "Down," but if "Down" means lie down, it can't also mean "Don't jump up on people" or "Get off the couch." In your dog's world, one word should mean only one thing.

Training "Come"

All dog owners want their dog to come when called, and a solid recall (as the command is known) is certainly an essential tool to have. But while it's fairly easy to get your dog to come to you most of the time, it takes great dedication to have a recall that works in challenging circumstances. Even then, you can't guarantee 100-percent reliability—don't bet your Yorkie's life on the power of your recall. Use a leash to keep your dog safe.

Opportunity Recalls

To start, you do things a little differently with "Come" than you did with "Sit" and "Down." Rather than using a lure in formal training sessions, you start adding a cue in circumstances where you know your dog is going to want to come to you anyway. So think of all the things that make your dog run to you—filling the food bowl, opening a bag of potato chips, jingling car keys, taking a leash down from a holder, whatever works for your dog. Before you do any of those things, say "Angel, come!" Then jingle the car keys (or whatever you choose), praise your dog when she appears beside you, then go for the ride you were planning on anyway. Your Yorkie gets rewarded with praise and with the original motivation—dinner, a walk, or whatever else.

Collar Grabs

Having a dog that reliably runs to you, but then shoots on by or dances out of reach isn't all that useful. You want to be able to attach your leash, or hold your Yorkie out of the way for a minute, or pull a twig loose before it gets tangled in that lavish coat. So you want to practice collar grabs as a separate exercise. The sequence of events is important. Reach out and gently take hold of your Yorkie's collar, say your marker word ("Yes"), and give a treat. If you are consistent about the order of things, the collar grab will come to predict a treat, and your Yorkie will be less shy about having you reach for her.

After you've done opportunity recalls and collar grabs separately for a week or so, you can occasionally include a collar grab in your opportunity come sequence. So it's "come," jingle car keys, dog comes, collar grab, yes, treat, praise, go for a car ride.

The "Real" Recall

Your Yorkie has had a chance to hear your recall cue ("Come" or whatever you're using) quite a few times. Now you can start using it a little more as you'd like to.

Enlist another family member or a friend to help. Go into a rather uninteresting semiconfined part of the house—hallways work great. Each of you should position yourselves at one end of the hall, with the dog between you and with a good supply of treats. Whichever person the dog is facing should call the dog. Don't worry about being formal—you can be squatting, sitting on the floor, or kneeling. Smile and call as if you were greeting a friend. Pat the floor, wiggle a toy, or do whatever it takes. When your Yorkie gets to you, mark ("Yes"), give a treat, and praise and pet your dog. When you stop petting, the other person should call the Yorkie and do the same thing. Move the dog back and forth between you for several repetitions.

 Essential

If your Yorkie should ever somehow escape you in an open area, do not run after your dog. This only encourages running away. Instead, use your recall in a happy voice, and move away from your dog, clapping and acting excited. Many dogs, driven by curiosity, will come to see what you're so excited about. Do not scold your dog once you get hold of her.

Next, move to a more open, more interesting room with more options and do the same thing. Sometimes throw in a collar grab. After you've practiced in various rooms, go outside, in a safely fenced area, and do the same thing again. The more successful repetitions you build up, the more likely your recall is to work out in the real world.

Now practice on your own. When your Yorkie is nearby somewhere, mildly engaged in doing something else, call your dog. Be ready to praise and reward. Gradually make it more challenging—you're in another room, or your Yorkie is watching birds out the window. Try not to make too big a jump, because you want to set your Yorkie up for success.

Some "Come" Cautions

A wonderful result from your dog can be ruined if you insist that your dog sit straight in front of you. Unless you're going to compete in the sport of obedience, you should be delighted that your dog comes when called and leave it at that. Reward the act of coming to you without putting unnecessary details and delays between the response and the reward.

Don't use your recall to get your dog to you for something the dog considers bad. If your Yorkie doesn't like his nails trimmed, don't use your recall and then trim his nails. He may see this as punishment for coming when called, and he will not be so eager to comply the next time. Instead, go and get your Yorkie without saying anything.

Also, don't use your recall to end good times such as playing with other dogs, running in an off-leash area, or playing in the yard. If you only call your Yorkie to come when play time is over, he'll quickly figure that out and will be less and less likely to come. Instead, call him to you several times during play, when you can praise and reward him for coming, and then send him back to play some more. If "Come" only ends play a small percentage of the time, it will be more likely to remain a strong skill.

Walk Nicely on Leash

Yorkie owners aren't quite as dependent on this skill as people who own much larger dogs, but many would still like their dogs to walk without pulling. There are actually two variations of good walking on leash: formal heeling, in which the dog stays at the handler's left side, aligned with the leg, and informal walking without pulling, in which the dog can be in any position as long as the leash doesn't tighten.

Loose Leash Walking

You have to be fairly dedicated to accomplish this. Remember, behavior that is rewarded at random becomes strong, so if you sometimes reward pulling on the leash (by continuing to walk forward), you will reinforce the pulling behavior.

To eliminate pulling on the leash, stop walking as soon as the leash goes tight. Wait for the leash to go slack, whether it's because the Yorkie comes back to you, turns to look at you, or sets off in another direction. As soon as there is slack in the leash, say "Yes" to mark the behavior you want, and resume walking forward. If your Yorkie comes to you for a treat upon hearing "Yes," give a small treat and then walk forward.

Alert!

Do not jerk on the leash to get the dog to move back toward you. This will muddy your training message and make success unlikely. If you get tired of waiting for your Yorkie to put slack in the leash, say his name or make some interesting sound, and when he turns to look at you, mark and move forward.

If the leash-pulling behavior is already well established, your walks won't get anywhere very quickly for a while. You'll have to use some other method to exercise your Yorkie while you're retraining how to walk on leash.

Heeling

Most people don't really care about a formal heel position, but if you want to compete in some of the dog sports, or you have some other reason for wanting your Yorkie to move in sync with you at your left side, then read on. Heeling used to be taught in a very negative manner, by yanking on a choke chain whenever the dog moved out of position. But you'll get better results, and both of you will enjoy training more, if you instead reward the position you want.

This is best done indoors, in a room large enough for you to move around freely, with the dog off leash. Clear the room of any distractions such as toys. Just walk happily around the room, keeping one eye on your Yorkie, and whenever the dog happens to appear on your left side, near your leg, say "Yes" and give a treat. Keep moving and wait for your Yorkie to move into position again. Say yes and give a treat. Keep this up for a few minutes, then quit. Have another session later in the day.

When your Yorkie is starting to stick close to your left leg, put down some distractions or move to another safe off-leash location, and do the same thing some more. When you're fairly sure that your Yorkie is going to be right there, prancing happily alongside you, start saying "Heel" before you start moving.

Practice turns and changes of speed. Tell your Yorkie to sit when you stop moving, until the sit becomes automatic. Practice on leash in the great outdoors. Before long your dog will get the idea and be able to heel consistently.

Continuing Training

Don't make the mistake of thinking that once a dog learns a skill and performs it consistently for a matter of time, you never have to have practice sessions again. Practicing these skills with your dog as a matter of routine will provide you with a steady opportunity to bond with your dog, and it will give your Yorkie a chance to show off for you. Dogs love to perform for their owners (and for treats), so continued training sessions will be fun for your dog. As time progresses, you can add new skills and teach your dog to perform as many different acts on cue as you like.

The same principles work for almost anything you'd like to teach your Yorkie. Choose a behavior, and think about how you could use a lure to shape it. To have a sitting dog stand up, for example, hold a treat near the dog's nose and then move it a short distance up and away. Or think about marking and rewarding some behavior that occurs naturally, such as lying down in a bed, and then putting it on cue. Continuing training with your Yorkie will keep her mentally sharp and engaged with you.

Traveling with Your Yorkie

ONE OF THE GREAT ADVANTAGES of Yorkshire terriers is that they're so portable. Their small size lets them accompany you in airplane cabins, stay out of the way on small boats, and take up minimal space in the car. It's one part of their great popularity. They're also entertaining travel companions, as they're interested in almost everything.

Car Travel

Most dogs love car rides and are eager to go on any trip, however short or long. A few suffer from carsickness as puppies, but most eventually grow out of it. As with most facets of a dog's life, car rides should come with rules. You may think it's cute to have your Yorkie riding in your lap with his head out the window, but this is a hazardous practice.

Restraint Rules

Yorkshire terriers riding in the car can endanger themselves or others. Standing up and leaning out the window might seem harmless, but particles in the air can lodge in the eyes, ears, or nose. Sudden stops could fling the Yorkie onto the floor of the car. A Yorkie is small enough to get in the way of gas and brake pedals. And a Yorkie on the seat back can be flung into the windshield in a sudden stop, while a Yorkie in the driver's lap could be killed by the airbag or the steering wheel in the event of a collision.

Many recommend a crate as the safest way for dogs to ride in cars, and it's a good choice. Be sure the crate itself is fastened down in some way. Or, if you'd like your Yorkie to be able to view the scenery, invest in a doggie-style car seat. This attaches to a car seat and raises your Yorkie to good viewing height, while fastening her in with a seat belt.

 **Essential**

Never put your Yorkie in the bed of a pickup truck. Larger dogs might be safely restrained by a tie-down, but Yorkies can be so easily injured by any piece of flying debris that the only safe place for them is in the cab.

If you want your Yorkie's car seat to be in the front passenger seat, use the switch included in many newer-model cars to turn off the airbag on that side. If your vehicle doesn't have such a switch, your Yorkie will be safer in the backseat.

Packing for the Road

If you're just going out for a day trip, then all you'll probably need are some plastic bags to pick up after your dog, a bottle of water and a water bowl (soft collapsible ones are great for travel), a few treats, a brush, and an old towel.

For longer, overnight trips, you'll need to add a food bowl and either pack a sufficient supply of food or know you can purchase it locally. You'll also want a crate or at least a dog bed or blanket. Bring some toys to occupy your Yorkie, especially if bad weather strikes, and a spare leash. Slip a copy of vaccination records and a health certificate, if you have one, into a secure pocket of some piece of luggage. They will be essential if you decide you want to cross a border or want to board your dog for a day so you can see some special sight that doesn't permit dogs.

While You're on the Road

Dogs are great at reminding you to stop and take a break, especially if you're a destination-driven driver. When traveling with a dog, you should stop every two or three hours. Most highway rest areas have pleasant dog-walking sections. Some even have short trails. Or take a longer break and visit a state or local park that's along your route. You just might find a park that becomes one of your favorite stops on the whole trip.

Be very safety conscious when on the road. Snap on your Yorkie's leash before unbuckling her seat belt, or only open one car door and block it with your body while opening the crate and attaching the leash. Never let your unleashed Yorkie jump out of the car in an unfamiliar location.

Locating Accommodations

Having a dog as a traveling companion complicates your life when it comes to finding a place to stay. It's better than it once was, and not as big a potential problem with a dog as small as a Yorkie. It might not be advisable to travel to some popular locale at the height of tourist season without hotel reservations in hand. But in less crowded times or places, you'll probably be all right.

 Fact

You can find books dedicated to travel with a dog within various states. Some focus on lodging, some cover only hiking opportunities, and some cover both of these plus much more. Look for a selection that might suit you if you're visiting a particular state.

You can also do a great deal of research from the comfort of your home computer. There are several dog-friendly travel sites, and all major hotel chains have their own sites. Many of the chains have a blanket policy on dogs, so you know they're welcome (or not) at some particular brand-name lodging.

Be a good guest so that others with dogs will continue to be welcomed. Don't leave your Yorkie in the room while you go out—barking is a frequent problem. Either keep your Yorkie off the bed, or cover the bedding with your own dog blanket. Be sure your dog doesn't relieve himself in the room; there may be lingering smells from previous canine visitors, so watch your dog to make sure he doesn't mark his temporary territory.

Combating Carsickness

If your Yorkie is under a year old and shows signs of carsickness, take heart. Many will simply outgrow the problem. Just give it a little time. If the Yorkie is older than a year and still showing signs of carsickness, you'll have to work on the problem. It does take some time, but is well worth it to have a lifelong traveling companion.

Essential

While you're working on your carsickness problem, your veterinarian can help with some motion sickness medications. Before you have to rely on the medication for a long trip, test these during a drive near home so you know how your dog reacts.

Start by having your Yorkie sit with you in your vehicle, without the motor running. Talk nicely to your little dog as you sit and look out the window. Praise quiet relaxed behavior from your dog. After a week of sessions sitting in the stationary car, start sitting there with the motor running. Continue to talk quietly, and give praise for relaxed behavior. After a week, make a very short drive each session—out of the driveway, up the street for less than a block, and back up the driveway. Repeat this for a week, and then gradually lengthen your drives. Watch for signs of distress—whining, drooling, or excessive yawning. Stop the car as soon as you can if you see any of these signs.

Sometimes it helps if the dog can see out the window, so if you haven't been using a car seat, you may want to try one. Having the window open slightly for some nice fresh air can also help.

Air Travel

With a Yorkie, you have the decided advantage of being able to bring your dog into the cabin with you. But don't expect to just walk on unannounced. Most airlines severely limit the number of animals they allow in the cabin—one or two per flight is common. You should have your reservations made well before your trip or else you'll risk having the cabin spaces for pets already booked.

You will have to pay for the privilege of having your dog with you, despite the fact that he will not take more space than anyone else's carry-on luggage. In fact, some airlines have increased this fee substantially in recent years. So be prepared to pay.

Alert!

Some people may suggest using tranquilizers to keep your Yorkie quiet while on the plane. However, this is a bad idea. Medications can work differently at high altitudes, and you would be risking an adverse effect.

Booking Your Flight

Before you book a flight, consider what will best suit your dog. A direct flight is convenient for you, but if it's going to be long and you think your Yorkie may get restless, or even need to relieve himself, you might want to book an itinerary with a substantial layover in the middle so that you can take your dog outside at the mid-trip airport. Airports are not the most dog-friendly locations, so you may even want to shop around a little for an airport that might have some accessible green space within walking distance.

If you don't mind, an overnight red-eye flight can also be a good option. Your Yorkie will be more inclined to go to sleep for the duration of the flight. These also tend to be less crowded, so you have the chance of having a row of seats to yourself. You wouldn't have to give up your foot space to your dog, and you could even lie down to be closer to your Yorkie. Again, be sure you have a confirmed reservation for yourself and for your dog.

In the Airport and in the Air

Before you get to the airport, make sure your Yorkie has relieved herself completely. There won't be much chance at the airport, and people won't take kindly to seeing your dog do her business where they have to walk or set down luggage.

Plan extra time for passing through security checkpoints. If you are asked to take your Yorkie out of her travel bag, take your time and be safe. Be sure you have a leash attached and have a firm hold on your Yorkie. Airports are big, noisy places, and if your dog gets loose, you might never see her again.

Once you arrive at your gate, try to stay out of the way. If the gate attendants don't mind, you may be able to have your Yorkie on your lap rather than in her carry bag. Be aware that some people may want to interact with your Yorkie, while others might be horrified at the prospect of sharing the cabin with a dog.

From the time you board the plane to the time you disembark, airline rules mandate that your Yorkie must be in her carry bag. The bag must be stowed under the seat for takeoff and landing, but in between, if you want to hold the entire bag on your lap, that's up to you.

◀ Always keep
your Yorkshire terrier
restrained when
traveling.

Photograph by Jean Fogle

Shipping by Air

If for some reason you ever have to ship your Yorkie as air cargo, in the hold of the plane, everything changes. First, your Yorkie will have to travel in a rigid plastic crate. Label it with "Live Animal" in large letters, and add arrows indicating which side is up. Place newspaper or a towel in the crate in case your dog has to relieve herself during the trip.

Book a nonstop flight if at all possible. You can oversee or at least check that your dog is loaded onto the plane, and if there are no stops before the final destination, you or someone else can be there to meet the plane. Only an unscheduled stop for some emergency could disrupt this plan. In the summer, book an overnight flight so it will be cooler for your Yorkie. In the winter, book an afternoon flight so it will be warmer.

Before the flight, take the cage cup from the crate, fill it with water, and freeze it. Put it in the crate just before you leave home. That way, the water won't spill while the crate is being loaded on the plane, and will thaw gradually during the trip. Also tape a bag of dog food to the crate top. This keeps the crate from being loaded upside down, discourages the crew from stacking other items on top of the crate, and guarantees food for your dog in the event of a long delay somewhere along the line.

 **Question?**

What if your Yorkie starts making noise during the flight?
This is a problem indeed. Try putting the carry bag on your lap, so your Yorkie can see your face. Hold your hand against part of the webbing so your scent is strong. Talk quietly to your dog. Eventually, she should settle down.

Label the crate with the destination of your Yorkie, and the name, address, and phone number of the person who will be collecting the dog at the end of the flight. Have a tag on your Yorkie with your cell-phone number or some other phone number where you can definitely be reached.

At the airport, let everyone possible know you're traveling with your dog, or, if you won't be on the plane, that your dog will be traveling alone. Tell everyone your Yorkie's name and where she's headed. You want as many people as personally involved as possible. Ask if you can watch the crate being loaded. This is less likely now than it once was, but there's still a chance, and it alerts everyone that you're concerned. If you're traveling on the same flight as your dog, you can ask the flight attendants to confirm that your dog has been loaded safely.

Boat Travel

Yorkshire terriers aren't particularly known as water dogs, but they're small enough not to take up much room on board a boat. Because they are small, they won't make much of a splash if they fall overboard, so you need to keep a careful eye on them.

 **Essential**

If you are boating on water with even small waves, a Yorkie that falls in will quickly disappear from view. She may be swimming gamely, but you won't be able to see where she is. To avoid this, keep a watchful eye on your Yorkie, and consider using a device, such as a bell attached to the dog, to help you know where she is at all times.

Getting Acclimated to a Boat

Plan on taking several short outings so you can assess your Yorkie's reaction to traveling by boat. Some dogs suffer from seasickness just as some people do, and the same medications help them both. Get the appropriate dose of Dramamine or Merazine from your veterinarian.

Also get your Yorkie accustomed to wearing a life vest. Most pet life-preservers are orange, semi-rigid jackets with a handle on top over the back for ease in plucking the dog out of the water. Of course your dog can swim, but the life vest is easy to see, will help you lift her back into the boat, and will keep her afloat if for some reason rescue is delayed. You might also want to consider putting up safety netting between the stanchions around the boat. That way, if your Yorkie loses her footing in rough seas, she won't just slide overboard.

Many dogs don't like walking down the gangways at marinas, or stepping into a moving boat. Your Yorkie is small enough that you can solve that by carrying her on board.

Longer Boat Trips

Once you've confirmed that your Yorkie can travel happily by boat, you may want to make some longer trips. This raises two major issues for your dog: boredom and relieving himself.

If you're sailing close to land or between nearby islands, stop and take your Yorkie ashore several times a day if possible. Many waterfront towns and cities have guest boat tie-ups somewhere along their shores. State parks along the coast often have their own docking facilities. Avail yourself of these amenities, and let your Yorkie have a good walk on dry ground.

Most marinas welcome well-behaved dogs. Be sure your Yorkie lives up to that designation. Don't let him bark excessively, especially later at night, and don't let him urinate on other people's possessions. If your boating takes your farther from shore, you'll have to provide somewhere for your dog to eliminate on board, and teach him to use it. You can utilize any of the choices you have at home, as described in Chapter 7—newspaper, a litter box, piddle pads, or even a strip of grass.

Saltwater dries out your Yorkie's skin and coat, so you may want to give your dog a rinse in fresh water often, and spray on some coat conditioner. If your Yorkie will be taking a lot of saltwater spray, you might also want to invest in some doggie goggles to protect his eyes from the salt.

Stainless steel food and water dishes that are weighted at the bottom are unbreakable and will tend to stay where you put them. Special plastic travel water bowls are constructed with a rim that curves in or a lid with a hole in the middle, both to keep the water from sloshing out. These are good choices for boat travel with your Yorkie.

Finally, bring some toys to occupy your Yorkie on board. Food puzzle toys are good self-entertainment. Fetch opportunities are rather limited on a boat, but your Yorkie may enjoy "killing" some favorite toy. And any birds or fish going by can provide plenty of viewing enjoyment.

Travel Abroad

International travel has become somewhat easier for dogs in the last few years, and they can now visit more countries with fewer quarantine requirements. But travel abroad with a dog is still nothing to be taken lightly. Meeting the new requirements can mean starting preparations nearly a year before you plan to travel, and several vaccinations and blood tests may be needed. For a one- or two-week vacation, you're probably better off leaving your Yorkie behind. But if you're going to be away for a month or more, or are traveling to one of the less-regulated countries, you'll probably want to bring your dog.

Alert!

Note that many countries require recent vaccinations. If your Yorkie has been sufficiently vaccinated and you're concerned about overdoing things, you may prefer to leave your Yorkie at home while you travel. This option might be better than having to pay for more (unnecessary) vaccinations and travel accommodations for your dog.

Canada, Mexico, and the Caribbean

The nearest neighbors to the United States are all relatively friendly toward visiting dogs. Canadian regulations call for a current health certificate and proof of vaccination within the last three years. If you drive across a border, you may not even be asked to show those.

In Mexico, rabies runs rampant in the dog and coyote populations, so you'd want to have your dog vaccinated anyway. Regulations require that the vaccination take place within a year before entering the country. You will also need a veterinary health certificate dated no more than a week prior to your visit.

The various islands of the Caribbean may differ slightly in their specific requirements. Puerto Rico simply asks for a veterinary health certificate and a rabies vaccination certificate. Bermuda requires a health certificate dated within ten days of entry and an import permit issued by Bermuda's Department of Agriculture and Fishers.

The European Union (EU)

Taking a dog to Great Britain used to be nearly impossible because of the six-month quarantine. Now it's merely difficult. Ireland and Sweden are similarly difficult to enter with a dog.

It will take more than six months to gather all the necessary paperwork. Your veterinarian will have to give your Yorkie a rabies vaccination, wait a specified time, then draw blood and send it to Kansas State University. The results of blood work and vaccination details then have to go to a veterinarian approved either by the United States or Canada, who will issue a special certificate. Your Yorkie will have to have an ISO-approved microchip (those commonly in use in the United States are not ISO approved). One or two days before you disembark, your veterinarian must treat your dog for ticks and tapeworms, and issue yet another certificate.

 **fact**

Every state has an official APHIS/USDA state veterinarian. You can find the office for your state at *www.aphis.usda.gov* or by calling USDA Veterinary Services at (301) 734-8364.

Other EU countries are a bit less forbidding in their requirements, though they still have hoops you must jump through. They require a microchip or tattoo to identify the animal. The dog must be accompanied by the owner, and the dog must have his own pet passport. For the passport, your veterinarian must complete and sign APHIS form 7001, detailing vaccination information and certifying that your Yorkie is free of parasites and in good health. You then have to deliver or mail this form to the APHIS/USDA veterinary office in your state. You will have to pay a fee for each form. Your veterinarian can list several dogs on one form. Once you arrive, many EU countries, most notably France and Germany, are extremely dog friendly, allowing them to accompany you almost everywhere.

Other Countries

It's a wide world out there, and this book can't cover every country you might choose to visit. But here are a few more examples to consider.

Australia and New Zealand both still maintain their mandatory quarantines, for a minimum of thirty days. Japan requires that visiting dogs receive a rabies vaccination within thirty days prior to arrival and have an International Health Certificate. Hong Kong has no quarantine provided the dog meets their specifications for age, health, and current vaccinations, but you do need an import permit.

Within the United States, Hawaii has long been known for its lengthy mandatory quarantine. This has now been shortened to five days, provided that dogs meet requirements for rabies vaccinations.

Boarding Kennels

Not every trip will be appropriate for your Yorkie to accompany you. Cruises are definite downers for dogs. A two-week jaunt to Hawaii will mean your dog spends almost half that time in quarantine. A spa vacation may pamper you but have no amenities for your dog. And foreign countries with longer quarantines are out unless you're taking a year's sabbatical.

Some people choose to arrange vacations and select places to visit based on their dog-friendly aspects. But many want to see and do specific things, which may mean leaving the dog behind.

In that case, you'll need somewhere to leave your dog where some-one can tend to your Yorkie while you're gone.

What a Boarding Kennel Can Offer

Good boarding kennels can actually be a welcome destination for your dog. They offer fresh sights and sounds, the opportunity to meet new canine friends, perhaps a romp in the country, and humans who delight in playing daily with dogs. Some also have groomers, nutritionists, or veterinarians as part of their staff.

At a boarding kennel, your Yorkie should be kept safe at all times, either in a kennel, in a securely fenced area, or on a leash. Playgroups should be carefully selected and fully supervised.

Finding a Boarding Kennel

The best way to find a boarding kennel is through personal rec-ommendations. Ask your veterinarian, your trainer, your groomer, or friends with dogs. If you can't find a kennel through word of mouth, you can check your local Yellow Pages. You can also con-tact the American Boarding Kennels Association (ABKA). They can provide a list of any member kennels in your area. Once you've gathered a list of boarding kennels, however long or short, contact each to set up a time for you to visit and inspect the premises.

Don't narrow your search unnecessarily. If you live in the city, a boarding kennel out in the country might be a fun change of pace for your Yorkie while you're gone.

Evaluating a Boarding Kennel

Before you even leave home, you can contact the Better Business Bureau and find out if any complaints have been lodged against the kennels you're considering. On your tour of each board-ing kennel, keep your eyes, ears, and nose open. The premises should look and smell clean, and dogs shouldn't be barking con-stantly. (All that barking will stress the other dogs in the facility.)

Pay close attention to the runs. If they're indoor/outdoor, you know your Yorkie can choose to go outside if the weather is fine or stay warm and dry inside if the weather is bad. See that the runs are well ventilated and lighted, and that they're kept at a comfortable temperature. Ask if bedding is provided (and scrupulously cleaned between occupants) or if you should bring your own. If the runs are indoors only, ask how and how often dogs are exercised. If runs are outdoors only, this probably isn't the right place for your Yorkie.

Alert!

Don't leave your Yorkie at a boarding kennel you have not thoroughly checked out and visited personally. Dogs have been injured, lost, and killed at disreputable boarding kennels. To be sure your dog will be safe, try to use a kennel that has been recommended to you by a trusted friend or canine professional.

Observe the demeanor of any employees and how they interact with the dogs. You want the people who will be tending to your Yorkie to like being around dogs, not just doing a job for money. Also ask if the kennel is a member of the ABKA. Members commit to following the organization's code of ethics. Member kennels can also request an inspection, allowing them to be accredited.

Inquire about any paperwork you will have to supply to board your dog. Proof of vaccinations, including for bordetella (kennel cough), should be required. With vaccination schedules changing from annual to every three years or even less frequently, ask how they respond to dogs that have not been vaccinated in the last year. Do they accept veterinary health certificates, or blood titer levels?

Find out if they will feed the food your Yorkie is accustomed to and if you should provide a supply. Also inquire if they have a veterinarian on call in the event of unforeseen problems.

Pet Sitters

Another alternative to bringing your dog along when you travel is to have your Yorkie stay in your own home, and hire someone to come in and tend to her needs. You could use a neighbor, but only do this if you are absolutely certain that this person has the time and dedication to be there for exercise and feeding every day. The other choice is to hire a professional pet sitter.

Fact

There are a couple of organizations to which pet sitters can belong, and they can both provide you with the names of members in your area. Contact the National Association of Professional Pet Sitters or Pet Sitters International. Ask all your dog-enthusiast acquaintances for recommendations.

Some pet sitters visit your home once or twice a day, while others come and stay in your home the whole time that you are gone. Many will also water your plants, bring in your mail and newspaper, and generally deter intruders by being present in your home.

A pet sitter should be insured—he will be coming into your home, so you want to have some guarantee of his reliability—and carry commercial liability insurance. This person should have experience with dogs, and he should provide a written list of services and fees for those services. He should come to your home for a consultation, at which time you can give any specific instructions relating to your dog or your home.

CHAPTER 17

Dog Sports and Activities

YOUR YORKSHIRE TERRIER MAY BE SMALL, but he's a dog just the same. He can take part in a variety of dog sports and other activities. Perhaps he's not the best candidate for herding or field trials, but he'll fit right in if you want to have him try conformation, obedience, agility, freestyle, or go-to-ground competitions. Yorkies are rare in flyball, but there's nothing to stop them from competing. And your well-mannered Yorkie makes an excellent candidate for pet-therapy work.

 Essential

If you don't have papers for your Yorkie, you can apply for an ILP (indefinite listing privilege). This form of registration will allow you to compete in any sport other than conformation. Contact the AKC or UKC for more detailed information.

Conformation

This kind of competition is commonly known as the dog show, where your Yorkie will compete against others to determine which dog comes closest to matching perfection as described by the standard and determined by the judge. Classes are divided by age or experience. Winning a class sends you on to further competition. A win can earn your dog anywhere from one to five points, depending on how many dogs you defeat. Wins of three or more points are classified as majors. To qualify for the title "Champion," designated with "Ch." before the dog's name, you must gain a specified number of points under different judges, with some of the wins being majors.

What You Need to Compete in Conformation

First, you need a Yorkshire terrier that conforms reasonably well to the standard. Of course you find your Yorkie incredibly appealing, and no one should ever change your opinion, but the standard calls for specific attributes, especially relating to the head and coat. Failing to have the spectacular coat called for in the standard in no way decreases your dog's greatness—it just makes it unlikely you will win in the ring.

Dogs well suited to showing need to have self-assurance and an outgoing personality. If there are several individuals that conform well to the standard, it may be personality that determines the winner. The AKC requires that dogs be intact—not spayed or neutered—to compete in conformation. They consider dog shows to be venues for choosing breeding stock. The UKC (United Kennel Club) has a dog show program similar to the AKC's, but also has classes for spayed and neutered dogs.

 Fact

The one thing that is absolutely essential to enter your dog in conformation competition is registration. Your Yorkie must be registered as a purebred Yorkshire terrier in order to compete.

You can devote yourself to showing, spending every weekend on the road. Or you can spend the occasional weekend at a local show. It's up to you how much time and money you want to invest in the sport. Your Yorkie will likely be up for whatever you choose.

Grooming for Conformation

If you want to show, you'll need to do more than basic mainte-nance grooming, and you can't have your Yorkie's coat cut down. It should sweep the floor. But it can't be left to sweep the floor all the time, or the ends will be damaged and it will pick up dirt. So you need to keep the coat in wraps. If possible, have your breeder or an experienced groomer show you how to wrap the coat. You can also hire a groomer to do it, as the job can be rather involved the first few times you try it.

If you need to do it yourself, without benefit of hands-on instruction, here are the basics. You part the hair into sections as naturally as possible. The topknot gets a wrap, the side whiskers on each side get a wrap, and the beard whiskers get a wrap. The coat from under the ears to the back of the head can usually be divided into two wraps, one for each side. The outside of each leg gets a wrap. The body between the legs gets a couple of wraps on each side. There's usually one on each shoulder and one on the chest. The tail gets a wrap, and the britches behind each of the rear legs each get one.

So, what are these wraps, and what do they do? They don't somehow magically make the hair grow faster, though that's a common misconception. Wraps simply prevent the ends of the hairs from being broken, and they keep the hair, especially on the tail and britches, from getting soiled when the dog eliminates or moves around.

The wraps themselves are simply papers and rubber bands used to gather the hair and keep it out of the way. You can buy paper for wraps at some grooming shops. You can also use rect-angles of waxed paper, found at kitchen shops, or you can just buy a roll of waxed paper and cut your own. You can buy the rubber bands (small) from a grooming shop or an office-supply store. To actually wrap the coat, brush a section of hair, wrap the paper around the hair near the end, fold it in half and back over itself, and secure it there with one of your rubber bands.

Most Yorkies will have enough coat to start to have it wrapped at somewhere between nine months and one year of age. It's best to start wrapping just a few sections at first—the tail and britches and the topknot are the usual choices. And you can't just wrap a Yorkie and consider it done until your next bath or show. The wraps should be undone and brushed out every other day. As you can see, this is a major undertaking.

Alert!

When wrapping hair, be careful not to pull on the roots. If you've ever worn a too-tight ponytail, you know how uncomfortable it can be. Wrapping your Yorkie's hair too tightly will just make her more aware of the wraps and more likely to try to rub or scratch them off.

Types of Shows

The dog shows you may have seen on television are all-breed shows. The portions that are televised are the Group competitions. To reach the Group competition, dogs of each breed first compete against others of their kind to select Best of Breed. Best of Breed winners then move on to compete against the other Best of Breed winners in their group—as a member of the Toy Group, the Yorkshire terrier would compete against other toy dogs such as the Maltese, Pomeranian, and pug (to name a few). The AKC recognizes six other groups: Sporting, Hound, Working, Terrier, Nonsporting, Herding, and Miscellaneous. Winners of each Group competition move on to compete for Best in Show.

All-breed shows host all the breeds recognized by the kennel club. They are large, often multiday affairs. A few, scattered around the country, are still benched, meaning the dogs must be there, on public display, for the duration of the show. Some shows may concentrate on a single group (terrier specialties, for example), or a selected set of breeds. This is common practice with the UKC—less common with the AKC.

Finally, there is the Specialty. This show concentrates on one breed only. There can be regional specialties and a national specialty. Most of the top dogs of the breed will come to the national specialty to compete against other top winners. Extra classes are generally offered at specialties. Brood bitch and stud dog classes show off adults with their offspring, while sweepstakes classes focus on the puppies. Veteran classes honor older dogs.

Handling for Conformation

Both you and your dog have to be comfortable in the show ring. Your Yorkie has to be relaxed in order to show well. If you are stressed, your feelings will travel down the leash to your dog. To make things easier, you should understand how a show works prior to competing. This way, you'll know when to be at your ring, and what you'll be expected to do once you're there.

When you get to a show, first pick up your exhibitor armband and a show catalog. The armband identifies you and your dog, and the catalog will tell you the ring and time for your class. Once in the ring, you will usually stack or pose your Yorkie, along with all the others in the class, on the ground for the judge to get her first look at the dogs. She may ask everyone to move their dogs around the ring as a group, or she may start right in with the individual examinations.

You will put your Yorkie up on a table and pose him to present the best possible picture. The judge will go over your dog, looking in his mouth, feeling his structure under the coat, checking the coat texture. Your job is to stay out of the way while keeping your Yorkie still and composed.

After the exam, you'll put your Yorkie down on the ground and move him individually for the judge, usually directly away and back to the judge, then around in a circle to the back of the line. You should move so that your Yorkie performs a fast walk or slow trot. You and your dog will benefit from taking some handling classes before you show. Check with your local kennel club and area trainers for these opportunities.

Professional Handlers

Some owners prefer to hire professional handlers rather than show their dogs themselves. Be clear on what you expect before you take this route. If you would just like to earn a championship, your Yorkie will almost certainly be handled by one of the professional's assistants. The big pros concentrate on dogs that are specialing—have already earned their championships and are showing heavily to try to earn top-dog honors in the various ranking systems. They will bring a string of dogs to a show—one or two dozen—but they can't possibly handle them all.

 Essential

If your dog turns out to be capable of winning more often than not, you may be encouraged to special your dog. Understand that this means your Yorkie will be on the road attending shows for most of the year. Be sure this is what you want before you agree on it.

Before you give your dog over to a handler, be sure you agree on how your dog will be treated, where he will be housed, and so on. The easiest arrangement is for you to bring your Yorkie to a show and just have the handler take him into the ring. If the handler will be taking your dog on the road, ask to see how your dog will be housed in the inevitable RV, and who will feed, groom, and exercise the dog. Don't hand your dog over unless you're completely comfortable.

Obedience

Obedience competition tests the handler's training, the partnership between the handler and the dog, and the dog's willingness to work. Obedience trials may be offered as a part of conformation shows or as events on their own. You generally work your way up through classes of increasing difficulty, and titles usually require three qualifying scores, also known as legs.

Traditional Obedience Classes

The traditional titling classes are Novice, Open, and Utility. Novice includes on- and off-leash heeling, a stand for examination (your dog must stand still while the judge touches several places), a stay and recall (you sit your dog at one side of the ring, walk across the ring while your dog stays in place, and then call your dog), and group exercises. In the group exercises, as many as ten dogs are brought into the ring. Handlers and dogs line up on one side of the ring, and dogs must sit for one minute (with handlers across the ring), then lie down for three minutes.

Fact

Deb Gatchell's Yorkshire terrier, Rothby's Wrapped In Rainbows (Raney), has earned both the Obedience Championship (OTCH) and the Utility Dog Excellent (UDX) titles, both very difficult to achieve. He is only the third Yorkie to attain the OTCH.

In all levels of competition, you must score at least 170 points (out of a possible 200) and at least half the points available for each individual exercise in order to achieve a qualifying score.

The Open class performs only off-leash heeling, adds a drop (down) in the middle of the recall, and includes two retrieves. The retrieve on the flat means the dog stays at the handler's side while the handler throws the dumbbell, fetches it on cue, and holds it until the handler takes it. In the second retrieve, the dumbbell is thrown over a jump, which the dog has to clear both going and coming back. There is also a broad jump, and the group exercises are done with the handlers leaving the ring and going out of sight of their dogs.

The Utility class includes a completely different set of exercises. In the signals exercise, the handler must use visual signals only to have the dog stay, down, sit, and come. Scent discrimination uses a set of dumbbells, only one of which the handler touches. The dog is sent to find and retrieve the scented dumbbell. The directed retrieve uses three gloves spaced across the ring. The handler must have the dog retrieve whichever glove the judge indicates. For the moving stand, your dog is heeling and you must have him stand-stay while you continue walking. The judge examines the dog with you some distance away, and you then call the dog. The final exercise is directed jumping. You have to send the dog away from you, between two jumps, to the other end of the ring, then have her sit. The judge tells you which jump the dog is to take, and you signal your dog to come over that jump and return to you.

 **Essential**

Obedience has long been declining in popularity. The focus on earning points for the obedience championship has resulted in a drive for extreme precision, and both dogs and handlers have found other sports more fun. But you can still earn obedience titles without obsessing over minute details.

These are not full descriptions of the exercises but just enough details to give you some idea of what is expected. Other classes also exist, and dogs that have completed Utility can continue competing to earn points toward an obedience championship.

Rally-O

Rally obedience, or Rally-O, is a new variation on obedience, concocted to try to make obedience competition more fun and to compete with the fast-rising sport of agility. It's much less formal than traditional obedience. You can talk to and praise your dog throughout your time in the ring.

The exercises aren't set as they are in traditional obedience. Instead, fifteen to twenty exercises are chosen from a total of about thirty-five. An actual course is laid out, with a sign indicating each exercise ("270° turn to the right," for example), and numbers indicating the order in which to do the exercises. Handlers are given time to walk the course without their dogs, to familiarize themselves with the exercises they will be performing. Precision is still prized, and points are deducted for sloppiness, but this is also a timed event, so speed is important.

 **fact**

Arlene King and her Yorkie, Illusion's Jaws With Paws (JP), have already earned a perfect score in Rally-O, and a Rally-O title from the Association of Pet Dog Trainers. Along with JP, Arlene also performs in tracking with her other Yorkie, Fergie. Fergie is the first Yorkie to earn the Tracking Dog Excellent (TDX) title.

Agility

Agility has been the fastest-rising dog sport for a number of years. The dog must follow the handler's directions to negotiate a series of obstacles. Obstacles include a variety of jumps, tunnels, an elevated dog walk, a teeter-totter, an A-frame, and weave poles. Each run is timed, and the fastest clean run (with no points off for knocked bars or other miscues) wins.

Training for Agility

Be cautious about doing too much agility training too early. Yorkie puppies should not practice weave poles or do a lot of jumping before they are physically mature at one year of age. But that need not keep you from training. You can use poles lying on the ground between uprights as jumps and work on lowered versions of the teeter-totter and dog walk. Tunnels are no problem.

Before you get too involved with obstacles, you should concentrate on groundwork. This means teaching your Yorkie other skills she will need on the agility course, such as directional cues (go, out, left, right, close). You can also teach a foot target to be used in working on contact zones (the last few feet of an obstacle such as the dog walk, which the dog must touch to avoid a penalty).

Find a trainer who uses positive methods and understands that it doesn't pay to rush into competition training before laying down the basics. Private lessons may be safer and less stressful for your Yorkie. Many group agility trainers do not screen class members effectively, and both handlers and dogs may cause problems, particularly for toy dogs.

Question?

Are smaller obstacles used for toy dogs?
No. Jump heights are adjusted, but nothing else. But while the A-frame may be a harder climb for a Yorkshire terrier than a Border collie, think how difficult a tunnel is for really big dogs. Each breed has different advantages and disadvantages, and the weaknesses can be overcome with plenty of practice.

Competing in Agility

This is one sport that definitely tests the skills of both handler and dog. Before a class starts, handlers are given a few minutes to walk the course without their dogs. In this time, you will have to memorize the course of seventeen to twenty obstacles, and plan how you are going to handle your dog through it. You may then have to wait some time before it's your turn to run. You can watch others run the course, but you need to keep your own plans firmly in mind.

Warm up both your dog and yourself before a run. Do some stretching to limber up those muscles. You can have your Yorkie spin in circles or weave between your legs to do bending exercises. Some dogs like a long walk around, while others get too excited and need to be kept away from the hubbub until it's almost time to go.

Photograph by Pamela Shelby

▲ Competing in agility is a great way to keep your Yorkie in shape.

On the course, never forget that this is a partnership. Always keep your dog's safety in mind—don't turn so tight to the A-frame that your Yorkie won't have enough momentum to scramble up it easily. Don't pull her off the teeter-totter before the end has touched down by moving away too soon. Most of all, don't rush into competition. This is a sport that definitely takes time to master.

Freestyle

Freestyle is an even newer sport than agility. It's also called "dancing with dogs" for its human-canine routines set to music. No one has to be particularly athletic to take part in freestyle events—you just have to be willing to get out there in front of everyone and perform.

The Human Half of the Team

You're the one who has to choose the music and choreograph the routine. But you should keep your Yorkie's attitude and preferences in mind, too. Some dogs love fast movement, while others might enjoy a slower beat. A cute theme seems a natural for a Yorkshire terrier, but more serious individuals might appreciate drama instead.

You can choose among different divisions of the sport. Heelwork to music doesn't use all the flashy trick moves of a full-blown freestyle routine, relying instead on heel positions on either side, in front, and in back of the handler. A new innovation, K9 Dressage, is a freestyle version of Rally-O, with a course laid out with predetermined moves to perform according to signs. Neither of these requires costuming or a lot of dance moves for you.

Alert!

While competition, specifically agility training and competition, is sometimes recommended to help bring shy dogs out of their shells, freestyle works best for more confident dogs (and people). The crowd surrounding the ring and loud applause may be a bit too intimidating for shy individuals.

The mainstay of the sport, however, wants showmanship. The early judges had backgrounds in figure skating, so think of yourself as doing a pairs performance—only you're in a ring rather than on the ice and with a dog as your partner. You don't have to be Fred Astaire (though it wouldn't hurt), but you will have to do more than walk around the ring. The routines incorporate any number of trick moves—jumping over your leg, weaving through your legs, running circles around you, or backing up. Partners can separate, so working at a distance can be important.

The Canine Half of the Team

Performances are in a ring, often with the judges on one side and public spectators on two or three other sides. Freestyle may not be the right choice for a shy dog. But for the typical outgoing Yorkie, this is a chance to shine.

Because your dog is so small, you'll have to be careful of your footwork to be sure you don't step on any of your partner's toes. Dogs do seem to have musical preferences, so try out some different song styles while just moving around with your dog to see what suits him.

You can buy videos of others' routines to help get some ideas for your own moves. Clubs also hold seminars, often in conjunction with competitions. Just keep your dog's strong and weak points in mind when working up routines. Also make sure to take plenty of time to practice. The more self-assured you can feel when you enter the ring, the less you're likely to upset your dog.

Go-to-Ground Competition

This is the natural pursuit of the small terriers. Remember that the Yorkshire terrier was originally a ratter, chasing and cornering its prey in mines and mills. Though they haven't been bred for such work for a good many years, some still retain the instinct.

 **Fact**

Go-to-ground competitions are also called Earthdog trials. The word terrier comes from the Latin *terra*, for earth. The nearly universal short, sturdy upright tails of the small terriers were once used to pull dogs out of tunnels.

If you decide to take part in go-to-ground competitions, you'll likely find yourself surrounded by Jack Russell (or, as the AKC now calls them, Parson Russell) terriers, and an occasional smooth fox terrier. Not many Yorkies are willing to sully themselves going into tunnels in the dirt. But your dog might enjoy it, so why not try?

In go-to-ground competitions, a tunnel is dug and a scent trail of some rodent such as a rat is laid. Dead-end tunnels without the scent trail may lead a dog astray. The rodent is safely caged at the end of the tunnel. The dog is expected to go down the hole, follow the scent to the rodent, and then "worry" the prey by barking.

Pet Therapy

If you'd rather do some good for others instead of compete with your dog, maybe you'd like to try your hand (and paws) at pet therapy. Clean, well-mannered dogs accompany their humans to such places as convalescent hospitals, senior care facilities, and pediatric wards to bring some canine cheer to patients or residents. Other programs take dogs to schools and have children read to them.

 **fact**

Tami Grinstead and her Yorkie, Cleo, made monthly visits to both a nursing home and an Alzheimer's facility, bringing cheer to all they visited. Cleo has partially retired due to her own health problems, but she still checks in with the staff of the facilities from time to time.

The Organizations

For liability reasons, you and your dog should be registered with one of the several organizations formed for this purpose. The Delta Society's Pet Partners program is the most stringent, but you'll also learn the most about what to expect and how to behave. Therapy

Dogs, Inc., and Therapy Dogs International both use the CGC (described in Chapter 14) or something very close to it to test the dog, and they provide no instruction to the human. What all the organizations do provide their members is group liability insurance in case an incident ever arises while you are visiting.

Organizations can also put you in touch with other members in your area. There may even be an official group that goes on visits together.

What to Expect on a Visit

You can visit in several ways. Some go to large common areas and put on demonstrations with their dogs, doing tricks, obedience exercises, or even agility. Others go person-to-person, allowing people to pet their dogs. Be a little cautious with your Yorkie the first time you visit individuals. You don't want anyone pounding on him or pulling his hair. People probably don't mean to hurt him, but some may have impaired mobility or functionality.

You're likely to hear a lot of stories about people's own pets. If you visit regularly, you'll probably hear the same stories over and over. Some people relating their memories may cry. Others will smile and laugh. You should be prepared for either. Pet therapy can be an emotional hobby, but your small contribution can make a huge difference in people's lives.

Doing pet-therapy work can be tiring for your dog. Some facilities can also be a bit warm or not as well ventilated as your dog is used to. Watch your Yorkie for panting of signs of stress. And be sure to end a visit early if necessary. To be effective at therapy work, dogs must be relaxed, healthy, and in a good frame of mind.

CHAPTER 18

Behavior Problems

Y ORKSHIRE TERRIERS, LIKE MOST PUREBREDS, are susceptible to several behavioral conditions. Because of their natural in-charge attitude, you'll have to be a firm authority in order to keep your dog under control. They will run your household if you let them, and can become manipulative and demanding if they're used to getting their way. However, they can just as easily be perfectly wonderful companions. The way you treat them, and what you expect of them, has a significant effect on how they behave.

The Instinct to Spoil

Dogs in human society sometimes serve as child substitutes—small dogs more than most. There's nothing wrong with treating your Yorkie as a full member of your household. In fact, it's a good idea. But you probably wouldn't let your human child eat only ice cream and cake for dinner, hit visitors, scream over nothing, and declare ownership over family possessions. Nor would you lock a human child in a room and go off and forget about him. These parenting styles don't work particularly well with Yorkie "children" either.

Being Overindulgent

People make the mistake of letting puppies get away with things that they'd rather not have the adult dog do. Yes, puppies are very cute, and it's hard to discipline them. But it's much easier to start as you mean to continue rather than to change the rules six months down the road. If you don't want your adult Yorkie occupying the furniture, don't put your puppy on the couch, and correct him if he manages to get there on his own. (Put him back on the floor and give him something to do down there, such as play with a toy.) Don't tolerate puppies chewing on your fingers or hair or pants leg. It's important for them to learn bite inhibition and to keep their mouths off humans. Don't cuddle and pet your Yorkie every time he barks or whines or paws for your attention. Ignore it until it stops, and be sure you consistently give attention when your Yorkie is just lying quietly.

Essential

If your puppy mouths your hands or other body parts, respond by yelping in a high-pitched voice and removing your hand and your attention. This is how other puppies respond to too-rough play and it works with the majority of puppies. You want to convince your pup that humans are very fragile and must be treated tenderly.

Also be firm about food. It's perfectly natural for small dogs to skip a meal occasionally, or not finish everything that's given to them. But don't rush to add delicacies to convince your Yorkie to eat—you may well create a finicky tyrant that demands smoked turkey one day and filet mignon the next.

Being Neglectful
You can't expect to just put down food a couple of times a day and ignore your Yorkie the rest of the time or pick her up only when you feel like cuddling. Yorkshire terriers may be a small-sized responsibility, but they're still a responsibility. Puppies require near-constant supervision to keep out of trouble and learn

housetraining. Even older dogs need training, exercise, and companionship. If your time is already fully taken up, you probably shouldn't have a dog.

Because Yorkshire terriers are so small, they are easy to stuff into a Sherpa bag or a crate and relegate to a corner, out of the way. This is abuse. A dog, however small, is a pack animal that needs to be with his family as much as possible. Dogs require time and attention—don't get a dog if you don't have these things to give. Puppies are cute and a novelty in the family, so their transgressions are usually forgiven. But when the dog reaches adolescence and isn't a puppy anymore, but still takes up considerable time, the dog is often shuffled out of the family to live a lonely, unloved life. You must understand that a dog is a commitment *for life* before you get one.

Shyness

Think about how large everything in your home is compared to your Yorkshire terrier and you'll understand how easy it is for your Yorkie to be a bit shy and fearful of new things or people. A little caution isn't necessarily a bad thing, but you don't want a dog that's afraid to meet new people or see new sights.

Puppy Classes

A good puppy class not only lets you and your pup have a good time and begin formal training, it also lets your puppy know that it may be a big, wide world, but you'll be sure it's a safe one. If your Yorkie learns early to look to you for how to react to some novel situation, you can help her lead a happy, self-assured life.

Shy puppies should not be forced into the midst of play in a puppy class. That will only convince them that you're a dangerous leader who will put them in danger. Instead, let them observe from the sidelines. Remain calm and relaxed, and praise and reward any desired behavior such as stepping forward into the room. The trainer may invite you to come early or stay late to give your pup the opportunity to explore without all the other dogs around. The trainer may also suggest you try a scent called Rescue Remedy that seems to have a soothing effect on many dogs (and people). There's also an item called a DAP dispenser that some training centers use. DAP stands for dog-appeasing pheromone—it's a scent that's comforting to dogs.

Loud Noises

Dogs that tremble, whine, and try to hide at the sound of sirens, fireworks, or thunderstorms can be a real worry for their humans. As a first line of prevention, try not to be reactive yourself. It's normal to jump at a sudden loud sound, but it's crucial to then make light of it rather than rushing to comfort your Yorkie. Remember the jolly routine from Chapter 13.

Dogs that become noise phobic can become destructive, climbing the drapes or chewing up possessions in a frantic attempt to make themselves feel better. Phobic dogs are also prone to running aimlessly, so you have to be careful to keep them safely indoors.

As a temporary measure, you can ask your veterinarian about using some tranquilizers. Always get the correct medication and dosage from your veterinarian. Because the breed is so small, you could easily overdose a Yorkshire terrier.

Alert!

If you happen to have some Zoloft or Effexor or any of the other common human antidepressants in your medicine cabinet, don't just reach for one for your Yorkie. While canines and humans do share some medications, others can be deadly for dogs. It's a standard rule that no one (whether human or canine) should take anyone else's prescription medication.

As a longer-term measure, use desensitization and counter-conditioning. You can buy tapes or CDs of the common noise triggers. Play them at such a low volume that your Yorkie doesn't react, and do pleasurable things such as play with toys or practice some training, with plenty of treats. Over a span of sessions, increase the volume just a tiny bit at a time. You want to do this so gradually that your dog never reacts badly. If you see any signs of nervousness, stop the session. Lower the volume for the next session.

This is a lengthy process, made more difficult if the fear-triggering noises can occur without warning while you're trying to desensitize. So don't wait until the end of June to start working on fireworks. Use tranquilizers if you know a thunderstorm is approaching.

Shyness with People

You might see two levels of shyness—actual reluctance to approach strange people or hand shyness. If your Yorkie is hand-shy, she may be perfectly happy around anyone until a hand reaches toward her. You can avoid hand-shyness by practicing collar grabs with positive results (see Chapter 15), avoiding patting on top of the head, and not allowing anyone to grab your Yorkie roughly or without warning.

For people-shyness, you need to enlist friends and family to provide your Yorkie with as many positive interactions as possible. Don't force her to approach people. Instead, have someone sit on the floor with a handful of treats. Ask her to look away from your Yorkie, engage in pleasant conversation with you, and occasionally toss a treat toward the dog. As long as the dog will get the treat, the person should toss it a little closer to herself each time, while continuing to ignore the dog. Repeat this procedure with as many people as possible. Over time, your Yorkie will start to associate approaching people with getting treats.

Aggression

Aggression is an unfortunate tendency that now occurs across all breeds and breed mixes. A dog doesn't have to launch a full-blown attack to exhibit aggression. Issuing a warning growl, curling a lip to show teeth, snarling, and biting are all acts of aggression. However, do not get caught up in all the references to dominance and alpha in dog literature. A dog exhibiting aggression is not automatically bent on taking over the household. In fact, fear aggression is more common than dominance aggression.

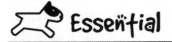 **Essential**

Don't assume you don't have to worry about aggression simply because your dog is so small. There are households in which people are afraid to move around their aggressive Yorkie. Aggression is not acceptable no matter what size the dog may be and action must be taken to eliminate all aggressive behavior.

Types of Aggression

Aggression can arise out of many circumstances, some less troublesome than others. Maternal aggression that only occurs when a mother has pups is not a major problem. The mother can be lured away from the nest with her food bowl or treats when the puppies need to be handled. (Though perhaps this mother should not be bred again, as nervous mothers can create nervous puppies.) The problem becomes more serious if the female starts exhibiting protective behavior over stuffed toys or other surrogate puppies.

As mentioned, fear is the most common basis of aggression. In human society, frightened dogs often aren't free to just run away. So they default to their second option: warning the scary thing to stay away. Frightened dogs would rather avoid the conflict, but if cornered they may feel that they are fighting for their lives. They are quite likely to bite if pushed.

Possession aggression occurs because canine rules differ from human rules when it comes to owning things. Even low-ranking members of canine packs own some object that is in their possession, and fights are rare. To be constantly fighting over scraps of food would be counterproductive to the pack's survival. Yet humans expect their dogs to willingly give up possessions to them. It doesn't happen automatically.

Dealing with Aggression

No form of aggression should be tolerated, but responses to the different underlying causes indicate different solutions. For example, if snarling or snapping arises suddenly, a visit to the veterinarian is in order. The sudden aggression may be in response to pain from an injury or illness.

Never punish a dog for growling. First, aggression by you (punishment can be viewed as aggression) begets more aggression, so you're making the problem worse. Second, growling is a warning, and if you eliminate the growling without correcting the underlying problem, you may create a dog that bites without warning.

Photograph by Jean Fogle

▲ **Curb aggression early to prevent unmanageable problems later on.**

To avoid possession aggression, convince your dog that giving things to you results in receiving even better things. While your dog is eating, drop an extra-special treat in the bowl. Gradually bring your hand closer to the bowl to drop the treat, until you are actually placing the treat in the bowl.

Also do trades for toys, having a second toy of equal or greater value than the one the dog has, and making it more interesting by showcasing your interaction with it. While you are working on possession aggression, keep human-valued objects such as the remote control safely out of reach of the dog, or at least tie a long string to them so you can get them back without confrontation.

 **fact**

Unfortunately, board-certified veterinary behaviorists are rare in the United States. They number only in the few dozens. However, many trainers educate themselves remarkably well. Be sure to ask your trainer about his experience in dealing with aggression.

Fear aggression can largely be avoided with proper socialization. Be sure your young Yorkie meets other people of all shapes and sizes and other dogs (in safe conditions), and encounters bicycles, school buses, park benches, mirrors, elevators, roller skaters, horses, and other possibly distressing stimuli. Make a game of it—try to introduce your dog to five new people or things every week.

If you've rescued an older Yorkie, or neglected this early socialization and now have a dog with fear issues, or you think you have a truly dominant-aggressive dog, you need face-to-face help from a trainer or behaviorist skilled in such problems. Look for someone who will use positive reinforcement with what is called classical conditioning—associating a good thing with the scary thing over and over.

Barking and Whining

Much of a dog's communication is through silent body language, but canines have plenty of vocal abilities at their disposal as well. Some dogs use their vocal repertoire freely, to the distress of their humans. "How do I stop him from barking?" is a frequently asked question.

Controlling Barking

Dogs bark in response to goings-on in their environment (company arriving, a dog going by on the street, a squirrel perching in a tree), because they're bored and it's something to do, or because they've learned it gets attention. Yelling at your dog is not only futile; it may actually work against you. From the dog's point of view, you're joining in with raising the alert, so it's confirmed that there is something to bark about.

Many people are happy to have a dog alert them to someone approaching the house, and Yorkshire terriers excel at this watchdog function. But they'd like the barking to stop relatively quickly. This is something you can work on through training.

Try to enlist a friend to help, so you can predict when barking will happen and be ready for it. If it's someone ringing the doorbell or walking past with a dog that sets your dog off, set up that situation. Have some really good treats at your disposal. When your dog reacts and starts barking, wait for her to be quiet for a split second (she does have to inhale at some point), and offer her one of your treats. She has to stop barking to eat. Your helper should disappear as quickly as possible so your dog doesn't feel compelled to start barking again.

When you begin to have a little control—the dog barks, but looks to you for that yummy treat—say some cue that will be your signal to the dog to stop barking. "Thank you" works nicely. Then give the treat. With practice, you can have a dog that barks at something, but runs to you for a treat when you say "Thank you."

Controlling Whining

Whining can mean various things. First, be sure that it doesn't indicate pain or physical distress. This form would generally exhibit itself as soft, almost continuous whining. Seek veterinary attention if this occurs.

The other reasons for whining are usually fairly apparent—a crated dog wants to be let out or a dog sitting by the table during dinner wants some of your food. If you succumb to the whining and give your Yorkie what he wants, you will encourage him to whine some more the next time. Instead, pay no attention to your Yorkie when he is whining. It may go on for some time, but wait it out. Because most whining is directed at getting attention of one sort or another, keeping your attention away from your Yorkie is the best response. Wait until he's quiet to let him out of the crate. And don't feed him from the table at all.

Digging

With their terrier heritage, it's understandable that some Yorkies feel a distinct need to dig. Your pup's excavations will likely conflict with the landscaping plan you've mapped out. But this drive to dig need not be a source of conflict between you and your Yorkie. Read on to understand why your little dog digs and what you can do about it.

Reasons for Digging

Dogs dig for a variety of reasons. The terriers may do it out of instinct, or the movement of prey animals underground may actually trigger the act. Other dogs as well as terriers may dig to reach cool dirt to lie in, especially during hot summer weather. Bored dogs, such as those left alone in the yard all day, may dig out of boredom or to escape and find something to do. In order to find the right solution, you have to identify your dog's reason for digging.

Dealing with Digging

If your dog is digging out of boredom, the solution should be obvious—to make life more entertaining for your dog! First, bring her inside. A Yorkshire terrier should not be stuck outdoors all day with no one around. These dogs are small enough to be seen as prey by hawks, coyotes, and raccoons. They are also observant and reactive enough to develop into a barking nuisance. If your Yorkie is stuck outdoors because you have housetraining or destruction issues, then work to resolve those issues rather than taking the "easy" route.

Question?

Why shouldn't you just stop your Yorkie from digging? He gets so dirty!

With dogs, compromise is a far better plan that stopping innate behaviors. In trying to stop one behavior, you may find yourself with others you like even less. Digging is part of the Yorkshire terrier's nature. If you fill a pit with loose sand for him to dig, you'll find that most of the sand falls off your Yorkie. You need to brush him daily anyway.

Second, exercise your dog more. Get up earlier and take a longer walk. Hire someone to come in at midday to play with your pup if you're not home. Have a training-and-play session when you get home from work. Well-exercised dogs are less trouble in general.

Third, give your Yorkie some home-alone activities. Buy a Buster Cube and put part of your dog's daily kibble in it before you leave. The dog has to turn the cube over and over to get a piece of food or two to tumble out. Or just toss some kibble around the house for the dog to hunt down and eat. You can also put a treat in a brown paper bag or a box and tie them closed, and let your Yorkie rip them open to get the treat—though this may encourage him to tear open actual packages in the future.

Of course, your Yorkie will still spend some time in the yard and may still want to dig. Rather than trying to stop the digging, which could result in stress and other unwanted behavior such as constant barking, give your Yorkie a place where digging is allowed. Dig a pit or build up walls. Fill the space with sand and loose dirt. Bury some treats and toys in the pit. To help your dog get the idea, run with him to the digging pit, dig up a toy, and play with him with it. Bury it again and encourage him to dig for it. If you see your Yorkie digging anywhere but the special digging pit, clap your hands to interrupt him and call him over to the digging pit. Keep digging in the designated area a rewarding experience by stocking the pit with treats and toys, and give him lots of time to play there.

Separation Anxiety

There's no way to tell which individual dogs might develop separation anxiety, so it's best to desensitize all dogs to their family's comings and goings. If you're starting with a puppy, you have a clean slate and should be able to progress through the program with no problems. If you've adopted an older Yorkie, the dog could already have a case of separation anxiety. Your training will be a little harder, and your dog's life will require a higher degree of management (leaving him alone as little as possible) while training is ongoing, but you can still succeed in the end.

 **Essential**

A dog suffering from separation anxiety needs to learn two things: she can be alone without anything bad happening, and you will always return. So it's crucial that you don't leave her alone for extended periods while you are working on the problem. Take her with you on errands whenever possible.

Symptoms of Separation Anxiety

Dogs suffering separation anxiety experience a high level of stress. They often lose control of their bodily functions, and you may find a puddle or a pile when you return home, generally close to the door through which you departed. This is not a willful act of disobedience and should definitely not be punished.

A dog suffering separation anxiety may scratch or bite at the door through which the person departed. Or he may go to wherever his human's smell is strong, often the couch, and engage in destructive chewing of cushions or pillows. This is another effort to relieve stress. You may also hear from neighbors that your dog howls or barks from the time you leave until exhaustion sets in. Even a dog left inside the house can often be heard outside.

If your puppy insists on following you and being close to you all the time (after you've untethered her), and cries when you're separated, this may be a warning of a tendency toward separation anxiety.

Dealing with Separation Anxiety

Whether you're starting fresh or dealing with a dog already showing signs of separation anxiety, the program is the same. First, use baby gates or an exercise pen to confine the dog close by, where she can see you but not reach you. Ignore her if she cries or whines. Release her when she's being quiet. Only confine her for a few minutes at first, and work up to an hour. Don't be emotional about confining her or releasing her—just go about it matter of factly. When she can be settled for an hour within view of you, confine her where she can't see you, but can still hear you talking. Start over with a short confinement time, and again gradually work up to an hour.

When your Yorkie can be calmly out of sight of you for an hour, begin actually leaving the house. If you haven't had any problems to date, you don't have to confine your Yorkie (provided she's old enough to be responsible). Just pick up your keys, put on your coat, calmly tell your dog goodbye, go out, close the door, wait a few seconds, and come back in. Do this several times a day. Then begin to gradually extend the time you're outside. When you get up to a minute or two, walk away from the house so your scent diminishes. When you get up to five minutes or so, get in the car and drive away, circle the block, and come back. You want your dog to stay calm through this entire process. Keep your departures and returns low-key and unemotional, and build up time slowly, so that your dog can cope.

CHAPTER 19

Emergency Health Care

EMERGENCIES HAPPEN with dogs, just as they do with people, but there isn't always a hospital available to your dog at all hours. Check on how your veterinarian handles emergencies before the need arises. Knowing his procedures, and having some idea of how to respond to such traumas as choking, hypothermia, or broken bones, will help you keep your wits about you should an emergency situation ever arise.

Your Canine First-Aid Kit

First-aid kits for dogs and humans can share many common components. Dogs don't have much use for adhesive bandages, and humans might not need ear cleaner, but both can use antibiotic cream, tweezers, gauze pads, an Ace bandage, scissors, an eyedropper, and sterile eye wash. For a dog, the thermometer needs to be rectal (rarely seen for human use anymore).

Contents of Your First Aid Kit

Some pet supply stores and veterinarians offer canine first aid kits, but you can also make your own. Your dog's first aid kit should include:

- Antibiotic cream
- Disinfectant, whether liquid (Betadine) or encased in swab-tipped vials

- Petroleum jelly
- Sterile eye wash
- Ear cleaner
- Antihistamine tablets
- Aspirin
- Ace bandage
- Gauze pads and/or rolls
- Adhesive tape (not bandages, but a roll of tape)
- Scissors (blunt-tipped are best)
- Tweezers
- Eyedropper
- Cotton balls and/or Q-tips
- Compressed activated charcoal
- Rectal thermometer
- Small, tightly-focused flashlight (to help examine eyes, ears, and mouth, or look for splinters)
- Pantyhose or soft rope to use as muzzle

Location of Your First-Aid Kit

At home, keep your kit in some easily accessible location—next to your fire extinguisher, perhaps. Or you could put it under your bathroom sink, if it won't become buried behind toilet paper and shampoo. Know where your first-aid kit is located, be able to access it easily, and be sure it's always kept well stocked. If you use supplies from it, replace them as soon as possible.

 Alert!

Before you might ever need them, know the correct dosages for any medications, such as an antihistamine. While this can be a wonderful thing to have if your dog suffers a bee sting, you don't want to accidentally overdose your Yorkie. This is easy to do because of the breed's small size.

Photograph by Cheryl A. Ertelt

▲ **It is essential to prepare a canine first aid kit in case of emergencies.**

If you travel a lot with your Yorkie, you may also want to keep a first-aid kit in your car. If kept in the car it can serve for both humans and dogs whenever an emergency arises. You may also want to have some clean towels alongside your first aid kit, especially in the car. You can use them to help transport an injured Yorkie, for warmth, or for direct pressure on wounds.

Using a Muzzle

It may sound horrible to have your dog already in distress from some injury and then add the insult of a muzzle. If you trust your Yorkie, you may wonder why you would ever need a muzzle. But an injured dog is unpredictable and may bite out of pain or out of fright. If you're worried about being bitten, you can't move or treat the dog. The muzzle will help keep you both safe.

You could buy a muzzle to keep in your first aid kit. They come in several varieties, from a wire basket to a cloth tube. If you choose to have a muzzle handy, it isn't a bad idea to practice putting it on your dog when nothing is happening. Make a game of it so that the dog isn't as frightened when you have to use it in a real emergency situation.

If you don't want to keep a muzzle around, you can use any soft ropelike material to serve the same function. Place the midpoint of the material on top of your Yorkie's muzzle, bring one end around each side of the muzzle, cross them under the jaw, then take the ends behind the Yorkie's head below the base of the ears and tie a knot. The loop around the muzzle should keep the dog from biting, while the loop behind the head keeps the dog from pushing off the nose loop.

Don't try to put a muzzle on a dog that's actively trying to bite you. Throw a blanket over the dog instead. Also, don't muzzle a dog that is unconscious, coughing, vomiting, or exhibiting trouble breathing.

 **Fact**

There are other options if you don't want to use a muzzle on your dog. Tying a soft rope around the snout can work, and there are other products on the market as well. While a head halter, such as a Gentle Leader, may look like a muzzle to some people, it doesn't keep a dog from biting.

CPR

CPR stands for "cardiopulmonary resuscitation." This procedure is used when the dog is not breathing and her heart has stopped beating. Don't rush to do CPR without first confirming that the heart really has stopped and the dog really isn't breathing. Performing CPR on a dog that doesn't need it can inflict further injury.

You should know beforehand how to check your dog's pulse. The easiest location is inside the dog's hind leg, near where it joins the body. The femoral artery is located there. Get used to finding it and feeling the pulse there so that you'll be practiced at it if you ever need to check the pulse in an emergency.

Also get used to checking your dog's breathing. You can watch for her side to rise and fall, but it can be a subtle motion if the dog is unconscious. Have a mirror handy to hold in front of the nose and mouth—watch it for fogging when the dog exhales.

Fact

Some CPR training includes practicing on a dummy human baby. While this is not equivalent to your Yorkshire terrier, it does give you at least a vague idea of the pressure required to massage the heart externally.

Rescue Breathing

If you determine that your Yorkie isn't breathing, first open her mouth, pull her tongue forward, and use your first two fingers to feel for any foreign objects in the mouth or throat. Clear any mucus or vomit. Wrap your hand around her muzzle to make an air seal, place your mouth against your hand, and blow into her nose. You should see the chest rise, then fall. If you don't see the chest rise, blow harder. It can help to have your Yorkie lying on her right side on an elevated flat surface. Continue rescue breathing until the dog starts breathing on her own or until the heart starts beating.

Chest Compressions

If your dog's heart isn't beating, place her on a flat surface on her right side. Put the heel of your dominant hand over the widest part of the rib cage. Put the heel of your other hand on top of the first hand, lace your fingers together and pull them back, so only the heel of your hand is on the dog. Keep your elbows straight and press down firmly, then release. Try to do this rhythmically, at a rate of about eighty compressions per minute.

There is great potential for injuring your Yorkie when performing chest compressions. First, be sure it's necessary. Then, use only as much force as necessary. Some CPR training events include dog models on which to practice, though they're usually larger dogs. See if one of these seminars might be offered in your area. If not, then as long as you're sure your Yorkie's heart isn't beating, your intervention is her only chance, and any injuries can be dealt with later if you succeed in reviving your dog. Ten minutes of chest compression should be enough to either restart the heart or let you know it's too late.

Putting Them Together

CPR is simply a combination of rescue breathing and chest compression. If you are by yourself, this is exhausting work, as you should do five chest compressions and then one rescue breath, and shifting between positions is difficult. If two people are present, one should do five chest compressions then pause while the other person does one rescue breath.

Stop every minute to check for a pulse and a breath, or you won't know if your Yorkie's heart has started beating on its own or breathing has resumed. If you continue doing CPR after the dog has been revived, you could cause further problems.

Moving an Injured Dog

While it's certainly easier to move an injured Yorkshire terrier than an injured Great Dane, the act still requires some thought and care. Remember that an injured dog may bite out of pain or fear, and you're liable to react without thinking if you're suddenly bitten. So for the safety of both of you, fashion a muzzle before you move the dog.

The most important thing when moving a dog is to keep the dog's whole body as stable as possible. You don't know what part or parts may be injured, so you want to avoid moving any joints at all. Use both your hands to cradle your Yorkie, or even use something solid that you may have handy, such as a piece of plywood, as a rigid surface under your Yorkie. If possible, place someone in charge of keeping the dog quiet and still while someone else drives to the veterinarian's office.

 **Essential**

> If your dog is injured but you don't know the details or the extent of the injuries (perhaps you were not present when he was hit by a car), you should assume that every part of the body is possibly harmed. The dog could have broken bones, internal bleeding, or lacerations hidden by the coat. Handle every part of the dog carefully as you load him into your vehicle to be taken to an emergency facility.

Specific Emergencies

Dogs can face a variety of serious ailments and injuries over their lifetimes, just as children can. Due to the nature of an emergency, you won't be expecting these problems, but you can be prepared to deal with them to the best of your abilities. Your task when facing an emergency is to keep your Yorkie alive and to avoid further injury while seeking professional help.

Broken Bones

Because of the Yorkshire terrier's size, dogs of this breed risk breaking bones when jumping or falling off even seemingly small heights. Decks, balconies, stairway landings, tables, and sofa backs are inappropriate launching sites. Yorkies are also frequently underfoot, and they're difficult to see if you're carrying packages. They can be injured by being tripped over or having something dropped on them. They can also be hard for drivers to see, and obviously aren't going to fare well in a collision with a vehicle.

If your Yorkie suffers an accident and you see bone sticking out through broken skin, your Yorkie won't put weight on a leg, or appears to be paralyzed, suspect a possible broken bone. You need to do as little damage as possible while moving the dog, and get to a veterinarian as quickly as possible.

 **Fact**

The only canine body parts you can effectively splint are legs. Take the time to splint only if you're far from your car and will have to carry your Yorkie a considerable distance. Branches and an Ace bandage or rolled-up newspaper and adhesive tape are effective splint-making materials.

Bleeding

Bleeding is nearly always a serious problem for a Yorkshire terrier, unless it's just a scratch. A small dog can bleed to death rather quickly. Arterial bleeding, where the blood is bright red and spurts in time with the heartbeat, is the most serious situation. To staunch bleeding, place a gauze pad or a clean piece of material over the wound and apply direct pressure. Do not lift the material to check on how things are going because you may reopen the wound. If the material soaks through with blood, add more material on top of it.

If arterial bleeding is from a leg and you can't stop the flow with direct pressure, you may want to try using a tourniquet above the wound. This is somewhat risky, as you can cut off all blood flow to the leg. Tourniquets need to be relaxed at least every five minutes to allow blood to flow to the extremity. Tighten one only enough to stop arterial blood from spurting or to slow the flow of venous blood. Because of its complications, use a tourniquet only in an absolute emergency, and get to a veterinarian as quickly as possible.

Bleeding can also occur internally, due to trauma or poisoning. The dog might cough up blood, or blood may ooze from the nose or mouth. There could be blood in the urine as well. It's also possible that there will be no signs of internal bleeding—the dog will just collapse. Pale gums are a sure sign of internal bleeding and necessitate an emergency trip to the vet's office.

Choking

Dogs tend to gulp their food in large chunks, and they can get pieces of rawhide or other hard chews caught in their throats. A dog with food caught in her throat may paw at her muzzle, will probably cough and gag, and could have difficulty breathing. As long as your Yorkie is breathing, get to a veterinarian to have the object removed.

If your Yorkie loses consciousness, try to remove the object yourself. See if you can reach it with your fingers, but be careful not to push it farther in. If you can't pull it free, try the canine version of the Heimlich maneuver. Hold your Yorkie with her back against your chest. Make one hand into a fist and position it just beneath the Yorkie's last rib. Place your other hand over the fist and thrust the fist in and up, directing the force under the rib cage, sending a burst of air up through the larynx. Thrust a half-dozen times at most. If this hasn't worked by then, it isn't likely to. Just get your Yorkie to a veterinarian right away.

Hypothermia/Frostbite

Remember, Yorkshire terriers can be prone to hypothermia. Cold temperatures can be hazardous to their health, especially if they're also wet. Frostbite happens most often to the extremities, such as ears or toes, when tissue becomes frozen. Older Yorkies are particularly prone to problems with low temperatures.

Avoid the problem by keeping your Yorkie indoors in exceptionally cold weather. If you must go out, dress your Yorkie accordingly, and don't stay out longer than necessary. Play indoor games for exercise and entertainment.

If you've been out in the cold and your dog seems lethargic, or starts to shiver, take his temperature. A reading of 95° or lower indicates hypothermia. Wrap your Yorkie in blankets to warm him up. If he's wet, dry him thoroughly. (Still use only a low-heat setting on a regular hair dryer—burning him with high heat won't help.) Call your veterinarian for further advice.

Suspect frostbite if skin appears pale or blue, especially on the extremities. Do not rub such areas in an attempt to warm them up—that can cause additional damage. If your hands are warm, cup them around the affected area, or apply warm compresses. Get to a veterinarian for further treatment.

Question?

How can a Yorkie get cold so easily with all that hair?
The Yorkie has a large surface area compared to body mass, and loses body heat through radiation. Yorkies kept appropriately lean don't have a lot of body fat as insulation. Also, the Yorkie's coat is akin to human hair and lacks the fluffy heat-conserving undercoat of other dogs.

Heatstroke

Yorkshire terriers are not prone to problems with warmer temperatures, but extreme heat or heavy exercise in heat can result in heatstroke. Leaving your Yorkie in a car in hot weather is certainly risky behavior. Signs of heatstroke are mostly opposite those of hypothermia—temperature rises, often above 104°. The gums and tongue are bright red. Your Yorkie may drool or vomit.

Heatstroke is a dire emergency, leading quickly to death if untreated. Do not plunge the dog into cold water—the shock could be too great. Instead, spray the dog with cool water, or place cool wet towels over him. Take him into an air-conditioned location if one is available nearby. Keep taking his temperature so that you know when it's fallen below 103°. At that point, you can transport your Yorkie to your veterinarian. Transporting him when his temperature is too high could cause him additional stress. Even if all seems well, secondary problems can develop after your dog's temperature has returned to normal.

Insect Stings and Bites

Minor reactions to insect stings, such as a rash or moderate swelling, aren't a true emergency. Scrape away the stinger, if you see one, apply a cold compress, and give the dog the appropriate dose of an antihistamine. But multiple stings, or stings on the face or neck, can create severe swelling that blocks off the airway. Dogs with a hypersensitivity to the sting can go into anaphylactic shock, with difficulty breathing or even loss of consciousness. This requires a speedy trip to the veterinarian.

Poisoning

Many substances can poison your Yorkie. Snail bait and antifreeze are two of the more common poisons, but animal carcasses, garbage, rat poison, toxic plants, herbicides or insecticides, and human medications are also possibilities. Of course, you should remove all potential problems, but antifreeze drops in the street or slug bait in someone else's front yard could fall within your Yorkie's reach.

 Fact

Pet-friendly alternatives to toxic snail bait and antifreeze have been available for years. You can certainly use them in your home, but you can't yet depend on others to use them. So always be cautious when taking your dog out of the safety zone you have prepared.

If you see your Yorkie eat some toxic material, and your veterinarian is more than a few minutes' drive away, call the National Animal Poison Control Center (see Appendix C). If you can tell them what your Yorkie has ingested, they can advise you on what course of action to take. They may tell you to force the dog to vomit with a hydrogen peroxide solution, or to give a dose of compressed activated charcoal, and then hurry to your own veterinarian.

Electrocution

The most common cause of electrocution is a dog biting into an electrical cord. You may find your dog unconscious, lying near the cord. In case there is still current flowing through your dog, throw the circuit breaker for that outlet, or throw the main breaker if it will take too long to find the correct one. Then check your dog for breathing and a heartbeat, and perform CPR as necessary.

Some dogs may get shocked without losing consciousness. But they will appear stunned, may cough and drool, and exhibit difficulty breathing. You may smell a strange electrical fire odor around the dog's mouth as well. In either case, take your dog to the veterinarian for further treatment.

Emergency Clinics and After-Hours Care

In the midst of the adrenaline rush of an emergency is not the time to find out that your veterinarian doesn't have a twenty-four-hour referral number of some kind. Before anything bad ever happens, be sure you know what options exist if an emergency crops up in the middle of the night or on a Sunday afternoon.

After-Hours Care

Many veterinarians who don't have office hours around the clock or through the weekend do have some method for responding to emergencies. Find out beforehand if your veterinary clinic provides an emergency number for all hours when the office is closed. Also ask what happens when the veterinarian knows he won't be at that emergency number.

Veterinary practices often cover for each other, so that one or the other is always available. If your own veterinarian will be away, your emergency call will automatically be connected with the cover vet, or the answering service will contact the other vet. Find out who your vet's cover vet is, and visit that practice so you know where it is and how to get there. If an emergency ever arises, you'll be glad you did.

Emergency Clinics

Some areas are served by an animal hospital emergency clinic. This can be a clinic in its own right, or it can share space with a regular veterinary clinic. Whichever position this clinic assumes, it is open when normal clinics are closed. It operates on the same principles as a hospital emergency room, seeing patients without appointments and, when necessary, taking the most serious cases first.

Make it a priority to find out if an emergency clinic operates in your area. If there is a clinic nearby, be sure to find out its hours, its location, and directions on how to get there. Prominently display this information (on the refrigerator, perhaps) or keep it with the canine first-aid kit. Be sure everyone in the household knows where to find this information.

As Your Yorkie Grows Older

DOGS ARE INDIVIDUALS. Some may show signs of aging at eight, while others still behave like pups at twelve. Fourteen years is a typical lifespan for a Yorkshire terrier, though some have lived into their twenties. As your Yorkie ages, her housing and nutritional needs may change, and she may develop some health problems. Regular health checkups assume even greater importance, as new problems caught early are easier to resolve.

When Is a Yorkie a Senior?

While larger dogs are said to enter their golden years at age seven, smaller dogs delay that until age ten. Of course, this is a generalization. Here are a few signs that your Yorkie is entering her senior years:

- Slower growing, thinning hair
- Graying on the muzzle and/or over the eyes
- Lower energy level, more time spent sleeping
- Increased reluctance to go out when it's cold
- Hazy or bluish eyes
- Increased dental problems
- Hearing loss
- Stiffness in legs

You could also see a sudden increase or decrease in appetite, a need to urinate more frequently, increased water consumption, or skin problems. All of these can be signs of disease processes common to older dogs, so if you see any of them, you should schedule a veterinary exam.

 Essential

Make note of any changes you observe in your Yorkie. If she seems to drink a lot on one day, but then goes back to normal, it's not a problem. But if the increased drinking recurs, you'll be able to check your notes and tell your veterinarian when the behavior first showed up.

More Frequent Health Exams

As humans get older, they are urged by their physicians to have more and more diagnostic procedures, such as colonoscopies and stress tests to find and treat any problems before they progress. You have to be the health advocate for your Yorkshire terrier. Your veterinarian might recommend twice-annual visits. If he doesn't, you should schedule them yourself.

Vaccinations

While you want more frequent examinations, you should also want less frequent vaccinations. If you've been having them done annually, you might consider changing to every three years. Some people stop vaccinations altogether once the dog becomes a senior. Dogs seem to become more reactive to the vaccinations as they age, so the vaccinations are not entirely benign. Ongoing research is showing vaccination effectiveness continues for several years—one manufacturer announced full antibody response four years beyond vaccination.

Examinations

As your Yorkie ages, you will be seeing more of your veterinarian, not less. Those twice-yearly visits might include a few more tests than in previous years. Your veterinarian will probably want to do blood work, first to establish a baseline, and then to check that nothing has changed. The blood work results can reveal any infection and check on the functioning of many of the internal organs.

Your veterinarian will also perform a physical examination. This can locate dental problems, any new or changed lumps, skin problems, and joints developing arthritis. Special veterinary diets, a wide variety of prescription drugs, and ever-more sophisticated surgery can help with many of the problems of aging.

Nutrition

Nutritional needs can change as your Yorkie grows older. Dental problems may necessitate a change to a softer diet, while kidney or digestive problems could lead to a prescription veterinary diet. Even healthy older Yorkies may need fewer calories, or a little help to revive a waning appetite.

 Fact

Some dog foods are developed using a process that breaks protein molecules down into smaller units. Though created to help dogs with food allergies, these foods may also be useful when a highly digestible protein is required for your older Yorkie.

Protein Quantity and Quality

You may hear that older dogs should consume less protein because of concerns with kidney function. This may be true for dogs actually suffering kidney disease, but it's not the case for healthy older dogs. Protein does not cause kidney disease; it merely becomes more difficult for diseased kidneys to process. So don't shy away from protein for your older Yorkie without reason.

What you do want to check is protein digestibility. Aging digestive systems may not be quite as efficient as they once were, so easily digestible protein is essential. Look for 22- to 25-percent protein, and call the manufacturer's toll-free number to ask about digestibility.

Calories

While you need to keep supplying a good level of protein, if your Yorkie is slowing down a bit, you'll need to provide fewer calories. You can look for a food lower in fat, but too little fat means the food will not be very palatable. Look for a moderate amount.

Your other choice is to feed a little less. This may leave your Yorkie feeling a bit hungry. You can look for a food with a little more fiber, to help create a feeling of fullness. Or you can add a little canned pumpkin (the plain kind, not for pie) as your own fiber addition.

Keep doing rib checks on your dog to know if you need to adjust calories. If your senior Yorkie needs more calories to maintain his weight, ask your veterinarian to find out why this is happening.

Alert!

Don't just start giving your Yorkshire terrier supplements whenever you want. Some supplements conflict with medications, and many are just a waste of your money. Some don't even contain the ingredients they claim, so be cautious when investing in these products.

Supplements

While supplements usually aren't necessary throughout most of your Yorkie's life, a few might be helpful for senior dogs. Older

Yorkies can suffer dry, itchy skin. Your veterinarian might recommend vitamin E or fatty acids to help. If your Yorkie is having trouble metabolizing any nutrients, other specific supplements might be indicated. Other options exist for easing aching joints.

Decreased Appetite

As they get older, some Yorkshire terriers may be less inclined to eat, or they may eat only a bite or two. This might be due to your Yorkie experiencing a decreased sense of smell. Food that doesn't smell good isn't very appetizing. If this is the case, you can help by warming the food in the microwave—not so it's hot, but just slightly warm, to release more aroma. Add a little chicken broth before warming for even more effect.

Sudden weight loss is always a cause for concern. If your Yorkie is eating well but suddenly starts losing weight, a veterinary checkup is in order.

The Problems of Aging

All creatures, including humans, have health problems of one sort or another as they get older, and Yorkshire terriers are no exception. The wear and tear of a lifetime of movement can lead to joint problems. Kidneys can become less efficient, any or all of the senses can decrease or fail, and coat and skin problems can arise. Modern veterinary medicine can help with many of the common canine conditions associated with aging.

Joint Problems

If your Yorkie has always jumped onto the couch or climbed stairs but is reluctant to do so as she ages, she may be experiencing arthritis. It's a common problem among older dogs of all breeds. Help make life easier for your senior by lifting her in and out of the car, onto the couch (if she's allowed there), and carrying her up and down stairs. If she lags on walks, take it slow and shorten the distance you travel.

Arthritis can also make joints painful to touch, so watch your Yorkie for any signs that she is in pain. If you ignore warning signs, your Yorkie may feel obliged to bite to tell you to stop hurting her.

Stiffness can make grooming more difficult for your dog. So you may need to take a larger role in helping her keep clean. Use a damp cloth to clean where urine may dribble or feces gets stuck in hair. Baby wipes are ideal for both purposes.

Essential

You may not bite if someone kept poking you in some sore swollen spot, but you'd certainly tell them to knock it off in no uncertain terms. If your Yorkie stiffens when you touch a certain place, or even growls, it doesn't mean she's turned into a dangerous dog—she's telling you it hurts.

There are both supplements and anti-inflammatories that may help ease the problem. Supplements might include glucosamine, chondroitin, MSM, or ester C. Glucosamine, specifically extract of green-lipped mussels (a natural source of glucosamine), has the most scientific study behind it. It's not a quick fix, however. Building up to therapeutic levels can take two months, so don't expect instant results.

Nonsteroidal anti-inflammatory drugs (NSAIDs) can help ease the swelling and pain. But they're not innocuous. Side effects can be serious and might include vomiting, diarrhea, and damage to the kidneys or liver. If your Yorkie is taking NSAIDs, you should have blood work done regularly to check liver and kidney function. And whatever you do, do *not* share your own NSAIDs with your Yorkie. Ibuprofen and acetaminophen can be toxic to dogs. Aspirin at the appropriate dose isn't toxic, but it can have its own side-effect problems.

Cancer

It's hard to hear the "C" word without flinching, but many forms of cancer are treatable. The incidence of cancer in dogs increases with age. Also, of course, the earlier it's caught the better, so it's wise to check for warning signs. Some possible signs of cancer include:

- Any new lumps or bumps, or changes in existing ones
- Sores that won't heal
- Sudden or unexplained weight loss
- Swelling, especially in areas other than joints
- Prolonged lack of appetite
- Bleeding or unusual discharge from the nose, mouth, or other body openings
- A bad or strange smell coming from any part of the dog
- Lack of energy
- Difficulty swallowing or eating
- Difficulty urinating or defecating
- Difficulty breathing

Don't panic and assume it's cancer if you see any of these signs. There are other explanations for most of them, and even if they are signs of the disease, the condition may be relatively easy to treat.

 Fact

Dogs can receive radiation treatment, chemotherapy, and other common cancer treatments, the same as humans. As they don't have the worry of knowing they have cancer, they often do very well with treatment.

The most common types of cancer in dogs are mammary (breast cancer), skin tumors, testicular cancer, lymphoma, and cancers of the mouth or nose. You can avoid testicular cancer by neutering your Yorkie and greatly lower the risk of mammary cancer by spaying before the first heat.

Cognitive Dysfunction Syndrome (CDS)

This is the canine equivalent of Alzheimer's disease. As in humans, the dysfunction progresses over time. A dog with CDS will often appear disoriented or confused. He might stand staring into space, almost as if he's forgotten what he was about to do, or wander aimlessly through familiar surroundings. Their interaction with the family usually diminishes. The dog's sleep patterns may change, and you may hear him wandering about at night. Often, he will start having housetraining accidents.

If you see any of the signs—disorientation, changes in sleep or activity, less interaction, housetraining problems—in a Yorkie aged eight or more, have a full checkup done on the dog. Problems with the thyroid, kidneys, or adrenal gland can mimic the symptoms of CDS, so it's important to establish a definitive diagnosis.

Supplements may help alleviate CDS, and medications have been developed to combat the disease. And remember that it's very important not to punish your Yorkie for any of these behavior changes—it's not his fault.

Essential

Giving your dog an injection is not as frightening a task as you may think. The shot is given subcutaneously (under the skin), so you don't have to find a vein. The loose skin over the back of the shoulder is easy to gather up and slide a needle into.

Diabetes

Diabetes is fairly common in older dogs. There might be a genetic predisposition, and obesity is a definite contributing factor. With diabetics, the pancreas doesn't produce enough insulin to send blood glucose into the body's cells. Glucose levels in the blood rise to abnormally high levels. Untreated diabetes can lead to a variety of complications and eventually death. Fortunately, it's a manageable condition.

Signs of diabetes include increased drinking, which, in turn, leads to increased urination. A diabetic dog may eat ravenously and yet still lose weight. Your veterinarian will perform a blood test and urinalysis to make a diagnosis of diabetes.

If your Yorkie is overweight, you'll have to help her lose those extra pounds. To keep glucose from spiking, meals should be given at regular times, and exercise should be as regular as possible. You'll likely have to give your Yorkie insulin injections once or twice a day. This is easy to do—your veterinarian can show you how to use the loose skin at the back of the neck. Most dogs don't object to the shots.

Dental Problems

Even if you have been lucky enough to escape dental problems when your Yorkshire terrier was younger, you may see them now that she's aging. It's hard to fit the normal number of canine teeth into that downsized mouth, and a less-than-perfect bite means that tartar and plaque tend to accumulate. You can help prevent problems by brushing regularly and having your Yorkie's teeth cleaned as necessary. But you still may see problems arise.

Dogs don't tend to get cavities, but teeth can fracture (mainly the canines) or loosen (mainly the incisors, the front teeth). Extractions may sometimes be necessary. Fewer teeth in a comfortable mouth is definitely preferable to pain.

Hearing Loss

Both humans and canines tend to become hard of hearing as they age. The delicate mechanisms of the inner ear gradually degenerate. Some dogs may go totally deaf. It's not much of a problem for them. Using hand signals during training means you can continue to communicate with your Yorkie even if he loses his hearing completely. You will only have to be mindful not to sneak up on him from behind. Some nearly deaf dogs can still hear sharp sounds such as clapping or a clicker, and you can use those to announce your presence. Otherwise, you can stomp on the floor or ground so your Yorkie can feel the vibrations.

Your responsibility to keep your dog safe increases if he is deaf. Never let him off leash outside your home or fenced yard because he can't react to any warning sounds of traffic.

 **Fact**

Dogs cope very well with the loss of one of their senses. Their hearing, sight, and sense of smell are all so effective that two senses together can compensate for the loss of the other one. With basic precautions, your deaf or blind dog can continue to do most of the things she's used to doing.

Vision Loss

The most common cause of vision impairment in dogs is nuclear sclerosis. As the lens of the eye ages, it thickens and loses elasticity. The eye appears hazy or bluish-gray when you look at it. Though it can impair vision somewhat, especially close up, it rarely causes blindness.

Cataracts also occur in older age, especially in diabetic dogs. The lens starts to become opaque at the center, and then the cataract spreads outward. Dogs can receive cataract surgery, but blind dogs can continue to live a happy life with their humans. Avoid moving the furniture around indoors, and keep your Yorkie on leash outdoors, and he should be just fine.

Kidney Disease

Healthy dogs have a lot more kidney function than they require, so obvious signs of kidney disease don't show up until three-quarters or more of kidney function has been lost. However, your veterinarian can perform tests that will spot problems earlier. You may want to make the early renal disease (ERD) test part of your Yorkie's regular health checkup.

Protein becomes an issue for dogs with kidney disease. The impaired kidneys can't process protein as efficiently as they once could, and metabolism by-products become an issue. Yet the dog continues to require protein. Your best bet is to feed the most easily digestible protein available.

Hypothyroidism

Hypothyroidism is a common hormonal disorder among middle-aged to senior dogs. The thyroid ceases to make a sufficient level of hormones, and the dog may suddenly gain weight, show skin and coat problems, and suffer ear infections.

Fortunately, hypothyroidism can be managed by giving replacement thyroid hormone. Your veterinarian will determine the amount needed and may require periodic blood tests to check that appropriate levels are maintained.

Accommodating Changes in Your Older Yorkie

As your Yorkshire terrier ages, keep alert for any changes. Sudden grumpiness when touched might indicate arthritis, and barking at people coming up from behind might be a sign of hearing loss. You can adjust some of your interactions and your home environment to help keep your Yorkie happy and comfortable. Some suggestions include:

- Provide soft bedding, and consider a heated bed for arthritic dogs
- Pet and massage more gently, avoiding painful areas
- Provide steps or a ramp, if needed, to reach previously accessible areas

- Keep walks shorter and games gentler, but do continue exercise
- Provide plenty of fresh water, and increased opportunities to eliminate
- Keep up grooming, and be sure to check for any changes in skin or coat
- Allow the dog to sleep more, but still include him in family activities

Spayed females may face an increased chance of becoming incontinent as they age. Your veterinarian may recommend a drug to help counteract this. Remember that this is not a housetraining lapse. In fact, it often happens when the dog is asleep.

Saying Goodbye

Every dog owner hopes her furry friend will live a long and healthy life, and when his time comes, the ideal is a quiet passing in his sleep. It happens this way for a lucky few. But for many others, health deteriorates and the question of quality of life arises. Choosing whether or not to put your dog to sleep is one of the most difficult decisions you will ever have to make.

If your dog has a terminal disease, it's a little easier to decide to put your dog's suffering to an end. However, any loving owner will be terribly attached to her dog and will be hesitant to let go. Try your best to step back and assess your Yorkie's quality of life. Does she still enjoy interacting with her family, eating, and going for a ride or stroll? When the bad days start to outnumber the good, it's time to do some soul-searching. Dog owners are responsible for releasing their friends from their failing bodies when the going gets too rough. You know your Yorkie better than anyone, and you can best assess her quality of life.

When the time comes, try to hold yourself together for the sake of your dog. Some veterinarians will come to your home, while others will have you come to their office. Whatever the location, the dog receives a tranquilizer, so he is relaxed and may even fall asleep, and then the final injection is given to stop the heart. It's a painless death, made easier by your presence.

Photograph by Pamela Shelby

▲ **When you lose your Yorkie, try to focus on all the great times you had together.**

Some may not understand your grief over "only" a dog, but others will empathize, having faced their own canine departures. Though the world may seem dark for a time, try to remember all the good times together, and hold your Yorkie forever in your heart.

Appendix A

Glossary of Terms

Amino acids The building blocks of proteins. Dogs require ten specific amino acids for a complete diet and good health.

Bite The way the teeth of the upper jaw meet the teeth of the lower jaw. With a level bite, the teeth meet edge to edge. With a scissors bite, the lower teeth slide just behind the upper teeth.

Buster Cube A food puzzle activity toy for dogs. It's a cube with a maze of tunnels inside. You pour in some kibble and turn the cube around, and the dog then has to move the cube about to get some pieces of food to dribble out.

Collapsing trachea A tendency of the windpipe to collapse in on itself, often due to a failure of the cartilage rings to develop properly. The condition can be worsened through pressure on the throat, as from a collar.

Color dilution alopecia Alopecia is hair loss. Color dilution is the fading of what would be a black coat to the blue of the Yorkshire terrier. Color dilution can be a genetic cause of alopecia.

Dewclaws The extra "toes" often seen on dogs a short distance up the leg from the foot.

Docking The artificial shortening of the dog's tail via surgery, usually done when puppies are very young.

Duck dryer A hair dryer specifically meant for dogs, with a stand to leave your hands free and only low heat to keep your dog safe.

Dysplasia Faulty development of a joint, most often a hip.

Enzymatic cleanser A cleaning agent specifically meant to counteract the smells of urine or feces, so the dog is not attracted back to the same spot.

Exercise pen A portable enclosure that collapses flat and opens to a rectangle or circle, and that can be used as a playpen. Most often seen in heavy wire, but also available with aluminum framing and mesh panels.

Forced-air dryer A dryer that uses a powerful blast of air to blow water out of the hair rather than heat to evaporate it.

Group judging The best dogs representing each breed in a single group, such as the Toy Group, are brought together and the top four dogs are chosen. Best in Group goes on to compete for Best in Show.

Harshness A coat quality, undesirable in a Yorkshire terrier, of roughness or coarseness. Wirehaired terriers should have harsh coats. A Yorkie's coat should be silky.

Heat The twice-yearly estrus of the female dog, generally lasting about three weeks each time it occurs, during which she is both highly attractive to males and sexually receptive.

KC Britain's Kennel Club, known simply as "the" kennel club.

Kong A hard rubber toy, shaped like a pinecone, with a hollow core that can be stuffed with various food treats.

Major A dog show win over a sufficient number of dogs to earn three or more points. The number of dogs varies by breed and area of the country.

Microchip A glass-encased computer chip the size of a grain of rice, injected into the dog's shoulder muscle as an identification device. The unique number can be read by a scanner passed over the dog's body.

Pancreatitis An inflammation of the pancreas, often caused by eating foods high in fats.

Papers Certificate necessary to register a dog with the AKC or other registry, attesting to the dog's purebred parentage.

Patellar luxation The slipping of the patella, or kneecap, out of the joint in which it should be seated. Severity of the slippage varies.

Performance sports Dog competitions other than the conformation ring, including agility, obedience, tracking, and others.

Pica The eating of nonfood items, such as rocks or cloth.

Piddle pads Absorbent rectangles of material intended to be provided as a surface for elimination.

Polydipsia/polyuria Increased drinking of water and increased urination, often in association with diabetes or renal failure.

Portosystemic shunt Blood vessel bypassing the liver, which ordinarily closes off to direct blood through the liver when puppies are young. Failure to close requires surgical intervention. Genetics can predispose a Yorkshire terrier to shunt problems.

Separation anxiety Elevated stress over being left alone or separated from a specific person. Can result in destructive behavior, constant vocalization. Requires a program of behavior modification.

Standard The written description of a breed, provided by the parent club of a breed.

Toy group AKC-defined group of dog breeds to which the Yorkshire terrier belongs, consisting completely of small dogs.

Withers The highest point of the shoulder, which can be felt just below and to the side of the base of the neck. Point at which a dog's height is measured.

Wrappings Papers and rubber bands into which a Yorkshire terrier's coat is rolled to keep it from being soiled or broken.

Additional Written Resources

Books

Dog Sports and Activities

The Absolute Beginner's Guide to Showing Your Dog, by Cheryl S. Smith (Crown Publishing, 2001)

All About Agility, by Jacqueline O'Neil (Howell Book House, 1998)

Clicker Training for Obedience, by Morgan Spector (Sunshine Books, 1998)

Competitive Obedience Training for the Small Dog, by Barbara Cecil and Gerianne Darnell (T9E Publishing, 1994)

Dancing with Your Dog, by Sandra Davis (Dancing Dogs, 1999—book and 3 videos)

Earthdog Ins & Outs, by JoAnn Frier-Murza (self-published, 1999)

Gone to Ground: Jack Russell Terrier (Canine Training Systems, 1997—video)

New Secrets of Show Dog Handling, by Peter Green and Mario Migliorini (Alpine Publishing, 2002)

Recreational Agility, by Warren Patitz (Doggone Connection, 1999)

Show Me!, by D. Caroline Coile (Barron's Educational Series, 1997)

Successful Obedience Handling, by Barbara Handler (Alpine Publishing, 2003)

Therapy Dogs, by Kathy Diamond Davis (Dogwise, 2002)

Grooming

Simple Guide to Grooming Your Dog, by Eve Adamson and Sandy Roth (TFH, 2003)

Stone Guide to Dog Grooming, by Ben and Pearl Stone (Howell Book House, 1988)

Ultimate Dog Grooming, by Eileen Geeson (Firefly Books, 2004)

Adoption and Rescue

The Adoption Option, by Eliza Rubenstein and Shari Kalina (Howell Book House, 1996)

Before You Get Your Puppy and After You Get Your Puppy, both by Ian Dunbar (James & Kenneth Publishers, 2001)

Health

The Angell Memorial Animal Hospital Book of Wellness and Preventive Care for Dogs, by Darlene Arden (McGraw Hill, 2003)

The Dog Owner's Home Veterinary Handbook, by James M. Giffin, MD and Lisa D. Carlson, DVM (Howell Book House, 1999)

New Choices in Natural Healing for Dogs and Cats, by Amy D. Shojai (Rodale, 1999)

Behaviour and Training

Dog Behavior: A Guide to a Happy, Healthy Pet, by Ian Dunbar (Howell Book House, 1998)

How to Behave So Your Dog Behaves, by Sophia Yin (TFH, 2004)

Little Dogs: Training Your Pint Size Companion, by Deborah Wood (TFH, 2004)

Outwitting Dogs, by Terry Ryan and Kirsten Mortensen (The Lyons Press, 2004)

The Power of Positive Dog Training, by Pat Miller (Howell Book House, 2001)

Quick Clicks: 40 Fast and Fun Behaviors to Train with a Clicker, by Mandy Book and Cheryl S. Smith (Hanalei, 2001)

The Rosetta Bone: The Key to Communication Between Humans and Canines, by Cheryl S. Smith (Howell Book House, 2004)

The Trick Is in the Training: 25 Fun Tricks to Teach Your Dog, by Stephanie Taunton and Cheryl S. Smith (Barron's Educational Series, 1998)

Magazines and Newspapers

Dog World
(weekly newspaper)
Somerfield House, Wottan Road
Ashford, Kent TN23 6LW
Tel: 01233 621877
www.dogworld.co.uk
editorial@dogworld.co.uk

Dogs Today
(magazine)
Town Mill, Bagshot Road
Chobham, Surrey GU24 8BZ
Tel: 01276 858860
dogstoday@dial.pipex.com

Dogs Monthly
(magazine)
Ascot House, High Street
Ascot, Berkshire SL5 7UG
www.dogsmonthly.co.uk

K9 Magazine
i-Business Centre
Oakham Business Park, Mansfield
Nottinghamshire NG18 5BR
www.k9magazine.com

Appendix C

Organizations and Online Shopping

Useful Addresses

The Kennel Club
1–5 Clarges Street
London W1Y 8AB
Tel: 0870 606 6750
www.the-kennel-club.org.uk

The Irish Kennel Club
Unit 36, Greenmount Office Park
Harolds Cross Bridge, Dublin 6W
Republic of Ireland
www.ikc.ie

National Dog Tattoo Register
PO Box 572, Harwich CO12 3SY
Tel: 01255 552455
www.dog-register.co.uk
info@dog-register.co.uk

Pro-Dogs and Pets as Therapy
Rocky Bank, 4 New Road
Ditton, Kent ME20 6AD
Tel: 01732 848499
www.prodog.org.uk

British Veterinary Association
7 Mansfield Street
London W6 9NQ
Tel: 020 7636 6541
www.bva.co.uk

Breed Clubs and Societies

Cheshire & North Wales Yorkshire Terrier Society
Tel: 0151 3273376

Lincoln & Humberside Yorkshire Terrier Club
Tel: 01765 602265

Midland Yorkshire Terrier Club
Tel: 01283 226189

Northern Counties Yorkshire Terrier Club
Tel: 01226 781373

South Western Yorkshire Terrier Club
Tel: 0117 9601592

Ulster Yorkshire Terrier Club
Tel: 02893 378302

Yorkshire Terrier Club of Scotland
Tel: 01592 759277

Yorkshire Terrier Club of South Wales
Tel: 01443 431052

Dogs' Homes and Charities

Dogs Home, Battersea, London
Tel: 020 7622 3626

Dogs' Home, Birmingham
Tel: 0121 643 5211

Dogs' Home, Wood Green, Essex
Tel: 0176 383 8329

Dogs' Home, Lothian, Scotland
Tel: 0131 660 5842

Blue Cross
Tel: 0171 835 4224

National Boarding Kennel Federation
Tel: 020 8995 8331

Dogs' Trust
Tel: 020 7837 0006

PDSA
Tel: 01952 290999

RSPCA
Tel: 08705 555999

Shopping

C&V Pet Supplies
32 Kelburne Road
Cowley
Oxford
OX4 3SJ
www.petsupplies.co.uk

Champion Pet Supplies
8 Horeston Grange Shopping
Centre, Camborne Drive
Nuneaton
Warwickshire
CV11 6GU
www.championpetsonline.co.uk

dogstuff
Ty Cerrig, Tylwch Road
Llanidloes, Powys
Wales SY18 6JJ
Tel: 01686 412736
www.dogstuff.co.uk

PetPlanet
www.petplanet.co.uk

Pets24
www.pets24.co.uk

Index

Other titles in the series

EVERYTHING

YOU NEED TO KNOW ABOUT...

£9.99 ISBN: 0 7153 2060 2

£9.99 ISBN: 0 7153 2062 9

THE
EVERYTHING
Dog Breed Guides

£7.99 ISBN: 0 7153 2331 8

Available through all good bookshops, and through
D&C Direct, Freepost EX2 110, Newton Abbot, TQ12 4ZZ.
Telephone 0870 9908222.